His Ownself

His Ownself

A SEMI-MEMOIR

Dan Jenkins

DOUBLEDAY

NEW YORK LONDON TORONTO

SYDNEY AUCKLAND

Grateful acknowledgment is made to *Golf Digest* for permission to
reprint "Nice (Not) Knowing You" by Dan Jenkins. Reprinted by
permission of *Golf Digest*.

Jacket design by Michael J. Windsor
Jacket images © Shutterstock: golf club © ifong; football © Xtremest;
tee © donskarpo; grass © grzym; skywriting © frescomovie
Insert photographs are courtesy of the author.

LIBRARY OF CONGRESS CATALOGING-IN-PUBLICATION DATA
Jenkins, Dan.
His ownself : a semi-memoir / Dan Jenkins. — First edition.
pages cm
1. Jenkins, Dan. 2. Sportswriters—United States—Biography.
3. Authors—United States—Biography. I. Title.
GV742.42.J46A3 2014
070.4'49796092—dc23
[B]
2013013822

ISBN 978-0-385-53225-9 (hardcover)   ISBN 978-0-385-53226-6 (eBook)

MANUFACTURED IN THE UNITED STATES OF AMERICA

2 4 6 8 10 9 7 5 3

First Edition

Always for June Jenkins,
my dynamite lady, without
whom none of this would
have mattered much

I can tell you briefly what I think of newspapermen.
The hand of God reaching down into the mire couldn't
elevate one of them to the depths of degradation.
—Ben Hecht, from his screenplay *Nothing Sacred*

Newspaper people speak of a police reporter, a City Hall
man, and a Washington correspondent, but always of a sports
writer. The sports writer is not expected merely to tell what
happened. Upon small, coiled springs of fact, he builds up a
great padded mattress of words. His readers flop themselves
down on this Beautyrest and escape into a dream world where
most of the characters are titantic heroes, devouring monsters,
or gargantuan buffoons.
—A. J. Liebling, from *The New Yorker,* 1946

Don't write me nothin' that rhymes.
—Blackie Sherrod, sports editor of the
Fort Worth Press to a young staff writer in 1948

They went to Elaine's every night, then they came home and went to Europe.

—Danny Jenkins, to a Texas friend when asked what it was like for him and his brother and sister to be raised in New York City with Dan and June Jenkins for parents

Contents

His Ownself

Chapter 1

The Fine Art of Sitting Around
and Hanging Out

IT SEEMS TO ME THAT in my busiest years of writing for a living, I spent most of my free time in convivial bars. I didn't seek out the bars so much for the whiskey as I did for the atmosphere. A decent bar was a place where I could sip a cocktail, smoke a cigarette, have engrossing conversations with friends, and if there was music at all it was a jukebox with Sinatra and Judy and others on it with a regard for melody—in contrast to today's eruptions of Krakatoa. I could sit in comfort and eventually reach for a cheese stick or a deviled egg. Dinner at last.

There were a lot of bars like that. They were easy to find after I'd licked another deadline for—in order of my employment—the *Fort Worth Press*, *Dallas Times Herald*, *Sports Illustrated*, *Playboy*, and *Golf Digest*.

Hotels provided such hangouts. Downtowns offered them. Neighborhoods had them. They provided a calmness and sanity to life, travel, deadlines, and those occasions when an editor might mistake a machete for a pencil.

Truthfully, I can say that in sixty-five years of covering sports and sidelining as a book author, my stuff hasn't been raped and plundered too much. There were a few times at *Sports Illustrated* in the New York days when I'd feel that my stuff suffered cruel and unusual punishment. If an editor, for example, would insert "faster than a speeding bullet" in my copy, I'd resist the urge to throw his pot plant overboard. Instead, I'd take out my revenge by staying in another luxury hotel on the road.

Say it was the Beverly Hills. I'd reserve a cabana by the pool, relax over a cocktail, have a McCarthy Salad, and watch the fat music mogul in thongs and dark glasses yell at people on the phone.

Those were the days when it was almost impossible to abuse an *SI* expense account because the magazine was wallowing in coin. It enabled me to avoid discomfort and inconvenience.

IT WAS IN A BAR THAT I reconnected with the incomparable June Burrage, girl of my dreams since high school. The bar in Fort Worth was the Key Club in the Western Hills Hotel, and we dined later in the Branding Room. We were both between pictures.

After dinner I took out my gold Dunhill, lit her cigarette, stared into her eyes, and said, "I've got Texas with nine and a half over Syracuse in the Cotton Bowl—what do you think?"

She said, "Can I go?"

We should have married years earlier, but life got in the way. I made two earlier mistakes in the marriage game.

My first was Pattie, the high school girlfriend. We were married for, oh, thirty minutes, maybe forty-five. Just long enough for both of us to realize it was financially irresponsible.

The second was less of a marriage than two people finding themselves trapped in an Edward Albee play. Joan was a young English professor at TCU and she happened to come from a wealthy family, which made her twice as smart as me.

Both divorces were almost the same thing as affable. No kids or money involved. Each split fell into the category of You Take the Books, I'll Take the Records.

Flashback. It's 1997 at the Ryder Cup in Valderrama, Spain. I was in the press lounge, which could pass for a bar, when I was told that a lady from America was at the door and wanted to say hello. I went out and found a slender woman in dark glasses and graying hair.

"I'm sorry," I said. "Do we know each other?"

She said, "I'm Joan, you asshole."

Christ, I hadn't seen her in forty years.

I said, "It *is* you! What are you doing here? You used to hate golf. You used to throw clock radios at golf."

"Nice seeing you, too," she smiled.

We laughed and visited for twenty minutes about life itself, then she went back to Austin, Texas, and I went back to acting interested in Spain.

June married at nineteen in her folly of youth, and it didn't last for whatever reason, or reasons, some marriages don't last.

The fact is, I've been the luckiest sumbitch ever allowed to make a living as a writer. Luckier still that June and I found each other. We've produced three wonderful kids—Sally, Marty, and Danny. We enjoy great friends from high school, college, journalism, and sports. We're still laughing and loving our way through life after fifty-four years together.

It's hardly news that there's trouble, strife, and entanglements in everybody's life. But when messy things happen, I tend to fall back on the words of Billy Clyde Puckett.

Billy Clyde didn't go to Harvard, but he was still deep enough to say: "Laughter is the only thing that cuts trouble down to a size where you can talk to it."

MY DOWN TIME WAS MORE SATISFYING in civilized bars. A civilized bar is where it was discovered that the problem with sitting around is you never know when it's over.

Part of the appeal is that cynical wit exists in civilized bars where writers gather. As do suggestions on how editors with tin ears and blue pencils can be captured and put in straitjackets for making stories look like squirrels have been nibbling on them.

Incidentally, I have to say that bars looked more civilized before so many sportswriters began wearing shorts and sneakers. Today you can find dozens of them armed with bottles of funny-colored health drinks. Things that could pass for A-Rod's specimen.

Among them, there's always one who will take it to DEFCON 2 if anybody lights up a Marlboro.

Many are friends and while I'm pleased to see them looking fit and comfortably attired, it's not easy to envision the old heroes of my trade—John Lardner, Red Smith, Damon Runyon—walking around in public in shorts and sneakers.

It's a severe challenge today to find a bar that's not a war zone, even if I only want one Junior and water at this stage of my development. Granted, I used to require twenty to become witty and charming, or rich and powerful, or to make other people interesting.

The mindless din in a bar today renders it next to impossible to chat about worldly things. Like, you know, exactly how many Kardashians are there? Is Sean Penn still grieving over Che Guevara's execution? And how many NFL players will be tackled by their hair this season?

As for the music, melody has been replaced by something that brings to mind dueling leaf blowers, with lyrics written for juvenile delinquents.

A while back I was moved to raise my voice as I sat alone at the breakfast table. In the paper I came across this review of a rapper named Mucus something. I could have the name wrong. The critic wrote:

"A richly textured effort. The lyrics slip past in an elliptical blur. Heartbreak drifts to the surface, leaving only the beautifully conceived sound-scapes catapulting into staggering new dimensions."

To nobody I shouted, "Jesus H. God! It's not Irving Berlin, you pathetic moron!"

In most bars these days even a hold-it is part of the din. Yelling, chirping, screeching. Except she's not a hold-it anymore. Or a stove (over forty), a stovette (under forty), or a chick, a babe, or a shapely adorable. She's a young hotness.

"I note a deluge of young hotness in here tonight," I overheard a young man say shortly after the twenty-first century arrived.

In my day a young hotness was Debbie Reynolds in *Singin' in the Rain*. A mature hotness was Cyd Charisse in *Singin' in the Rain*. Today in my opinion a young hotness suffers from sundry defects. A ring in her nose, a zircon in her eyebrow, a diamond on her tongue, a safety pin in her navel, and a dragon on her back.

Up on the walls there are these TV announcers howling with their unbridled enthusiasm about nothing. Tiger Woods has made a two-foot putt. Tiger Woods has pumped his fist. Tiger Woods has finished 43rd in the tournament but will take away a lot of positives from the experience.

I recall a night in one of these places where a stranger tried to have a conversation with me at the peak of the din.

He said, "You headed to the British?"

"What fish?"

"I said British . . . the Open."

"I hate Oakland."

"I think it's at Birkdale."

"It's your birthday?"

"I liked your story on the Masters."

"You ask her—I think she's with someone."

In this age there are bars I avoid with the same nimble footwork that enables me to avoid fish tacos and kangaroo nachos.

I give you the arena where eight or more NFL games glisten on the TV screens as hordes of intellectuals in Dallas Cowboy jerseys or with blocks of cheese on their heads do fist bumps to celebrate an incomplete pass.

Then there's the rock-café emporium. Among the artifacts on the walls are a framed tooth that fell out of Mick Jagger's mouth when he turned 106 years old, a jar of Vaseline Jim Morrison autographed for Janis Joplin, and the leg of a corpse left over from a Led Zeppelin concert.

So what is a decent bar, you may ask?

To start, it's not political. If you grow loud discussing the issues

5

that divide us today, you have to go outside and stand in the blizzard with the smokers.

I frequently discussed politics with Bud Shrake, one of my oldest friends and a fellow writer—he the Communist infiltrator, me the Vast Right-Wing Conspiracy—but we never got angry. As Bud explained to his liberal Austin friends, "If it gets serious, we settle it at Ping-Pong."

A decent bar becomes a personal clubhouse. Many of the customers are friends. If there's music, it's tuneful. If there's no Sinatra or Judy on the jukebox, there are the anthems of Willie and Kris and Patsy. Which was when country music peaked. The writer Allison Glock summed up today's country in a piece in the *New York Times*. "Pop in cowboy hats," she called it. Damn, I wish I'd said that.

My personal clubhouse has good, simple food at all hours. The all-day breakfast is available. You'll never find quail eggs, avocado, or fois gras on the cheeseburgers. The place isn't fancy. Clean and comfortable does it. The lighting is right. Not too dark, not too bright, just sort of golden. Lighting that in my younger days made the occasional lady look like Barbara Jane Bookman and me look Witty and Charming, Part II.

IN THE *SI* DAYS when I was traveling constantly, there were special haunts that required my presence as soon as the plane landed, my ankles had been taped, and I'd rubbed on the eye black.

Club XIX in the Pebble Beach Lodge was one. It was from the same stool at the end of the bar in Club XIX that I covered four U.S. Opens, a PGA Championship, and twelve Crosby tournaments.

In the evenings the place would be awash with movie stars, golfing heroes, sports immortals. A man could sit there and watch it all come and go, including a variety of tricky ladies, some of whom were even wives. The time in there deserved the name I gave it.

I blurted it out one night in a moment of brilliance. It was when James Garner pushed into my corner to order an after-dinner beverage, and said, "Why am I not surprised you're still here?"

"I'm waiting for Lana Turner," I said. It stuck with friends.

Garner said, "I think I saw three earlier."

Another place that demanded my presence was the Polo Lounge in the Beverly Hills Hotel. I got there too late for Clark Gable, Marlene Dietrich, Will Rogers, and Jean Harlow, but the Polo Lounge was—and still is—a historic landmark for sitting around.

I would stay at "the Hills" when I'd go to L.A. for USC football games, UCLA football games, Ram games, Rose Bowls, Super Bowls, L.A. Opens, book tours, or urgent Hollywood confabs and pow-wows.

I would establish headquarters in the Polo Lounge. The use of a handy money clip earned me the devoted friendship of the three gentlemen who ran the room in those years—Dino, Walter, and Nino.

I couldn't guess how much whip-out it took for me to progress from "Good evening, Mr. Jessup" to "Good evening, Mr. Jamson" to "Ah, Mr. Jenkins, right this way."

I'd be led to one of the front booths on the left, dark green and cushiony. The guacamole, cheese dip, and chips would appear, and a plug-in phone—like I might need to return Paul Newman's call.

BACK IN MANHATTAN, home for thirty years, I'd settle into Elaine's, P. J. Clarke's, and Toots Shor's to relax and enjoy doing three of my favorite off-duty things—smoking, drinking, not giving a shit.

I called it "sailing to Europe" if I devoted a full evening to Elaine's, and found myself ordering backups for total strangers who'd joined my table. The check could equal the passage on an ocean liner to Cherbourg.

I relied on character and conditioning to see me through such nights.

Elaine was sitting with June and me and Mike Lupica of the *Daily News* the night she made the remark that was widely quoted in her obits. A first-time customer leaned in to ask her where the men's room was. She glanced down at the opposite end of the room, and said:

"Uh . . . go to Michael Caine and take a right."

In a joint where celebs were part of the woodwork, I took a celeb to

Elaine's on occasion. A Darrell Royal, a Jack Nicklaus. But my major celeb was David Merrick, the biggest Broadway tycoon in the days when Broadway was Broadway. We became friends when he bought *Semi-Tough* for the movies.

My wife and I often dined at Elaine's with Merrick, and with his associate Allen DeLynn. Allen was a walking book of theater, Hollywood, and sports anecdotes.

It's been written that Merrick was "feared by many, liked by few, but never disregarded." I have to say he was wonderful to us and our kids. He wanted to pay Sally's tuition when she was accepted at Stanford. It made June cry.

I said, "David, it'll be easier on my money clip if I handle the tuition. You can get the car, drugs, guns, and pizza."

It surprised me to discover that Merrick was a big sports fan. I got him a press credential and took him along when I covered the U.S. Open in 1980 at Baltusrol in New Jersey. I found a moment around the putting green to introduce him to Jack Nicklaus. He'd wanted to meet Jack, a fellow icon.

Not long after that, David said at dinner, "You know, actors are great mimics. They can be very talented. But most of them are quite stupid. They'll play a role in a film but not have any idea what it's about until they see it on the screen. They're rather like children. Theater and movies are entertaining, but they're just imagery. A sports event is the true showbiz—it's real."

He had a wicked sense of humor. I once asked him if there was any one thing that had given him the most satisfaction in his showbiz career.

I was thinking *Gypsy, Hello Dolly!, 42nd Street*.

With his usual straight face, he said, "Yes. Seeing to it that Anna Maria Alberghetti never worked again."

THE IDEAL BAR OF ALL TIME was P. J. Clarke's in the years when Danny Lavezzo owned it. The place was a reliable watering hole for the high and low folk of Broadway, Hollywood, TV, sports, politics, fashion, society, publishing, and the press. But the backroom regulars, who were in there three or four nights a week, remained the same. They would be the bookmaker, the homicide cop, the TV guy, the horseplayer, the airline purser, the out-of-work actor, the dilettante, the columnist, the press agent, the sportswriter.

Clarke's late was where June and I closed up shop after two of the most fascinating nights in our Manhattan lives.

One of those was on March 8, 1971. It was the night of the "Fight of the Century" at Madison Square Garden. The vibes were all over town, beginning at noon. It was the kind of night Toots Shor used to reminisce about. Joe Louis and Billy Conn in the Polo Grounds. Tony Zale and Rocky Graziano in Yankee Stadium. A real old-fashioned night in the Apple.

Personally, I enjoyed watching Smokin' Joe Frazier whip Muhammad Ali like a tied-up goat. But the fans were almost as much fun to gaze upon. Half the dudes wore full-length mink coats. Half the dolls from the waist up looked like *The Guns of Navarone*.

The other gala evening was August 23, 1980, when David Merrick took us to the grand opening of *42nd Street* at the Winter Garden. We'd never laid eyes on so much star power under one roof. Every guy in the audience who wasn't Leonard Bernstein was Neil Simon or Bob Fosse. Every dame who wasn't Lauren Bacall was Angela Lansbury. It came close to turning us into tourists from Des Moines.

The musical was a smash hit, but nobody was prepared for Merrick's appearance on the stage after the final curtain. He shockingly announced that Gower Champion, the show's director, had died that day at one o'clock. The audience gasped and fell back in their seats, many starting to sob. Real-life drama on Broadway.

At the cast party in a hotel ballroom, we were seated at David's table. Every star of stage or screen, young or old, stopped by to congratulate Merrick on another hit, and mourn the loss of Champion. The night didn't end until the cast did a number in honor of the director, proving once again that the show must go on.

———

IN CLARKE'S, THERE WAS ALWAYS SPACE for the regulars when a well-known person might be standing in line for a table in the back room, wondering when Frankie Ribando, the maître d', would recognize him or her. Frankie ran the back room like Bear Bryant ran Alabama.

Danny Lavezzo's table—the owner's table—was to the immediate left as you entered the back room. We were sitting there with Danny and Jack Whitaker the night we heard the sharp, unmistakable voice of Frankie saying, "Ten minutes, Arthur."

We looked around at the front of the line to see a distinguished gentleman standing and waiting. It was Justice Arthur Goldberg of the United States Supreme Court.

We were in there on another winter's night when Danny received a phone call telling him that Jackie and Aristotle Onassis were on their way over and would like a table. Danny picked a deuce in the middle room by the window looking out on 55th Street. He arranged for a bodyguard to occupy a table next to the couple.

The bodyguard was a regular, Billy Mack, a TWA purser and horseplayer who sounded like Walter Matthau when he spoke. Danny stood at the end of the long bar that stretched from the front entrance on Third Avenue to the middle room. He wanted to ensure protection from intruders or autograph hounds.

But less than ten minutes after Jackie and Onassis were seated, Billy Mack became the intruder he was supposed to guard them against. Billy pulled his chair over closer to their table, squeezed Onassis on the shoulder, and said: "Is it still snowing outside, Ari?"

I nominate that for the title if a book is ever written about Clarke's.

How did I get to all those good times and good places?

I guess I've reached the point where the author is supposed to say that things will maybe make more sense if he starts at the beginning, and proceeds to explain that he comes from humble origins, except I didn't.

Chapter 2

A Unique and Happy Compound—
with Homemade Biscuits

ONE OF THE BEST THINGS that ever happened to me was coming from a broken home.

It's a particularly good deal if you're an only child and there are loving folks on both sides of the family, which means I was spoiled rotten from every angle. A baby Lab couldn't have had it better.

The pulley bone and a drumstick were reserved for me at Sunday fried chicken dinners, and there were volunteers to make a choo-choo train out of my green beans. It was an even better deal that one side of the family liked sports and the other side liked money.

I have nothing but warm memories of being raised in a home by a self-sacrificing grandmother and granddad—on my dad's side. We lived in a white frame house with a porch swing, a lawn in front and on the side to romp around on, all of it in a modest neighborhood on the south side of Fort Worth, Texas. A caring aunt and uncle lived across the street. A fun-loving cousin and his wife lived next door. A divorced aunt lived with us off and on, as did an uncle in his single days. Nobody shouted or argued in my presence.

It was a happy compound.

I did have a mother and father, but I don't remember living with them. It must have happened—but it couldn't have lasted long. A few months? A year?

Getting to know them helped me understand why. They were uniquely who they were, and I've never thought they "deserted" me. For one reason or another, they just weren't around. That was okay. I had a better deal in the compound anyhow.

What is it with this mandatory law about grandmothers? They have to have names like Me-Me or Me-Maw or Mam-Maw. Mine was Mimmie. But she was Aunt Sally to others. Our daughter is named for her.

Mimmie was born in a covered wagon in Indian Territory, now Oklahoma. She was a teenage girl when the airplane was invented. She lived to fly on jet airliners and watch TV as men walked on the moon. What a window of life.

Like most grandmothers, she was the world's greatest cook. Every morning for breakfast there'd be homemade biscuits and gravy, eggs fried or scrambled, pattie sausage, crisp bacon, homemade preserves. Her banana layer cake with white icing would have solved most of the world's problems. She was still cooking family dinners on Sundays at the age of ninety, and quietly passed away in her sleep at ninety-six.

My granddad was "Pap" at home and "Jenks" to his coworkers. He was E. T. Jenkins Sr., the initials for Elzie Thomas. He was a United States deputy marshal, complete with a pearl-handled .38 and a large gold badge on his belt that looked like he'd won the Olympic shot put.

He was the court deputy when trials were in session at the federal courthouse downtown. I was often taken there to hear him say, "Hear ye, hear ye, hear ye. The honorable United States District Court for the Northern District of Texas is now in session. God save the United States and this honorable court."

Pap ate the big breakfast on weekends, but on workdays he'd have his "health drink." Pour himself a glass of tomato juice, doctor it with Tabasco, add salt and pepper, drop in a raw egg, and chug it down. I could only admire such courage. Afterward he'd have another cup of coffee, light up an Old Gold, peruse the morning paper, and go off to catch the crooks.

Occasionally he'd transport a prisoner in his Essex from Fort Worth to Huntsville, Gatesville, El Reno, Oklahoma, or some other indoor joint.

I was taken along on one trip. I was ten. We went to Huntsville. I sat in the front with Pap and looked at magazines when I wasn't sneaking a peek at the prisoner, a bank robber, I was told, but evidently not too good at it.

My cousin, Sid Whitley Jr.—Little Sid—packed heat and rode shotgun. He sat in back next to the chained-up guy, ready to turn him into a deer, a dove, or a quail at the slightest provocation. The prisoner was a scrawny white man in his late twenties, and had a bony face with red splotches on it. An "Oklahoma face," Pap called it.

I remember hearing the prisoner speak twice. He said, "I sure would like a smoke." And, "I could use me a sody pop."

"When we stop for gas," Pap replied both times.

The experience was intended to be an education for me. Mimmie didn't object to my going. My cousin was a good shot.

On the drive home Little Sid said to me, "You can grow up and go to school and make something of yourself, or you can wind up like that sorry sack of shit."

That may have been the moment I decided to be the first person in the family to earn a college degree. It was the least I could do for all the people who were raising me.

AUNT LOES (she spelled it that way) had a hand in the raising. She was the sister of my dad and my Uncle Mack, and naturally was known as Sister. She had gone through her flapper days and a marriage and divorce to an oilman in Oklahoma.

She was my adventurous aunt. After her divorce she worked for a time in the wardrobe department at Paramount Studios in Hollywood. We'd visit her in the summers.

The trips began when I was eight. Mimmie and I would stay a month with Sister in her apartment on Wilshire Boulevard. Uncles and cousins would drive us to California and back, but once Sister sent us home on the Santa Fe Super Chief.

Exciting deal. Eating in the dining car, sleeping in an upper berth in the Pullman, sitting in the club car with men in business suits and ladies in hats and pearls, and watching America go by.

There were occasions when Sister took me to the Paramount soundstages when movies were in production. In one soundstage they were making *The Plainsman*. I recall watching a scene where Gary Cooper and Jean Arthur argued with each other.

Gary Cooper was tall, Jean Arthur was pretty. I've never forgotten how she smiled at me when she walked past taking a break. Jean Arthur became my favorite actress for a year, despite the fact that she was wearing her Calamity Jane costume that day.

We took trips to San Francisco to see the Golden Gate Bridge, which I found to be orange, to Yosemite to look at huge trees, and to Catalina on the glass-bottom boat.

If I was exposed to anything as glamorous as California, it was the Texas Frontier Centennial back home. It opened in 1936 and glamorized Fort Worth—and entertained me—for four summers.

The idea was to honor the 100-year anniversary of Texas gaining its independence from Mexico. That issue was settled on the outskirts of what became Houston. That's where General Sam Houston's army defeated General Santa Anna's army while hollering, "Remember the Alamo! . . . and although it's never gotten as much publicity . . . remember Goliad!"

It's unfortunate these days that certain teachers and professors would have you believe General Sam Houston's men were nothing but greedy real estate developers, and the poor Mexican troops were chased back across the border only after we confiscated their recipes for tamale pie and cheese enchiladas.

Fort Worth's celebration was Amon Carter Sr.'s revenge on Dallas, which had been selected by politicians as the "official" centennial site. Carter was known as "the Father of Fort Worth." He owned the *Star-*

Telegram and radio station WBAP, was a close friend of FDR and Will Rogers, and even a friend of my grandparents, I'm happy to report.

It was Amon Carter who hired Billy Rose, the flamboyant Broadway showman, to put on an extravaganza that would make Dallas residents learn to cuss properly.

Billy Rose came up with the slogan that was plastered on billboards in both cities and on signposts in between: DALLAS FOR CULTURE, FORT WORTH FOR FUN.

And it was Billy Rose who hired Sally Rand, the platinum-blond fan dancer, to add zest to the Fort Worth celebration. It made big news when Sally Rand arrived on an American Airways plane at Meacham Field, and stepped off to say, "Hi-ya, Texas!"

The Fort Worth Frontier Centennial was anchored by an astonishing showplace, Casa Mañana, a 4,000-seat open-air supper club with a revolving stage. It presented splashy revues where 200 scantily clad Texas showgirls mingled with Broadway stars in "dream sequences."

The centennial grounds offered Jumbo, a musical circus, the Last Frontier, a Wild West show complete with live cavalry, Indians, and a herd of buffalo, the Sunset Trail, a re-created Old West town, Sally Rand's Nude Ranch, and Pioneer Palace, a big rowdy saloon with vaudeville acts and burlesque performers.

Sister would take a leave from Paramount each year to assist in wardrobe for Pioneer Palace and Casa Mañana. This meant that the Centennial baby-sat me on many a summer evening.

Mimmie and I would roam the premises, which were located five minutes west of downtown, an area known today as "the cultural district," where you can find the Kimbell, Modern, and Carter museums. They provide lodging for the richest people in the world—dead artists.

We were given free access to the shows and often attended while waiting for Sister to get off work. In the Pioneer Palace I never tired of watching Pat Rooney Jr. launch his happy feet and vocal chords into "The Daughter of Rosie O'Grady."

I wasn't supposed to be intrigued by another act, a striptease lady named Hinda Wausau. She would disrobe slyly and bump and grind under blue lighting to the strains of "A Pretty Girl Is Like a Melody." The stripper's curves made a kid want to grow up faster than nature allowed.

Big name entertainers turned up at Casa Mañana. I saw Edgar Bergen and Charlie McCarthy, Eddie Cantor, who was slightly larger than Charlie McCarthy. I watched Ray Bolger high-jump more than he danced, and I heard Martha Raye yell louder than any mother in my neighborhood.

The *Star-Telegram*'s top writer, Bess Stephenson, did a loving obit to the Centennial when it shut down in '39. I think she captured what everybody thought about it when she wrote:

"It was a time of splendor and romance and incredible miracles. It was a time of dazzling beauty and warm-hearted gaiety and wholly magnificent gestures. It was a time of extravagance, too, and of picturesque memorable nonsense."

Sometimes I envy my own childhood.

UNCLE MACK TAUGHT ME TO DRIVE when I was twelve. Which is no big deal. Kids today know how to steal cars by the time they're twelve.

I learned in his dark green '36 Ford roadster convertible with a stick shift, clutch, and rumble seat. This was real driving. No hand available for texting.

Mack could do stuff, fix things. He added a bedroom to Mimmie and Pap's house, enlarged the screened-in back porch, built a guesthouse at the back of the side lawn. He was a civil engineer, which came in handy when the war started. Rejected for military service due to a heart murmur, he worked for the Civil Aeronautics Administration, which would become the FAA. He built runways for air bases.

Mack married his longtime sweetheart, Henrietta Taylor, a beautiful girl who became my youngest aunt. She joined the pack of those who were doing their best to spoil me.

I spent the summer of '42 with Mack and Henrietta in Oklahoma City. Mack was overseeing the building of runways at Will Rogers Air Base. One night the three of us saved the Ford roadster's life, or it saved ours. We walked out of a movie and into a tornado. If you've never been near a tornado, it sounds like fifty freight trains passing over your head.

Since this was nighttime we didn't know it but we were only three miles from the funnel. It claimed the lives of thirty-one people, injured hundreds of others, flattening a neighborhood.

Ironically, we'd just seen *Reap the Wild Wind* in the theater. But the movie wasn't about a tornado. It's the epic in which Paulette Goddard has a difficult time choosing between Ray Milland and John Wayne. It's settled for her when the Duke dons a deep-sea diving suit and gets himself devoured by the world's largest, ugliest squid.

Offer me calamari today, I say, "Do you take me for a fool? You never saw *Reap the Wild Wind*?"

THERE WERE OTHERS IN THE COMPOUND that demand a mention. Inez and Big Sid Whitley were the aunt and uncle who lived across the street from us in the red-brick house with thick carpet and the fish pond. They owned Whitley's Drugstore, a magical place for me to hang around. It offered everything from work clothes, guns, hardware, whiskey, and fishing tackle to milkshakes, plate lunches, pills, magazines, and permanent waves.

Next to my grandparents' home was the side lawn, where I created a par-3 golf course. I was the designer, greenskeeper, head pro. The Bermuda greens were three feet in circumference, cut by a hand-pushed lawn mower, watered by garden hose, closely cropped by scissors. The cups were soup cans sunk in the ground, and the flagsticks were the limbs off bushes with handkerchiefs tied to them.

The fifth and sixth holes were rugged. They required shots across the street to Aunt Inez's side lawn—over to the fifth, back to the sixth. But it wasn't enough to negotiate the sycamores along the sidewalks and the telephone wires stretching above the treetops. There were Miz Tarleton's flower beds to worry about, and I can tell you that Miz Tarleton was no fan of golf, boy.

That was junior golf in my day. The toughest challenge facing a junior golfer today is selecting the country club his parents should join, and it better be one where the practice range is acceptable to him.

The house on the other side of my golf course was where Little Sid and his wife, Betty, lived. My cousins. Little Sid was the pharmacist at the drugstore, and Betty was a lively blonde—she edged out Jean Arthur in the cute department. They helped raise me, and acted like it was fun, having no children of their own.

Little Sid and Betty were full of life and laughter and their many friends would drop by to drink and smoke and converse. At times I'd sit quietly off to the side and watch and listen and look forward to doing it myself someday.

ALL THIS WAS DURING THE DEPRESSION, a word I never heard spoken around the house.

Pap never came home at night and said, "Well, I got by another day in this Depression. How did everything go around the house in the middle of this Depression?"

I saw hobo camps, bread lines, and soup kitchens, but only in newsreels. The occasional "hobo" would knock on the front door and ask if there was any work he could do for food. No, Mimmie would tell him, but she'd make him a sandwich and give him a fruit jar of ice tea.

The thing is, everybody in my family had a job. Everybody in everybody else's family I knew had a job. Everybody had a house, everybody had a car, everybody had food. Obviously I didn't realize how fortunate we were because there was this Depression going on.

I'm sure I would have become a better writer if I'd grown up eating pickled pigs feet, worn calluses on my hands from heavy lifting, and traveled by freight train.

I could have written something meaningful instead of sports stories and all those darn novels with happy endings.

Chapter 3

If Dad's Back in Town There Must Be
a Big Sports Event Coming Up

NOW TO SPEAK OF BUD JENKINS, one of the two people who couldn't possibly have raised me. My dad.

He was actually E. T. (Bud) Jenkins Jr., a handsome fellow, man about town, fancier of snappy attire, devout golfer, fierce sports fan, enjoyed the social life—gambling, dining, dancing.

Family historians claimed he won a Charleston contest at the Majestic Theatre downtown with Fort Worth's sixteen-year-old Ginger Rogers, who was Virginia Katherine McMath then, a student at Paschal High, which was Central High in her day, and originally Fort Worth High.

Years later, I asked him about it. He said it was her, but she didn't look like *Top Hat* then. I asked him what he was doing in a dance contest in the first place. He said it was a popular thing in the '20s. They were held often, and you could win prize money.

Everybody said Bud Jenkins was a natural-born salesman. They also said he might sell more furniture if he played less golf. There's a good chance my mother said that before anyone else.

Maybe that's why my dad took a quick powder in their marriage, him being, from all reports, a no-heat kind of guy.

My dad and mother, Catherine Louise O'Hern, were married in

1928, and although it must have happened I don't recall seeing him in the flesh, or feasting my eyes on one of his checkered sport coats, until the fall of 1935, well after he and my mother were divorced. He had come back for a visit. He was living in California, which was where he'd taken a powder to.

I had discovered a piece of evidence revealing that he was a pretty fair amateur golfer. It was a trophy stuck away behind some figurines on a shelf in Mimmie's living room. The engraving on the trophy said that Bud Jenkins and three other guys won the 1934 Fort Worth City Team Championship for Katy Lake, their home course.

Katy Lake was a nine-hole public course with sand greens built by the Missouri-Kansas-Texas Railroad. Aside from catching golf balls, the lake was for fishing, swimming, boating, and there was a lighted dance pavilion. The course was six blocks from my grandparents' house. I played my first round of golf at Katy Lake when I was eight years old.

If I wanted to get ahead of myself, I'd mention that Katy Lake was where a kid named Ben Hogan had taken up the game. That I would get to know Ben Hogan and write tons of words about him while covering his triumphs and losses, and spend more time with him on the golf courses than I did with my own father—well, it's enough to make a man lean back in his chair and say, "Life's a funny old dog, ain't she?"

THE REASON BUD JENKINS DROPPED IN from California was that Slingin' Sam Baugh was slinging touchdown passes for the TCU Horned Frogs and my dad wasn't about to miss the two biggest games of the season that were coming up in his hometown.

When he stopped by in November he let drop the news that he and two buddies had acquired a handful of tickets to the sold-out TCU-Rice game and the even more sold-out TCU-SMU game a week later.

They were going to fill up their flasks and have a high time watching the Frogs defeat the Rice Owls and SMU Mustangs and win the national championship of the United States and all the ships at sea.

I wanted to go to those games, but I'd have been content to listen to them on the radio and use my imagination while Kern Tips handled the broadcast for the Humble Oil and Refining Company. Kern Tips was popular with fans because he said things like, "He's a rolling bundle of butcher knives . . . out there around TCU they call him Joltin' Jimmy Lawrence."

My grandmother settled the issue. She said to my dad, "You're not going to those games without taking this little boy with you. He'll remember it the rest of his life."

TCU's concrete stadium looked bigger than downtown to me, although it held only 30,000 then. Our seats were high up on the 20-yard line of the west side, the press box side. My dad and his pals, Tony and Bob, were each in a dandy sport coat and a fedora worn jauntily. I was the kid in the sweater wearing a large round purple and white button pinned over my heart. The button had a football player's photo on it, a souvenir Bud Jenkins bought for me at a concession stand.

The button said:

I AM FOR

SLINGIN' SAM BAUGH

AND THE

FIGHTING FROGS

I still have it. Never throw anything away.

While Sam was slinging three touchdown passes and pulverizing the Owls, I made the mistake of saying Rice had better uniforms.

The Frogs wore plain white jerseys with purple numerals, khaki pants, and black leather helmets. Dull compared to the Owls in their dashing bright blue jerseys, gold satin pants, and shiny gold-and-blue helmets.

"You don't know what the hell you're talking about," my dad said.

It was on the way home in Bob's car that my dad told the first joke I'd ever heard a human tell. I've never forgotten it.

My dad said, "Knock knock."

I was told to say, "Who's there?"

"Spinach," he said.

I was told to say, "Spinach who?"

He said, "Spin itchin' all night."

I don't believe I laughed as hard as Tony and Bob did.

The following Saturday lives on as one of the most memorable in the history of Fort Worth. Right in there with the meatpacking plants opening in 1902, transforming a cattle town into a thriving city. Right in there with the death of Vernon Castle, the internationally famous ballroom dancer, who died in the crash of his training plane at Benbrook Field in 1917 during the First World War.

The crowd for the SMU game was estimated at 42,000. Temporary bleachers were set up in both end zones, and I remember seeing fans without tickets ram their cars through the wire fence that surrounded the stadium.

TCU and SMU each went into the game with 10–0 records. The national championship was at stake, as was a bid to the Rose Bowl. This brought to town Grantland Rice and the nation's sportswriting elite, and Bill Stern and the nation's broadcasting elite.

None of that was known to me then. What I did know was that the Frogs were wearing the same dull uniforms, and SMU's were better, although I kept that to myself. The Mustangs looked dazzling in their red helmets, two-tone pants of red and tan, and red jerseys with blue numerals and blue stripes running up the rib cages.

I'll let Grantland Rice tell you about the game. I tracked down his story later in life.

FORT WORTH, Texas, Nov. 30—In the most desperate football this season has seen from coast to coast, Southern Methodist beat Texas Christian 20 to 14 today, and carved out a clear-cut highway into the Rose Bowl beyond any argument or doubt.

In the Fort Worth stadium that seated 30,000 spectators over 40,000 wildly excited Texans and visitors from every corner of the map packed, jammed and fought their way into every square foot of standing and seating space to see one of the greatest football games ever played.

With the Rose Bowl at stake, Southern Methodist got the big jump by taking a lead of 14 to 0 behind speedy little All-America Bobby Wilson, the greatest running back of 1935.

Facing this smothering margin Texas Christian came back from the middle of the second period with a counter charge led by Jimmy Lawrence, a rollicking halfback, and Slingin' Sam Baugh, perhaps the greatest passer the game has known.

Tied up 14 to 14 as the game entered the fourth quarter, the big crowd sensed a T.C.U. victory over a fading S.M.U. team, but it was the Mustangs who had the winning drive left. Facing fourth down and eight yards to go and the ball on T.C.U.'s 37-yard line, and under seven minutes to play, Southern Methodist pulled off the most daring play of a daring game. From punt formation fullback Bob Finley instead of kicking dropped far back and pegged a prodigious 48-yard pass deep into the northeast corner of the field.

Bobby Wilson was racing for the ball with two T.C.U. defenders in close pursuit. As the ball cleared his shoulder, Wilson made a leaping, circus catch that swept him into the end zone for the winning touchdown.

Fighting with desperation to the end, T.C.U. twice drove within 25 yards of the Mustangs' goal. As the final whistle blew, Sam Baugh was again putting on a passing attack that was eating up ground and S.M.U. supporters were almost in a panic from Baugh's deathly machine-gun fire.

A bitter Bud Jenkins drained his flask. So did a depressed Tony. So did a disgusted Bob. We sat in the stands for an hour after the game. I listened to them discuss the criminally unlucky ways in which the best team lost—and heard them wish plagues, incurable diseases, and deformed children on every asshole who lived in Dallas.

My dad went back to California after the game, so I could only imagine how happy he must have been with the results of the bowl games on New Year's Day. TCU defeated a strong LSU team in the Sugar Bowl by the baseball score of 3 to 2 while SMU fumbled its way to an embarrassing 7–0 loss to an underdog Stanford team in the Rose Bowl.

Those two results gave the Frogs the No. 1 spot in the Williamson System's final rankings. SMU had already been named No. 1 by the Dickinson Ratings based on the regular season results. Two national champions from Texas, and I'd seen them play.

Every kid should have a big sports event in his life.

FOR THE NEXT SIX YEARS I saw my dad on trips to California to visit Sister in the summers. That's when he lived in Fresno and was married to Patsy, who wore her dark hair short and may have been trying to look like Mary Astor in *Dodsworth*.

He came back to town in June of 1941, a visit arranged to coincide with another big sports event. For the first time, the U.S. Open golf championship was going to be played in Texas, and it was taking place in Fort Worth at Colonial Country Club. Bud Jenkins wasn't about to miss it.

I didn't miss it either. My dad managed tickets for me and Uncle Mack and Little Sid. In my polo shirts, khaki pants, and moccasins, I wandered around Colonial for four straight days. I was sent off on my own with a map of the course, and was told to show up at the putting green around six o'clock to go home.

Wednesday's last practice round found me following the foursome of Byron Nelson, Lawson Little, Gene Sarazen, and Tommy Armour. A photo appeared in the *Star-Telegram* the next day of the four pros striding side by side down the first fairway, and there I am in the background. I still have a print of the shot that Mimmie bought. It hangs on my office wall at home. Long ago I captioned it. Gene Sarazen is saying: "If that little kid back there behind us in the striped shirt grows up to be a golf writer this game is in big trouble."

My dad told me to follow Ben Hogan and Byron Nelson because they were the two greatest golfers in captivity, and they were from right here in by God Fort Worth, and he knew them personally.

The attire of the big-time pros intrigued me. They dressed like a combination of gangsters and movie stars. They wore straw hats with bright hat bands, James Cagney caps, berets, fedoras. They wore shirts with neckties, slipover sport shirts, two-tone shoes, and strange beltless slacks, which hadn't come to my neighborhood yet.

Colonial's bent grass greens were mysterious. The pros made the ball spin backwards when it hit the smooth greens where the grass lay down flat. I'd never seen a golf ball spin backwards, or grass that could lie down flat. Bent grass. Made me wonder who bent it.

I watched Craig Wood play two or three holes, and was told he was winning the Open. He wore a yellow straw hat with a blue and white flowered band, a long-sleeve striped dress shirt, a pair of tan beltless slacks, and constantly swung at the ball with a cigarette in his mouth.

I was disappointed that Ben Hogan or Byron Nelson didn't win. I'd followed them most of the time, having learned they were the two greatest golfers in the world. Hogan came close, finishing third, but Nelson was further back.

I asked my dad how come Hogan and Nelson had lost, considering they were the two greatest players in the world?

"That's golf," he said.

I didn't grasp the depth of his explanation until I was old enough to gamble on golf courses for my own money.

Every kid should have two big sports events in his life.

ONCE AGAIN BUD JENKINS WASN'T SEEN for a while. This was during World War II. He was too old for military service but worked in the defense industry at Lockheed Aircraft in Burbank. Not knowing exactly what his job was at Lockheed, I chose to romanticize that he was helping build P-38s, the fighter plane that was spraying Jap Zeros like insects.

When he did return after the war he arrived with another wife—Margie had replaced Patsy—and another family of two young boys, Ron and Randy, and his golf clubs.

The golf clubs meant that he didn't spend all of his time selling furniture and carpet. He could often be found at Glen Garden Country Club on the southeast side of town, the club where Ben Hogan and Byron Nelson had caddied as teenagers around the time I was getting born.

He continued to sell furniture and carpet until he retired, separated from Margie, and spent his last years living in an apartment in a gated community between Fort Worth and Dallas. He played golf with new friends in the community, had a cat that listened to his birdies and bogeys, and passed away from a stroke at the age of eighty-seven.

My dad may have flunked the child-rearing course, but I'd always be grateful to him for introducing me to college football and pro golf, the two sports that continue to arouse my passion and have given me so much to write about.

Chapter 4

Cigarettes, Coffee, Antiques, and
Looking for Mr. Harger

AT THE TOP OF HER GAME, Catherine Louise O'Hern Jenkins was a stylish lady. She laughed easily and thought she resembled Wallis Simpson if the Duchess of Windsor would smile more often. Or perhaps a brunette version of Carole Lombard when she—my mother—slipped into her full-length leopard coat and slouch hat.

She introduced me to grown-up movies—Bette Davis movies—and they happened to appeal to me more than Westerns of the era. I refer to those Westerns in which cowboys in stylish shirts sat on their horses and sang songs, and galloped their horses fast enough to catch the villains in speeding roadsters.

She chain-smoked Lucky Strikes, drank black coffee day and night, loved playing bridge, surrounded herself for business and pleasure with stacks of newspapers, magazines, and rotogravure sections, built a successful business as an antique dealer and buyer of houses to remodel and sell, and ultimately invented the migraine headache.

If all that didn't disqualify her as a mother consider that making toast and coffee on the maid's day off was only slightly more difficult for her than trying to operate a construction crane.

I was handed over to Mimmie to raise from the age of two. One reason was that I suffered all-conference asthma from birth. My mother was only eighteen when I was born, and had no idea what to do about asthma, other than light up a Lucky and call a doctor. A nurse looked after me the first six months of my life.

My breathing apparently sounded like three squad cars chasing John Dillinger. I spent a good deal of time sleeping under a tent, inhaling fumes from a home remedy of Mimmie's. It slowly cured me, and by the fifth grade I'd outrun the asthma completely.

My mother paid for my upkeep and wisely allowed me to live in the sane surroundings of Mimmie and Pap's home. I'd try to spend weekends with her when she wasn't off on buying trips to Chicago or New York.

Catherine Jenkins was no fan of discomfort. In her two-story red-brick house on Hemphill, the first floor served as her antique shop. Her bedroom was upstairs with a wood-burning fireplace, wall-to-wall carpet, radio, RCA Victor phonograph, desk, sofa, a wall of books, adjoining bath, terrace off the bedroom offering a view of the city's skyline—and cartons of Luckies. My mother said cigarettes kept her from ever being bored.

I envied that bedroom and dreamed of having one like it someday.

By the time I was in the fifth grade I'd discovered the wonders of her RCA Victor phonograph. My regard for melody and lyrics in popular music may have started when I learned to put Decca records on the turntable and listen to the Mills Brothers having their way with "Lazy River," "You're Nobody's Sweetheart Now," and "Paper Doll."

While I was in high school I dropped by to visit her one afternoon, and out of nowhere she announced that I needed a "safer" car. My car was the Ford roadster Uncle Mack had given me. I'd been driving it since my senior year at McLean Junior High.

The fact that I had a car at all was thought by my pals to be obscene, although they didn't think it was obscene when they had a chance to double-date with me.

We were sitting in her living room surrounded by antiques when she decided that since the war was over I should have a Ford sedan with a sturdy roof, air-conditioning, and "fluid drive."

I shrugged an okay, thinking the air-conditioned part had its appeal.

She made a phone call as she smoked, and said, "Lucille, do you still want that blue vase?"

The response was obviously a yes. She hung up and gestured with her Lucky toward a tall antique blue vase with gold trim sitting on a table.

"There's your new car," she smiled.

The way she refilled the fluid in her cigarette lighter has long passed into family legend.

She'd call Goolsby's, Renfro's, or Park Hill Pharmacy, or which-ever drugstore was closest to the house currently under remodeling, and ask them to send someone over to fill her lighter, and as soon as possible, please.

They would.

She would order a taxi if she didn't care to drive herself some-where on business if the address sounded suspicious. It might be in an undesirable neighborhood.

She'd dial Yellow Cab and say, "This is Catherine Jenkins. I'd like a cab, please." And hang up.

The cabs would find her.

June Jenkins delights in these stories. They remind her that I've inherited some of the traits of Catherine Louise O'Hern Jenkins when it comes to problems around the house. Apart from being able to change a light bulb, it's common knowledge that I'm not a handy-man, but I do know how to buy new.

My mother was raised a Catholic. She wasn't a militant Catholic, although the thought of remarrying never entered her mind after my dad jumped ship. She would have dinner dates and bridge partners, but I have no idea if anything happened beyond that.

She made an effort to interest me in her religion by taking me to mass one Sunday when I was, I believe, in the second grade or there-abouts at E. M. Daggett Elementary. The service was at St. Mary's Cathedral and was completely in Latin. I was intrigued by the cos-tumes but didn't understand a thing that went on.

I remember reporting to Mimmie that I never knew God couldn't speak English.

Mimmie was alarmed. She didn't know what to think of Roman Catholicism and its mysteries. She took me to what she thought was a normal church service. It was at the First Baptist Church.

In a stuffy boiling hall downtown, I sat among hundreds of worshippers furiously fanning themselves as Rev. J. Frank Norris stood on a stage in a black suit and shouted at the crowd for an hour.

Rev. J. Frank Norris, in his thundering voice, sternly assured everyone that they were going to burn in hell for an eternity, if not longer. I couldn't help wondering why this should include *me*. I was only seven, and burning in hell for an eternity sounded like rather harsh punishment for somebody who'd done nothing worse than refuse to eat liver.

Congregational religion was saved for me by my Aunt Inez. She introduced me to *her* church, Magnolia Avenue Christian. I found it to be calm and reassuring. The flip side of hellfire and brimstone. For the record, June and I are members of University Christian Church, a splendid structure across the street from the TCU campus, where I dipped my toe into higher education—when I wasn't sitting around.

A TRAGEDY STRUCK IN MY MOTHER'S LIFE when she was a young lady of seventeen. She was in an automobile accident that took the life of her best friend and that of a young heir to one of Texas's cattle and oil fortunes.

Catherine Louise O'Hern had traveled by train to Hollywood to be with Dorothy Scott, her best friend, on the occasion of Dorothy's wedding to Guy Waggoner Jr., the grandson of W. T. (Pappy) Waggoner, a legend among Texas cattle ranchers and oil barons.

On the trip home the afternoon of March 24, 1927, there were five passengers in the car driven by Guy Jr. The other three were my mother and two of Guy Jr.'s buddies. The accident occurred when a tire blew out near Douglas, Arizona. The car spun out of control and crashed.

Dorothy and Guy Jr., the newlyweds, were killed, but Catherine Louise O'Hern and the two male friends were thrown free to the side of the highway. They suffered major cuts and bruises, but lived.

My mother was haunted by the accident the rest of her life, and could never speak of it in length. I had to research it to learn the details.

IN MY VIEW ANOTHER UNFORTUNATE THING happened in my mother's life. It was having Eugenia Harger for her own mother.

Genie, my "bad grandmother," was a small, delicate woman, but she carried a big stick. It was called money. The way she tried to manipulate Catherine, I would have sworn her role model was Gladys Cooper, the actress who played Bette Davis's mother in *Now, Voyager*. I believe Genie was ultimately responsible for my mother inventing the migraine headache.

When my mother and Genie would visit me at Mimmie's, Genie would embarrassingly produce a wad of bills, and peel off a dollar to give me, and say that if I was a good little boy, she would buy me a pony one of these days.

A pony? I didn't want a pony. Where would I keep the dumb thing anyway?

Genie had been left flush by her husband, Thomas O'Hern, the granddad I never knew. He died before I was born. He'd been some sort of executive at the Swift and Armour meatpacking plants. He'd been sent to Fort Worth from Chicago sometime after the plants opened.

By the time I came along Genie had opened a furniture store and found herself another husband, a Mr. Harger. He was her store manager. A heavy-set fellow with a thick mustache, he chewed on a cigar every waking moment. Everyone called him Mr. Harger, including Genie.

I can't remember ever hearing him speak, other than to say a word that sounded like a cross between a grunt and a maybe.

Mr. Harger was responsible for a family game. On Sunday afternoons everybody would pile into my mother's burgundy Packard sedan and go looking for Mr. Harger. When the car was full, everybody meant Genie; Catherine; my mother's older sister, Mary Treadway; her daughter, Betty Treadway, my first cousin; and me. As we grew older, it was Betty Treadway who taught me to laugh at Genie instead of despising her.

It was known that Mr. Harger would be frequenting saloons on Sundays in search of people who wouldn't care to lecture him or order him to move 700 pounds of furniture from this corner to that one over there.

The Packard would take the family along the Dallas Pike, Jacksboro Highway, Camp Bowie Boulevard, Mansfield Highway, Weatherford Highway, Cleburne Road, Granbury Road, Burleson Road, and even one or two roads that weren't named for Confederate generals.

We would cruise past Lola's Paradise, Reba's Hideaway, Coconut Grove, Homer's Lounge, Jenny Lind, Four Deuces, Top of the Hill, and establishments less chic, like Buck's Tavern and the It'll Do.

We never spotted his car on the trips where I was a passenger. Sly old Mr. Harger.

I am named for him. He was Dan Harger, my step-granddad. I am also named for the dead granddad I never knew. I am Dan Thomas Jenkins. Years passed before I realized Genie's money had given her naming rights.

I was amused with their conversations when I'd visit that side of the family, and find myself in a room with Eugenia Harger, Catherine Jenkins, and Mary Treadway. Herewith, a one-act play based on the memories of an idle listener.

INTERIOR. Eugenia and her daughters, Catherine and Mary, sit in an overdecorated living room. Catherine smokes.

CATHERINE: I hear Blanche King is filing for divorce. She'll be better off. Ralph is an oaf.
EUGENIA: Land sakes, Catherine. I've told you a hundred times never to use names and tales together.

CATHERINE: She's still better off. She has her looks.

EUGENIA: Catherine, dear, you really shouldn't smoke so much.

CATHERINE: Mama, how old am I?

EUGENIA: Oh, I wish Mr. Nolan would come on. I do want that sink fixed so badly.

CATHERINE: Mr. Nolan works for *me*, Mama. You're supposed to use Mr. Taylor or Mr. Johnson.

EUGENIA: Catherine, sweetheart, I believe you're boiling too much water for one cup of coffee.

MARY: If Catherine hadn't wanted to stop for coffee last week when we drove to Austin, I wouldn't have locked the keys in the car and had to break a window.

CATHERINE: Austin has scorpions as big as my shoe.

EUGENIA: Lord of mercy, the smoke. If I had my strength I could open a window.

CATHERINE: Mr. Nolan can open it after he fixes your sink.

MARY: I'm going to put a big fountain in the backyard of the next house I do.

EUGENIA: My word, Mary. A child could drown.

MARY: What child?

EUGENIA: Oh, the lawsuits that would come of it.

MARY: Mama, I'm putting in a fountain, not a swimming pool.

EUGENIA: Catherine, darling, you know when you were married to Buddy, I never had to look for a handyman. He was so good at lifting things.

CATHERINE: Mama, nobody ever called him "Buddy" but *you*. He hated it. He thought it sounded like a dog. I'm sure it was one of the reasons he left me.

EUGENIA: I do so wish I could hear better.

MARY: Bud never liked me or Mama.

EUGENIA: I'm so afraid the brewery bill won't pass. It would do so much for my property.

CATHERINE: Mama, you have never approved of drinking. Why would you be in favor of a brewery?

EUGENIA: My lands, dear. It's business.

MARY: Mama has always had a good mind for business. She keeps perfect books. She never rents to colored.

CATHERINE: My God, she lays in wait for an audit.

EUGENIA: Never use the Lord's name in vain, sweetheart.

MARY: I can't wait to start my next house. I've learned that mustard walls never go with anyone's hair. It's one of the things you learn from reading.

EUGENIA: If I had my strength, I could fix the sink myself.

CATHERINE: Mama, you've always thought a partition can be moved in twenty minutes. Mr. Nolan has carried my last slab of marble. Mary, you and Mama can live in a mess. I no longer can.

MARY: I was thinking the other day about the edge I have over other decorators. I've done thirty-seven houses on my own.

CATHERINE: The only reason you may have done thirty-seven houses on your own is because you've never been particular about neighborhoods.

MARY: I have absolutely done thirty-seven. I counted them last night.

CATHERINE: Did you really? I played bridge last night.

Catherine goes to the kitchen for coffee as the CURTAIN FALLS.

Need I say Genie liked to rewrite history?

She would brag about sending Catherine "sailing around the world" to enhance her education when she was young. Not just to Europe. *Around the world.*

What happened was that my mother, at the age of fifteen, and in the company of an aunt and an uncle, sailed to Europe on the SS *Reliance*, a Hamburg-American ocean liner, to visit another uncle, a priest named Charles, who worked in the Vatican in some capacity for Pope Pius XI.

The way Genie told it, Catherine had been granted a private audience with the pope. She said Catherine even "sat on the pope's knee when she was a young girl."

I accepted that last bit of information as fact until I was old enough to realize that if Pope Pius XI had allowed a pretty teenage girl to sit on his knee, somebody missed a scoop.

Chapter 5

I Learned More from Radio and Movies
Than I Did in Any Schoolroom

IF IT'S TRUE THAT LIFE really begins with your first memories, mine consist of a big magnolia tree I wanted to climb, a smooth green lawn I scampered on, and the first action photo of a football game I cut out of a newspaper to put in a scrapbook.

But my first vivid memory, I swear, was when I was five years old. It was watching Mimmie rush around to lock the doors and windows of the house on a night in 1934 only moments after we heard on the radio that Bonnie Parker and Clyde Barrow were in town.

Three months later we heard on the same radio that Bonnie and Clyde were dead.

This was during the Depression I missed.

As I measure it, the 1930s began with the Wall Street crash on Black Tuesday, October 29, 1929, and lasted until the Pearl Harbor attack on December 7, 1941. Life's longest decade, as I see it.

I savor the 1930s. Yeah, I know. It was tough hitchhiking and rugged dust-bowling for the Steinbeck people, but it's the decade I grew up in, and the one I remember with unapologetic affection.

I like to say everything was better in the '30s, but that's not true. It just seems like it when my TV cable goes out. That's when I yearn for the newspapers of the era—they were incredibly more abundant—

and other treasures. Like magazines, movies, movie stars, circuses, white sidewall tires, department stores, gangsters, radio shows, rodeos, detectives, drugstores, soda fountains, swing, jazz, songwriters, tap dancers, Amelia Earharts, nightclubs, drive-ins, carhops, diners, home cooking, passenger trains, and automobiles—how about that sexy '37 Cord with the louvered wraparound grille?

To put it another way, I'll see your Sarah Jessica Parker and raise you four Irene Dunnes. And if you're in need of a leading man, I'd like to suggest Clark Gable or Cary Grant.

In the '30s, Joaquin Phoenix wouldn't get the girl, he'd get the luggage.

Radio and movies had everything to do with my infatuation with journalism. I was more impressed with wisecracking newspaper people on the screen than I was with swashbuckling swordfighters, soldiers in sun helmets, daring aviators in biplane dogfights, ship captains braving storms, and leather-slappin' gunslingers in the Old West.

I wanted to grow up to be:

Peter Warne (Clark Gable), reporter, chasing after heiress Ellie Andrews (Claudette Colbert) in *It Happened One Night.*

Wally Cook (Fredric March), reporter, falling for Hazel Flagg (Carole Lombard) in *Nothing Sacred.*

Walter Burns (Cary Grant), editor of *The Morning Post*, trying to win back ace reporter Hildy Johnson (Rosalind Russell) in *His Girl Friday,* the classic remake of *The Front Page.*

John Jones/Huntley Haverstock (Joel McCrea) coping with Nazis and Carol Fisher (Laraine Day) in *Foreign Correspondent.*

Sam Craig (Spencer Tracy), sportswriter, trying to deal with Tess Harding (Katharine Hepburn), powerful columnist on the same New York paper, in *Woman of the Year.*

I collect "dialogue" movies today. My all-timers, if you insist:

Casablanca, of course. Humphrey Bogart—"I remember every
detail. The Germans wore gray, you wore blue."

All About Eve. Hugh Marlowe—"It's about time the piano
learned it did not write the concerto!"

Dr. Strangelove. Sterling Hayden—"I don't avoid women,
Mandrake, but I do deny them my essence."

Sunset Boulevard. William Holden—"The last one I wrote was
about Okies in the Dust Bowl. You'd never know because,
when it reached the screen, the whole thing played on a
torpedo boat."

Command Decision. Clark Gable—"Right now they're on
oxygen 25,000 feet over Germany. Some of them will be
dancing at the Savoy tonight. Some of them will still be in
Germany."

His Girl Friday. Rosalind Russell—"I'm no surburban bridge
player, Bruce. I'm a newspaperman!"

The Philadelphia Story. Katharine Hepburn—"South Bend? It
sounds like dancing."

The Americanization of Emily. James Garner—"All right, fink.
How do you want me to play it, shy and self-effacing?"

Radio had as much influence on me as the movies. Radio was the
indispensable tonic of the '30s and '40s. It brought drama and laughter into the lives of its listeners, made personal friends of fictional
characters, and often made staying home more fun than going out.

I was a slave to *Big Town*—it was about journalism. Edward G.
Robinson played Steve Wilson, managing editor of the *Illustrated
Press*, and Claire Trevor was Lorelei Kilbourne, Steve's trusty side-
kick. The two of them crusaded against corruption and all things
unsavory every Tuesday night at eight for the benefit of Ironized Yeast
and Lifebuoy soap.

Big Town's signature was an announcer's serious voice telling the
world, "Freedom of the press is a flaming sword! Use it justly, hold it
high, guard it well!"

Journalism aside, I was a sucker for *I Love a Mystery*, an adventure serial that frightened listeners of all ages even if they didn't buy Fleischmann's Yeast. Jack Packard, Doc Long, and Reggie Yorke of the A-1 Detective Agency tracked down evil everywhere on the globe in episodes with creepy titles like "The Terror of Frozen Corpse Lodge" and "The Decapitation of Jefferson Monk." Youngsters less stable than I were known to turn the volume down low and cover their heads with a blanket when *I Love a Mystery* came on.

Friday nights, if I hadn't been taken to a high school football game in the fall, which I usually had, I could count on Pillsbury Cake Flour at nine o'clock to provide this opening:

As a bullet seeks its target, shining rails in every part of our great country are aimed at the heart of the nation's greatest city. Drawn by the magnetic force of the fantastic metropolis, day and night great trains rush toward the Hudson River, sweep down its eastern bank for 140 miles, flash briefly by the long red row of tenement houses south of 125th Street, dive with a roar into the two-and-a-half-mile tunnel which burrows beneath the glitter and swank of Park Avenue, and then . . . Grand Central Station . . .

Years later, the wife and kids and I once found ourselves living on Park Avenue for a couple of decades. This was in the *SI* days. I didn't think of it so much as living amid the glitter and swank as I thought of it as Looking for a Cab.

Barring a natural disaster, Saturday night at eight was reserved for *Your Hit Parade*. Brought to you by Lucky Strikes, the music by Mark Warnow and His Hit Parade Orchestra, the tobacco auctioneers were L. A. (Speed) Riggs of Goldsboro, North Carolina, and F. E. Boone of Lexington, Kentucky. The announcer was Basil Ruysdael, who would say:

Who's No. 1 on the Hit Parade this week? Once again the voice of the people has spoken. You've told us by your purchases of sheet music and records, by your requests to orchestra leaders in the places where you've danced, by the tunes you've listened to on the radio, and those you've played in the coin-operated machines.

Coin-operated machine. Would that be . . . maybe . . . I don't know . . . like a jukebox?

Tension would build toward the close of the show before Bea Wain or Wee Bonnie Baker warbled "Deep Purple," which had fought off "Jeepers Creepers" for No. 1. A bow tie guy named Frank Sinatra didn't join the show until 1943, but he brought his screaming bobby-soxers with him, and when he sang "In the Blue of Evening," throngs of them were known to faint. Some were hired help, it came out later.

At 8:30 on Sunday evenings people caught NOT listening to *One Man's Family* could be expelled from their own family. The program ran forever, to the delight of Tenderleaf Tea. Geezers remember that it was "dedicated to the mothers and fathers of the younger generation, and to their bewildering offspring."

It was the story of the Barbour family, which lived in the Sea Cliff area of San Francisco. Allow me to set the lineup for you defensively. Father Barbour was always in the study saying, "Yes, yes, Fanny," if Fanny ever spoke. Hazel, the divorced older sister, would be baking something in the kitchen while her kids, Hank and Pinky, were up at the Sky Ranch. Paul, the oldest brother and World War I flying ace, was forever in the library, poking around. Jack, the youngest brother, would generally be wondering what he wanted to be in life. And Clifford and Claudia, the twins, were usually sitting down on the sea wall discussing the peaceful sky, the restless ocean, whither existence.

Clifford's and Claudia's penetrating questions about life came to mind one morning as I sat in a booth in the TCU Drug having coffee and a cigarette when a student acquaintance, a guy named Hubert from a town in West Texas, invited himself to join me.

After the football talk, he asked in a weary voice: "Whur old boy gone git at?"

Good question. It was committed to memory, as was the pronunciation. It became a lament around the sports department of the *Press*, as well as in the lounges, bars, and cafés of our wanderings.

"Whur old boy gone git at?" a man would mutter, slumped over, lighting another cigarette, before going to cover a TCU football workout.

THERE WAS PLENTY OF COMEDY ON the radio to take everyone's mind off the hard times—those who were having any. Personally, I thought potato patties and potted meat sandwiches were delicacies.

Amos 'n' Andy was the most popular radio show in history—two white guys, Freeman Gosden and Charles Correll, performing gentle humor in black dialect.

"I'se regusted," "I'm layin' down to think," and "Ain't dat sumpin'" became part of the national dialogue.

Amos 'n' Andy reigned supreme for thirty years in behalf of Campbell Soups and Rinso White. This was despite a group of mongrels in the We-Know-What-Humor-Is-Best-for-You Society that petitioned vainly to sink the show, practicing an early form of political correctness.

For all of the humor of the nighttime shows, I was part of the cult that lifted daytime's *Vic and Sade* above them all. The show was created by a man named Paul Rhymer, and brought to you by the makers of Crisco and Ivory Snow. It was the reason I raced home—on foot or bicycle—by 3:30 every afternoon, Monday through Friday.

It was a daily slice of life rooted in America's heartland which so closely touched the truth of everyday people that the exaggerations were forgiven, if not beloved. Since the time slot was surrounded by soap operas, the announcer proudly called it "an island of delight in a sea of tears."

The show revolved around Vic and Sade Gook, "radio's home folks," played by Art Van Harvey and Bernardine Flynn, who lived in "the small house halfway up in the next block." With them in this town in Illinois was their son, Rush, played by Billy Idelson, who addressed his father as "Guv" on the occasions when Vic addressed Rush as "Egg-Crate" or "Brain-Fog." But the character that stole the show was Uncle Fletcher, played by Clarence Hartzell, the only other voice on the program.

Uncle Fletcher was the befuddled relative and uninvited drop-in visitor who droned on about people and places the Gooks didn't know or care about. Not to compete with Paul Rhymer, but one of Uncle Fletcher's rambles would go:

> Frank Gumlooper left Dixon in nineteen-ought-seven. Moved to Dismal Seepage, Ohio. Knew a feller committed suicide jumping off a piano. Married a woman four foot wide, had her committed to the Missouri State Home for the Freckled. Invented a fingernail file run by music. Later died. Yes, sir. Stuff happins.

Sade's best friend was Ruthie Stembottom. They collected washrags from sales at Yamilton's department store. Vic's pals included Hank Gutstop, Ike Kneesuffer, and Rishigan Fishigan from Sishigan, Michigan, who married Jane Bayne from Paine, Maine. Rush's pals were Blue-tooth Johnson, Smelly Clark, and Rotten Davis.

Rush was devoted to reading books about Third Lieutenant Stanley, who once picked up a camel by its hind legs and hammered a vile Arab sheik senseless. And he talked of going to the Bijou Moving Picture Theatre to see Gloria Golden and Four-Fisted Frank Fuddleman. They once starred in a movie that bore my favorite title: *You're the Cowpuncher of My Dreams, Foreman Hastings*.

TELEVISION HAS NEVER DONE IT FOR me the way radio did. First of all, I didn't watch TV the first twenty years it existed. Maybe a sports event or newscast. The occasional *Tonight* show when Steve Allen was the host and Steve and Eydie might appear. Glimpses at the *Show of Shows* with Sid Caesar. I tried sitcoms to see what others found so hilarious but gave up on their pie-in-the-face humor.

This was until *The Mary Tyler Moore Show* in the '70s. It's the best sitcom in the history of network TV. It's the only sitcom I ever saw interrupt a bunch of guys drinking in a bar. It happened at the Bel-Air Hotel when a group of us were in town for the L.A. Open. Somebody realized what night it was, and what time it was, and yelled at the barkeep to turn on *Mary Tyler Moore*. Could there be higher praise for a sitcom?

The best cable sitcom in history was *The Larry Sanders Show*. It was one of the reasons to go on living. Best BBC sitcom: *Fawlty Towers,* although there were only twelve episodes.

My viewing habits today settle comfortably into selective sports events, old movies, and the occasional saga—a *Tinker Tailor Soldier Spy, Smiley's People, Jewel in the Crown,* or *Downton Abbey.*

Oh, and Fox News, the only news program network that doesn't seem to hate America.

Esther Newberg, my friend and longtime literary agent, groans when I sneak in a political line. I give her a hug and say, "There, there, enjoy your chic Manhattan apartment and your second home in Sag Harbor that's worth a tidy sum. You're my favorite kind of lib."

I see that my entire TV life has flashed before your eyes.

HOW MANY OF US REMEMBER LEARNING to read? I don't recall sitting on someone's lap while they turned pages, saying, "Dog . . . cat . . . boat . . . touchdown." All I know is, one day I could read.

My folks may have started me out on comic strips. *The Adventures of Smilin' Jack* might have done it. Or it could have been something deeper. A Big Little Book. Say, *Flash Gordon and the Monster of Mongo.*

But after I learned to read, teachers did all they could to make me hate it. They made me read about reapers, sickles, and cotton gins. Show me a kid who likes to read about reapers, sickles, and cotton gins, and I'll show you a potential serial killer.

I don't remember the sex-obsessed classmate who put a copy of *God's Little Acre* in my hands, the novel disguised in a brown school-book cover. But reading about Darling Jill making herself naked for half the male population of North Carolina was considerably more interesting than reapers, sickles, and cotton gins.

The teachers could bore you in other ways. I told Miz Lewis in Daggett Elementary that in adult life I really wasn't going to need to know how many bushels of wheat I could load into one boxcar. I finally wore her down.

Today I reread for inspiration as much as I read for enjoyment. When I read for enjoyment it means plunging into Michael Connelly, Robert Crais, Lee Child, John Lescroart, Phillip Margolin, Daniel Silva, and friends John Sandford and Sandra Brown.

Not a lot of Chaucer and Milton on my shelves.

Tops on my reread list:

John Lardner. Finest sportswriter who ever lived. The two best Lardner collections are *Strong Cigars and Lovely Women* and *It Beats Working*. This son of Ring Lardner once wrote the greatest sports lead in history. This one first appeared in *True* magazine: "Stanley Ketchel was twenty-four years old when he was fatally shot in the back by the common-law husband of the lady who was cooking his breakfast." Red Smith called it "the greatest novel ever written in one sentence."

S. J. Perelman. *The Best of S. J. Perelman.*

James Thurber. *The Years with Ross.*

Noel Coward. Plays, short stories, and his only novel, *Pomp and Circumstance*, which is weepingly funny.

Damon Runyon. *The Damon Runyon Omnibus*. And dig up his newspaper piece on the Al Capone tax evasion trial, which brilliantly opens: "Al Capone was quietly dressed when he arrived at the courthouse this morning, bar a hat of pearly white, emblematic, no doubt, of purity."

Dorothy Parker. *The Portable Dorothy Parker.*

Raymond Chandler. *The Big Sleep* and the other Philip Marlowes.

George S. Kaufman and Moss Hart. *Six Plays* by Kaufman &
Hart.
Michael Shaara. *The Killer Angels*. If you only read one book
on the Civil War . . .
Herman Wouk. *The Winds of War* and *War and Remembrance*.
They give Tolstoy two-up a side.
Bryan Forbes. *The Rewrite Man*. Tops among Hollywood
novels.

There are these occasions when I'm asked by college kids what I
like to read and what authors have influenced me. I answer with some
of the usual suspects listed above. Lardner, Parker, Thurber, Perelman. But the minute I mention those names I notice their expres-
sions struggle to seek a balance between puzzlement and lost in the
forest.

I've actually had a student say to me, "When I graduate, I think I'll
write novels and make movies. That looks like fun."

Kids today.

Yes, sir. Stuff happens.

Chapter 6

Wherein the Outwitted Mentally Resort
to Physical Violence

AMERICA WENT TO WAR on December 7, 1941, while I was in the White Theatre on the south side of Fort Worth watching Richard Arlen and Eva Gabor in *Forced Landing*, a non–Academy Award nominee. No, I don't remember what forced the landing, or what kind of landing it was, but I do recall one line of dialogue: "Pull up!"

I'd seen everything else that looked promising the day before downtown on 7th Street, our street of dreams—three movie houses, a chili parlor, a coffee shop, a soda fountain, and a nightclub. After Cary Grant didn't push Joan Fontaine over the cliff at the Hollywood Theatre, I went on to the Palace to be overwhelmed by the performances of two remarkable thespians in a double feature.

First came the old Texas Aggie, John Kimbrough, in *Lone Star Ranger*. With a football under his arm, "Jarrin' John" trampled a Hupmobile, mistaking it for—this is just a guess, don't hold me to it—a pile of Rice Owls.

Then came the old Horned Frog, Sam Baugh, in *King of the Texas Rangers*. Here, Sam found himself in a fast-draw situation with a gunslinger. But Sam happened to have a football within reach, so the gunslinger's six-shooter was no match for Sam's bullet pass. Knocked the six-shooter right out of the gunslinger's hand, if you can believe it.

Now on that Sunday I found myself caught in the midst of a celebration when I left the White Theatre and went to slide my Cromer's Ace out of the rack and pedal home.

Buford and Grady, two older punks from the neighborhood, were happy about something. They were whooping and firing imaginary machine guns at the clouds, the sidewalks, the Texaco station, Opal's Beauty Shop, and each other.

"We're at war!" Buford hollered.

"We gonna keel all them yellow sumbitches," Grady yelled.

"What yellow sumbitches?" I asked.

"The Japs," Buford said.

"What Japs?"

Grady said, "The Japanese Japs, that's who. Sumbitches sunk our battleships. They bombed Pearl Harbor. It's on the radio."

I said, "Where's Pearl Harbor?"

"Aw, out there around Los Angeles somewhere," Buford said. Grady said, "Yeah, it's where we was keepin' our battleships and our Navy sailors. The Japs sneaked up on it."

Buford's burr haircut blended in with his filling station shirt and soiled corduroys. Grady's burr haircut went with the patterned sleeveless sweater with the Yo-Yo champion crest on the front. He claimed to have won it in the Yo-Yo contest at Bob's Grocery. He bragged that he'd done all the required tricks better than anybody with his Filipino Twirler—walk the dog, around the world, rock the baby, shoot the moon—and wrapped up the title by looping the loop sixty-seven times without missing.

I, however, knew that Blinky Murdock won the Yo-Yo contest at Bob's Grocery—he never lost one. Grady had wound up with the sweater after informing Blinky that he could give Grady that fuckin' sweater or his front teeth.

It was no secret that Grady and Buford were members of the Berry Street Bandits, a gang that wasn't good for anything but shoplifting, shooting pool, and puncturing automobile tires. They would grow up to realize their boyhood dreams. They went to Chicago, became hoodlums, got killed.

There were other gangs around town that were better known and more dangerous. The Cue Racks gained the most fame. Their members wore ducktails, carried switchblades, and did the best impressions of Billy Halop and Leo Gorcey.

I said to Buford and Grady, "I've been to Los Angeles, but I've never heard about a Pearl Harbor out there anywhere."

"You been to Los Angeles?"

"Yeah," I said. "Folks took me in the summers."

Grady said, "I guess you saw a lot of movie stars, huh?"

"I did," I said, watching Buford spray a city bus with imaginary machine-gun fire as it passed the corner of Hemphill and Berry.

"Like who?" said Grady.

"Gary Cooper."

"Bullshit!"

"I *did*. My aunt worked at Paramount and I was around there when they were making movies."

"Damn. What else did you see?"

"Oh, the ocean. Mountains. Lot of fancy cars. Big old houses. Tall palm trees everywhere."

Buford said, "Shit, Corpus Christi's got palm trees. You could have gone to Corpus Christi."

"I better head on home," I said, climbing on my bike.

Grady said, "Your folks got any guns? My daddy's got a .410 and a .22. Them yellow sumbitches could be in Amarillo by Wednesday."

THE FOLKS AT HOME HAD BEEN crying. Mimmie, Pap, and Sister were gathered around the radio, learning that three battleships had been sunk and others damaged, and the Japanese had bombed places named Hickam Field and Schofield Barracks.

I learned that Pearl Harbor was in Hawaii, so the possibility of the yellow sumbitches being in Amarillo by Wednesday seemed fairly remote.

The radio was saying President Roosevelt was going to declare war on Japan, Germany, and Italy tomorrow. Pap said Tojo and Hitler and Mussolini must really be dumb to pick on us, and there wasn't going to be anything left but their piss stains when the United States got through with the "slant-eyed shit-asses, goose-steppin' krauts, and greaseball wops."

Not a lot of political correctness during the war. The outwitted mentally had resorted to physical violence, and the USA was going to make their sorry butts pay for it.

Mimmie dabbed her eyes with a handkerchief, and said, "Lord, I never thought we would have to go through this again. Uncle Will fought in France the last time. It took him a good long while to get over it."

Uncle Will was one of her brothers. In our attic I had come across Uncle Will's "leggerns," canteen, campaign hat, and a jacket with the patch of the 36th Infantry Division on the sleeve. The 36th was the "Texas Division." Those doughboys had trained at Camp Bowie on the west side of Fort Worth before they sailed overseas to fight at a place called Château-Thierry.

As the reality of things kicked in on me, I turned to selfish interests. I wondered how many of my uncles and cousins and older guys I knew in the neighborhood would go off to war, and how many might not come back?

It never entered my mind the United States could lose the war. God would not let that happen. God was *not* going to let a bunch of Japs, Nazis, and Italians rule the world.

I mean, those people didn't even play college football.

MY WAR, the early part of it, was spent wearing rope-sole shoes, eating chicken burgers, playing golf instead of collecting coat hangers and tinfoil, and not sitting under the apple tree with anyone else but the Andrews Sisters.

Rope-sole shoes were the thing in '42 and '43. Leather had gone to war. So had Lucky Strike Green. This had inconvenienced my mother. She said Luckies in a white package didn't taste the same.

The rope-sole shoe was made of woven grass, straw, and weeds. They looked like a vegetarian's saddle oxfords.

A chicken burger was ground-up chicken—and who knew what else was in there with it—shaped into a pattie, fried in batter, and put on a bun like a hamburger. I can't believe I liked chicken burgers.

I didn't fall for the coat hanger and tinfoil trick. No guy did. It was the girls our age who went house to house collecting coat hangers and tinfoil, doing their patriotic duty while counting the days till they were fifteen or sixteen and could go to the Teen Canteen and jitterbug with soldiers and sailors.

I wondered what the coat hangers and tinfoil might be good for? When the Japs would charge our troops hollering, "Die, Yankee dog" or "Fooka Babe Ruth," would our troops pound them with balls of tinfoil? Lash them with their coat hangers? Why not just shoot their asses?

Not to make sport of those who served in World War II. They *were* the Greatest Generation. As far as that goes, anybody in the USA who wears a uniform, today or yesterday, is a hero to me. Their service makes it possible for me to observe fun and games for a living.

THE WAR SAW TO IT THAT 1943 was the worst year for sports in the history of America.

Every baseball and football team was depleted. Dozens of events were suspended for the "duration." Duration. Here was a word nobody had ever heard before, or used in conversation. Betty Jean Anderson, my fiancée from the fourth grade through the eighth, never heard me say, "Can I take you to a movie at the Parkway for the duration?"

There *was* a World Series in '43. Baseball was one of the things we were fighting for. The Yankees beat the Cardinals in five games, but only the seam-heads who covered baseball knew anyone in the line-ups. A Nick Etten with the Yanks, a Danny Litwhiler with the Cards.

College football was all about Notre Dame and service teams like the Iowa Pre-Flight Seahawks and the Great Lakes Naval Air Station Bluejackets. Notre Dame was voted No. 1 for beating war-weakened teams by 70 or 80 points every Saturday. Angelo Bertelli, the Notre Dame quarterback, won the Heisman Trophy while playing in only six games. Only a Notre Dame guy could pull that off.

Over in the blue-collar world of pro football the most interesting thing happened before the season started. For financial reasons the Philadelphia Eagles and Pittsburgh Steelers combined their teams to become the "Phil-Pitt Steagles." They were the worst of the NFL's eight teams, and undoubtedly the one with the funniest name.

As for the sport of golf, well, there wasn't much golf in '43.

On a personal level, Katy Lake closed. I may have been the last to play the course, and that was after it closed. I played it when the fairways were brown, bordered by weeds, the sand greens were cracked and hardened, and the lake was so stagnant a dinosaur wouldn't go near it.

The real story of golf in '43—and most of '44—was that the majority of the PGA Tour's brand names were in the service. This was a patriotic group I'm happy to list:

Lt. Ben Hogan, Seaman Sam Snead, Sgt. Lloyd Mangrum, Seaman Jimmy Demaret, Lt. Horton Smith, Cpl. Paul Runyan, Lt. j.g. Lawson Little, Sgt. Vic Ghezzi, Sgt. Dutch Harrison, Pvt. Tommy Bolt, Capt. Jay Hebert, Sgt. Clayton Heafner, Sgt. Skip Alexander, Pvt. Chick Harbert, Sgt. Jimmy Turnesa, Sgt. Ted Kroll, and Cpl. Jackie Burke.

Jay Hebert, a Marine captain, hit the beach at Iwo Jima; Army sergeant Ted Kroll was wounded three times in Italy; and Lloyd Mangrum saw action on D-Day and later at the Battle of the Bulge.

Mangrum's service record became fodder for Jimmy Demaret, a quote machine, one of golf's originals, a sportswriter's dream—like Lee Trevino in a later era. I enjoyed every minute I was around Demaret.

Demaret's classic remark about Mangrum was too risqué for the papers. He liked to say, "Man, I got tired of reading about 'Purple Heart Veteran Lloyd Mangrum.' Hell, he got one of 'em for stepping on a broken beer bottle running out of a Paris whorehouse."

Demaret spent his time in the Navy playing golf with the brass.

But he insisted that he made as big a contribution to the war effort as "Remember Pearl Harbor."

In Demaret's line of duty, he was often compelled to say: "That'll play, Admiral."

AS THE WAR WAS TAKING TURNS for the better, I came home from school one afternoon to find an old Royal standard typewriter on the dining room table. A stack of typing paper sat beside it.

My Aunt Loes—Sister—had rescued the Royal from Whitley's Drug. She'd found it in a storage room, had taken it to be worked on, and the machine was now mine.

When she returned that evening from her job at the U.S. Army Quartermaster Depot, a sprawl of prefab buildings south of town, she said, "If you want to work for a newspaper someday, you'll have to learn how to type. I can help you get started."

She did. Soon enough I'd semi-memorized the keyboard and found it rewarding to make words land on the paper and stay there. It became fun for me to copy war stories out of the *Star-Telegram* or *Press*, and pretend I'd written them. Then one day I started to rewrite them.

MOSCOW, Jan. 11 (AP)—The hard-charging Russians today pushed deeper into the Caucasus, which is in Russia or Germany or somewhere between the chest and the stomach.

LONDON, Sept. 8 (AP)—Gen. Dwight D. Eisenhower's headquarters announced today that Italy has surrendered to the Allies, and when last seen Benito Mussolini and his mistress were racing toward the Swiss Alps—with two orders of spaghetti and meatballs.

GUADALCANAL, Feb. 11 (UP)—The battle ended at sundown today in the first complete American victory in the South

Pacific. Old Glory flies unchallenged over this island—and there are a lot of yellow sumbitches lying dead around here.

Now I knew for sure that I wanted to be a newspaperman someday, preferably a sportswriter, even if I never got a chance to write anything but bowling agate.

Chapter 7

Fast Times at Paschal High on
the Way to a Career

SOMEBODY HAS SAID you're never more grown up than you are in high school. Might have been me. It basically applied to me.

Let's go over the checklist.

Had a car. Check. Only three or four of us did. The war, you see. I arrived at Paschal High in the fall of '44 in the green convertible roadster with the rumble seat, and departed in the spring of '48 in the black air-conditioned Ford sedan.

This gave rise to a remark from pals who were less fortunate than I in the area of transportation. It went, "Hey, Dan! Can I kiss your ass for a ride to town?"

Had pocket money. Check. The lavish $15 weekly allowance my mother gave me was embarrassing, but I bravely managed to deal with it.

Made close friends for a lifetime. Check. This included boys *and* girls. We chose each other. First, you had to pass the sense of humor test. One of the members of our group was June Burrage, blindingly gorgeous brunette, leader in the clubhouse of Fort Worth beauties, but even a better person. Only God could have arranged a future in which June would become my wife and the mother of our precious children. But first . . .

Had steady girlfriend. Check. Paschal was known for its shapely adorables. In my day Pattie Ann O'Dell—a close friend of June's, as it happened—was among them.

I'd first seen Pattie sitting on the trunk of an elephant in Jumbo, Billy Rose's musical circus at the Texas Frontier Centennial. She was four. I saw her again when she was ten on the stage of the Parkway Theatre at the weekly Saturday morning talent show. She was singing and tap-dancing to "Five Foot Two." But she was no Ginger Rogers, and wanted to be a normal person anyhow. We met in Paschal and went together all through school.

After our hasty, post–high school marriage we meandered off in different directions. She married again and raised a family of her own, but the three of us—June and I and Pattie—remained good friends for the rest of her life. She passed away a few years ago, and we were at her bedside in the hospital shortly before she took her leave. It was a Paschal thing.

Had our "Hoosiers moment." Check. In my freshman year the school won everything in the city that mattered—football, basketball, track, golf, tennis, band, school paper, pinball, partying, most rich kids. You could say it gave us a swagger.

The football team started it off in the fall of '44 when Guy Proctor, Danny Walker, Corky Groce, and other stalwarts led the Panthers to a 10–0 regular season and the school's first city championship in eleven years.

Then came our *Hoosiers* moment. A godlike figure named Jackie Robinson carried Paschal to the 1945 state basketball championship, the first that a Fort Worth high school had won in any sport.

Jackie was a handsome guy, and a commanding presence on the court. He was only six feet tall yet he could dunk the ball. That word hadn't reached our vocabulary yet. We said he could "stuff" it or "lay it in." Jackie could leap, fly, and hang, and he was white—may the politically correct not break out the windows in my car for mentioning that detail. Everybody in every Southern school back then was white. Not my fault.

The *Hoosiers* moment came in the state semifinals in Austin when

Paschal met Houston Milby, a tall, rangy team that had been favored to win the title. With a minute to play, Milby led by one point and controlled the ball. A shot clock wasn't in the rules then. Teams could stall.

I can still see what happened in slow motion. Milby's star, Billy Joe Steakley, is dribbling on the front line, stalling, the time clicking away. Jackie is guarding him. A group of us B team freshmen are sitting behind the Paschal bench and helping Coach Charlie Turner holler, "Get the ball, Jack . . . get the ball, Jack!"

The ball leaves Steakley's hand, but never gets back to him. Robinson strikes like a lightning bolt, steals the ball, and races down the court for the layup that puts Paschal ahead by one—and for good.

Robinson went on to Baylor and became a two-year All-American and led the Bears to the 1948 NCAA final—the first Southwest Conference school to go that far, and it was no embarrassment to lose to Coach Adolph Rupp's great Kentucky team. Later Jackie was on the U.S. squad that won the gold medal in the '48 Olympic Games in London. He became a Baptist pastor and theologian, and preached in more than eighty countries.

Most people have an unforgettable high school hero. Now you've heard about mine.

Lettered in sports. Check. Basketball and golf. Went out for football. Wanted to be a quarterback. Soon found out I had a skinny neck. You can't have a skinny neck and play football—unless you want to die in your teens.

Learned discipline from tyrannical coach. And learned pain, agony, humiliation, suffering, and embarrassment, plus, according to Coach Turner, a man I would always picture in gray sweats: "Nothing in this world is more important than WINNING—and this includes your family, your girlfriend, your health, and your car."

So we gave our all for this robust, thirty-year-old, prematurely bald coach armed with a paddle. We did it to earn a letter sweater and a gold charm championship basketball encrusted with a purple "P" on a key chain to prove we'd risen above the level of a "worthless shit-ass."

Anyone who played for Coach Turner, back in a feudal era when he built championship teams out of pampered, spoiled, arrogant snots by working you out until you suffered a near-death experience, and by using his two-foot-long wooden paddle on your gym-shorts ass, will testify that he made Coach Bob Knight look like Bing Crosby playing Father O'Malley in *Going My Way.*

There were many ways in which you could suffer Coach Turner's verbal abuse and the burning sting of his paddle. I offer these:

Five licks for being seen in the front hall talking to your girlfriend between classes.

"You better learn to guard your man the way you guard that tomato-mouth floozy who's got you by the balls. Bend over."

Ten licks for not running the weave properly in workout, even after he's thrown a chair at you from across the court.

"You do that one more time and I'm gonna tear off the top of your head and shit down your neck."

Ten licks for attempting a bounce pass into traffic.

"How many times I got to tell you bounce passes are made to get stolen? If you're a basketball player, I'm a Mexkin aviator."

Five licks for every layup you miss in a game.

"You couldn't hit the floor if you squatted down to pee on it."

Three of us on the '47 team would never forget the night we wrapped up the city championship with a squeaky win over the Riverside Eagles in their gym across town—I made the winning shot at the buzzer, cue the applause. I'd like to say it was a leaping jump shot, but it was more the case of my defender glancing at a set of tits in the crowd and me going around him for a layup.

There was one game left on our regular schedule, but that night three of us decided to celebrate. I went with Marty McAllister and Jim Rich, two of my good friends and teammates, to Herb Massey's restaurant on our side of town to reward ourselves with Herb's chicken-fried steak followed by pecan pie à la mode. The restaurant would later be immortalized as "Herb's Café" in my novel *Baja Oklahoma.*

We were into the pecan pie à la mode when we saw the front door open and Coach Turner enter the restaurant.

Jim Rich whispered, "Jee. Zus. Christ."

Marty McAllister whispered, "Ho. Lee. Shit."

I whispered, "Mother. Fuck. Me."

The coach came straight to our booth and glared at the plates of pie à la mode on the table. The look on Coach Turner's face told us he might as well have been staring down at glasses of whiskey and packs of Chesterfields.

In a weak voice Marty said, "We're celebrating our championship, Coach."

"Uh-huh," Turner said. "Well, I hope you enjoy it because your asses belong to me tomorrow."

The next day a math major couldn't have counted the number of licks we got, the laps we ran, and the fingertip push-ups we did.

Despite all the torture, we were proud to have played for Charlie Turner. He taught us discipline, teamwork, respect, all those "life lessons" you learn in sports. And he made us winners. The older we got, the more we appreciated what he'd done for us.

Worked on school paper. Check. Margaret Caskey was the nice lady who taught journalism, oversaw the publication of *The Pantherette*, and survived a period when she allowed four flippant students to kidnap freedom of the press and use it for their own amusement.

I plead guilty for my part in the crime, and enter a plea for Bud Shrake, Dick Growald, and Elston Brooks, all of them lifelong friends and talented writers. They can no longer speak for themselves, having been invited to join the Skipper in his newsroom upstairs.

The four of us had been pals since junior high, and if the group had any one thing in common, it was the notion that nothing was sacred when it came to humor, including anything in your personal life.

Elston Brooks went from writing a column called "Babbling Brooks" in the school paper to a long and illustrious career at the *Fort Worth Star-Telegram*. Fresh out of high school, he became a prize-winning crime reporter, and by nineteen he doubled as the paper's entertainment columnist.

Elston's major accomplishment in life was the book he wrote, *I've Heard Those Songs Before*. The songs were the Top Ten tunes from fifty years on *Your Hit Parade*, the radio show, to which he was incurably addicted. But well before the book's publication in 1981, Elston was memorizing the lists, and it became part of the entertainment when we'd gather at parties at someone's house or in hotel suites we'd rent for the night.

You could ask Elston what was the No. 1 song in the last week of April in 1942, and he'd sing the answer.

"Somebody else is taking my place," he'd sing. "Somebody else now shares your . . ."

Okay.

"While I was trying . . ."

I've got it.

". . . you go around with a smile on your . . ."

Then he'd say, "Ask me something hard."

All right. What about the last week in May 1932.

"It was only a shanty in old shanty . . ."

Okay, okay.

". . . just a tumbled down shack by the old railroad . . ."

I've got it, I've got it.

Dick Growald went from covering the Spanish language department for *The Pantherette*—"The Spanish class studied Spanish last week but mostly spoke English"—to becoming an acclaimed foreign correspondent for United Press. He grew a big black mustache and once lost fifty pounds on a six-week diet of black coffee and Anacin. The wire service sent him everywhere over a span of more than forty years as a correspondent or bureau chief—Paris, Berlin, China, Moscow, London, Vietnam, the White House.

He would draw humorous cartoons of himself on his exotic stops and send them to friends. The one I cherish most is Dick dining with what looks like Henry Kissinger in Beijing, and a waiter is saying to him: "And what will you be having with your fish head?"

No two ink-stained wretches were more firmly joined at the carriage return than Bud Shrake and I over so many decades I have to stop to count them. Six, is what it was.

We typed our way through *The Pantherette*, *The Skiff* at TCU, the

Fort Worth Press, fourteen months in Dallas on separate dailies, on up to *Sports Illustrated* in Manhattan.

We combined that last gig with writing novels and trying to master the craft of dumbing down screenplays for Hollywood producers who never read them, but had "coverage."

Their reaction to our collaborations or singular efforts was always instructive. A studio mogul once said to me, "Jesus, do you know how much that fucking dust storm would cost?"

Caught a career break. Check. I wrote a thing in *The Pantherette* that was noticed by a guy named Julian Read, a sportswriter on the *Fort Worth Press*. He passed it along to Blackie Sherrod, who was running the department for the aging Pop Boone. Blackie liked it enough to hire me for a speedy $25 a week. This was two weeks before I graduated from Paschal, and three months before I would enter TCU.

I'd written a takeoff on Amos Melton's "Purely Personal" column in the *Star-Telegram*. Sample of Amos:

"**Pete Donohue**, the old Frog hurler who jumped straight to the majors, has a funny yarn about **Rabbit Maranville**. I'll spin it for you one of these days. . . . Street nod to **Mayor Edgar Deen**. . . . **Dub Kirk** out Mineral Wells way reminds the Spa golf tourney is coming up. Twill be a honey. . . . **Harold Claunch** reports top prize in this year's Fishing Rodeo will be a big new automobile. Where's my pole? . . ."

A Marine platoon couldn't have kept me from writing "Purely Accidental" in *The Pantherette*:

"Word comes that **Ernie Hemingway** is spinnin' another yarn. Twill be a good 'un . . . Former Daggett Junior High Coach **Babe Henderson** said tuther day, 'Feller follows a blind man might fall in a ditch' . . . Howdy to ex **Pat Biggers**, head of a swell delivery department at Monnig's . . . Back slap on courthouse lawn from **Doug MacArthur**. Yep, he's quite a general . . . Hi, there, **Johnny Lujack** . . ."

Hey, it landed me a job, all right?

Chapter 8

A Quick Course in Grown-up Journalism
on a Daily Paper

I WENT TO COLLEGE with a byline.

A thing like that might make an eighteen-year-old arrogant if he hadn't received proper training in the home.

I wasn't required to report for work at the *Press* until the last week of August, ten days before I entered TCU. Could a man forget his first day at work on a daily newspaper? No way. I remember mine as if it were only sixty-five years ago.

Up at 5 a.m. that Monday. Shaved, showered, dressed in a white golf shirt, khakis, loafers, navy blue blazer. Arrived at the office downtown a little before six o'clock. This was how you put out an afternoon paper. Go to work at 6 a.m. to meet the 8:30 deadline for the first edition that would hit the streets by noon.

Normally, I'd be coming home at 6 a.m., but now I had a job. My social life would need adjustments.

I'd been told to cover the finals of the *Press*–Worth Hills golf tournament the day before I started to work. Easy. I'd spent half my youth at Worth Hills. I'd played in the tournament, lost a quarterfinal match, quite tragically, on the last hole, and was well acquainted with the two men in the finals, where Ed Revercomb won the 36-hole match over J. R. (Son) Taylor to grab the tall silver trophy.

I wrote the story at home that night, and when I arrived at the office I handed the copy to William Forrest (Blackie) Sherrod, native of Belton, Texas, named for his family's favorite Confederate general, Nathan Bedford Forrest, and nicknamed for his wavy black hair and olive complexion.

Blackie was *Silver Screen* handsome, a celebrity about town. He wrote swiftly with a cutting humor, even though the name of his daily column was "The Brawn Patrol." It would eventually follow a national trend and be called "Blackie Sherrod," which was convenient, we said, since that was his name.

He was five years removed from keeping the world safe for democracy as the rear gunner in a torpedo bomber; his plane operated in the Pacific off the carrier deck of the USS *Saratoga*. He was only shot down and pulled out of the sea once.

I stood at his desk while he read my story.

He said, "They didn't teach you the difference between AMs and PMs in Paschal?"

I said, "Of course. The AM paper comes to your front yard in the morning. The PM paper comes to your front yard in the afternoon."

"Aside from that," he said with a look.

I said, "I wrote it like this because the *Star-Telegram* didn't cover the tournament—it's a *Press* promotion. It'll be news to our readers, right?"

Feeling smart.

He said, "When you write for AMs, you concern yourself with who, what, when, where. For PMs, you concern yourself with how, why, and what's next. Put a little more in here about the winner. You know Ed Revercomb, I guess."

"I've played a lot of golf with him."

"Tell me about him."

I said, "Ed won't bet more than 50 cents if you put a gun to his head."

"Maybe we can spare the reader that news. What else?"

"He can't outdrive my grandmother, but he's always in the fairway . . . and his pitching wedge can make the ball sit up and talk to you."

"Go to work," Blackie said, handing the copy back to me.

I went to my knee-hole metal desk with the green fake leather top. I fooled around on the Remington typewriter the office had provided for me. I put in the story that Ed was the coach at Parker Junior High in real life, and he won the tournament by stiffing his wedges so close to the cups his golf ball chewed on the flagsticks.

I was happy Blackie stuck my byline on the story, even though it started off, "Recovering from a shaky start, scrappy Ed Rever-comb . . ."

After the first edition closed, Blackie gave me another tip on how to write for PMs. He didn't say, "Always pick an angle." He didn't say, "Recognize the defining moment and stomp on it." He didn't say, "Write like you talk." He didn't say, "Tell it to Aunt Edna."

What he said was, "See how many paragraphs you can go before you put the score in."

The *Press* was in a two-story cream-brick building on the corner of Fifth and Jones in downtown Fort Worth. The paper was born in 1921 and was considered a "scandal sheet." Reporters wore galluses and wrote stories that went after con men peddling fake oil leases to naive citizens throughout the booming '20s. Newsboys shouted, "*Press* catches another swindler!"

The paper had never lived down the image because it kept printing what it thought were valid exposés.

Once during my stay it produced a front-page spread with sequence photos and a blazing headline that accused a city council-man of double-parking on a downtown street. The story was not only ridiculous, it was embarrassing for me—the councilman's two daughters were friends from high school.

The *Press* was always fighting for circulation and advertising, chasing after Amon Carter's morning, evening, and big fat Sunday *Star-Telegram*. The *Press* didn't publish a Sunday edition until 1955, eight years after I got there.

It probably didn't help that the *Press* was part of the Scripps How-ard national chain. Locals didn't feel they had much in common with the *New York World-Telegram, Cleveland Press, Pittsburgh Press,* and other foreign products. The feeling persisted despite the fact that we offered a strong lineup of syndicated stars—Westbrook Pegler, Robert Ruark, Louella Parsons, Earl Wilson, Aline Mosby.

The paper's financial struggles led to it becoming a "community service" publication. This meant we had promotions out the ass—the Soap Box Derby, the Spelling Bee, the Jingle Contest, the Annual Freckles Contest, the Free Baseball School, the Santa Pals, the Handicraft Exposition, the National Snapshot Contest, the "Save the Soil and Save Texas" Awards Program, the Golden Wedding Anniver-sary Gala, the *Press* bowling tournament, and the *Press*–Worth Hills golf tournament.

I'm winded.

Advertising and circulation were on the ground floor, editorial was upstairs. Through a door to the rear of our floor was the composing room and the squeaking, whining sounds of the Linotypes.

A Linotype operator climbed into a contraption that looked like an electric chair connected to the world's largest erector set. He typed words in lead that went into a form. The form went onto a mat. The mat went onto a press. The press printed a paper that went into a truck. The truck dropped off a bundle that went into a bag. The bag went on the shoulder of a kid who tossed a paper into a front yard.

But we called it "writing."

Beneath a steady layer of cigarette and cigar smoke, the editorial floor consisted of the city editor's table, the news editor's table, and desks for the courthouse reporter, the police beat guy, the state poli-tics guy, and three general assignment writers, each of them rooting for a tornado—anything but another zoo story.

The city editor was Dave Hall when I arrived and Delbert Willis when I left fourteen years later. Dave was a balding, no-nonsense man who smiled twice a year. Delbert was a likable guy who'd lost a leg in combat during World War II. Neither could have functioned without Mary Crutcher, their assistant. Mary was a former police reporter, a lightning-fast rewrite lady, and known throughout the Scripps Howard chain as "the world's only beautiful city editor."

The news editor was hefty Sam Hunter. He was usually covered up in stories off the UP wire, a mound of local copy, and a decision to make on whether the 100,000 killed in the earthquake in Ecuador deserved Page One over the invention of Scrabble.

Surrounding all that were four waist-high, railed-off areas with swinging gates known as "cages."

The cage at the north end of the floor near the morgue, the two-man photo department, and the Acme Telephoto apparatus was where you could find Jack Gordon, the amusements columnist. He'd been at the *Press* forever. His cage had room for one extra chair in which he could entertain a Hollywood press agent, even a movie star. The day Dagmar walked in to see Jack was one of the most exciting in the history of the paper. I was there.

Jack was a dapper fellow who wore pin-striped suits, had a neatly trimmed Brian Aherne mustache, and when his coal black hair was slicked down, it reminded people of either Rudolph Valentino or shoe polish. His column never saw a movie it didn't like, mentioned the birth of babies, announced weddings, promoted restaurants, and helped find lost puppies.

He was a jovial guy, even though he rarely finished a sentence. "Fine, fine," he'd say. "Leslie Townes, Leslie Townes . . . Bob Hope's real name . . . Great guy . . . and here comes Bobby Bixler, Hope's great agent . . . How's Leslie doing, Bobby? Give him my regards . . . How's my girl Ann Sheridan? . . . Denton, Texas. Great Texas gal . . . the Oomph Girl . . . beautiful, beautiful . . . fine, fine."

On the west wall was the women's department. It housed Edith Alderman Dean and two girl assistants. Edith was a regal lady, the mayor's wife, and had been at the paper since 1924—like Jack Gordon and Pop Boone. She wrote columns that were largely about church ladies.

Walter Humphrey, the editor of the paper, didn't have a cage, he had a corner office with an air-conditioning unit. Walter was a kindly, soft-spoken man. He was cut from the mold of all Scripps Howard editors, I was informed. He smoked a pipe, turned off all the lights in the city room when he left for the day, and questioned my work only twice.

Once he politely asked what a reference to Bonnie and Clyde was doing in a story about a high school football game between Cleburne and Hillsboro. The other time he politely asked what a reference to Mussolini was doing in a story about a TCU quarterback.

Walter wrote a column called "The Home Towner" that concerned itself almost entirely with soil conservation.

Let me just say that I've encountered many boring topics in my life—global warming, health food, golf instruction, marathons, community theater, Major League Baseball realignment—but I'm here to tell you that soil conservation buries them all.

Walter had a partner to help him save the soil. He was Weldon Owens, the regional editor. Weldon was a cheerful fellow in a tan Eisenhower jacket, Stetson, and horn-rimmed glasses. He spent his time in regional hamlets talking to neighborly folks about the plight of the soil. The only good thing about soil conservation was Weldon's nickname—"the Loam Ranger."

On the wall backing up to the composing room was the desk where you could find the portly C. L. Douglas, managing editor. His career had known better days. He had written six books on Texas politics, and liked to say they sold less like hotcakes than they did like books on Texas politics. At lunchtime, Doug might be seen at his desk sticking a pocketknife into a can of cold green peas.

The sports department was the cage across the south wall. We were gratified to have the row of frosted windows you could crank open to give you a charming view of distant grain elevators. Built into the wall above the windows was a large ventilating unit that was supposed to supply warm or cool air, but mostly it blew soot down on our cashmere sweaters.

My arrival upped the staff to five. The kindly, gray-thatched Pop Boone, sports editor for a thousand years, still wrote a daily column called "Pop's Palaver." That title certainly sent me to the dictionary the first time I saw it when I was a kid. Blackie and Julian Read handled every chore known to journalism—write, edit, rewrite, headline, layout. I soon joined them in those endeavors.

Puss Ervin, a retired postman, a bent-over little man who wore suspenders under his shirt, was our grizzled but lovable bowling writer. Puss had a bottom line for everything.

I'd bought an oxford gray flannel suit because I'd been to New York City and seen every guy wearing one, but when I wore mine to work the first time, Puss said, "Who let the bullfighter in here?"

Blackie slumped over his typewriter in laughter.

One day I made the mistake of bringing my copy of *The Brothers Karamazov* to work. Puss stared at the jacket as the book sat on my desk.

"What's this Deedostydosty shit?" he asked.

I said it was a novel I was reading for my Continental Lit class.

"Communist turd," Puss said.

"I don't think so," I said. "It was written before the Revolution."

"Russian, ain't he?" said Puss, ending the conversation.

Two outside contributors brought marquee quality to the paper, or so our editor believed. Fort Worth's Polly Riley, a top lady amateur golfer, wrote about her own game, and Ki Aldrich, the All-America center on TCU's '38 national champions, and an All-Pro center on the Washington Redskins of Sam Baugh's era, wrote a column called "Memo from Ki."

We all agreed that Ki was going for a Pulitzer the day he broke this news in his lead: "The best thing you can ever see is a skillet bubbling over with hot grease, and the fish turning brown over an open fire. Man, you can't for the life of you beat a good old fish fry."

I used to joke that I didn't sleep the first forty years of my life, but it's close to the truth that I didn't sleep my first five years at the *Press*.

How could a man sleep when he was working full-time on a daily paper, working full-time on his degree at TCU, working full-time gambling on the golf course, and working full-time dating, dining, and sitting around?

I would get to the paper at dawn, smoke a pack by 8:30, drive eighty miles an hour to the TCU Drug, grab a donut and coffee, attend two classes, dash over to Worth Hills for 18 holes with the thieves, clean up, and take a date to a movie or Jack's jukebox joint on the Mansfield highway, then meet up with associates to sit around in an all-night hotel coffee shop to discuss the Cold War's effect on golf and football.

It would be negligent of me not to comment on the friendships that were formed at Worth Hills—"Goat Hills," we called it. Our wagering gangsomes roamed the course for around twelve years. A conversation today with two gentlemen who were once accomplished golfers—Dr. Donald Matheson (Matty) and Vance Minter (Magoo), current president of Colonial Country Club as I type, can't take place without a reference to Weldon the Oath, Foot the Free, John the Band-Aid, Cecil the Parachute, Grease Repellent, or Moron Tom, who talked backwards and in rhymes.

When Moron Tom spoke of "Cod E-Rack Fockledim" we knew it was Doc Cary Middlecoff spelled backwards. He would set up his wagers for the day with, "You, you, and you for two, two, two . . . cockadoodle do." Teeing up a drive, he'd say, "Think I can't, Cary Grant?" If his partner faced a critical putt, we might hear, "Up to thee, Don Ameche."

I did what I could to immortalize all that in a magazine piece in *SI*, and later in a hardcover collection, *The Dogged Victims of Inexorable Fate*.

My first fall on the paper, Friday nights meant covering regional high school football games to glorify a pine-knot scatback with a nose for the end zone, or simply let my presence be known to a town with ten subscribers.

But my game stories never measured up to the headlines Blackie put on them.

When I wrote that the Breckenridge Buckaroos crossed the goal line of the Weatherford Kangaroos more times than the wrong answers on a chemistry quiz, his headline said: "Buckaroos Swamparoo Kangaroos."

I only remember Blackie's headline when two backs from a school

I no longer recall ran wild over their opponent, whoever it was: "McKee, McCollum McMincemeat."

There was the time a couple of backs named Poe and White from McKinney or Gainsville or somewhere had a productive night against Highland Park, a school located in a wealthy Dallas neighborhood. Blackie saw it as a case where "Poe, White Trash Highland Park."

My choice for his best headline was the morning he sacrificed his own lead on a baseball story. The night before, a pitcher named Bob Austin of the Fort Worth Cats had hurled a no-hitter at LaGrave Field. Blackie's headline on the event: "Why Don't We Name the State Capital After Him?"

Blackie was my guru and godfather, and when he wasn't leading by example, he was pointing me toward the masters of our craft to study and learn from. This sent me into our morgue in idle hours to browse through the heavy binders of past issues of the paper.

There was a moment when a rare awakening was thrust upon me. It happened when I paused to read a UP column by Henry McLemore, who was covering the Berlin Olympics in 1936. His lead that day: "The Olympic Marathon was run on Tuesday. It is now Thursday and I'm still waiting for the Americans to finish."

It was a journalism degree in two sentences.

That's the way I wanted to do it, I thought. Let others write "a breath of flame, a streak of fire."

Blackie was responsible for lining me up as a fellow worshipper of John Lardner. When I read this Lardner lead in *Newsweek*, it was a master's degree in sports journalism:

"Take yacht racing, now. Why does it fascinate the sporting public so much that crowds will stand all night outside a newspaper office in Terre Haute or Des Moines waiting to hear the result of a regatta for F-Class Butterfly Sloops off Throg's Neck, L.I.? For that matter, who was Throg?"

Today, pitifully, there's some sportswriting admired by the literati among us. Fortunately, there's not too much around. It is (a) the New York writer who finds racism in every metaphor west of the Hudson

River, (b) the political writer who turns to sports to inform the public that a Mickey Mantle strikeout against Boston on the night of July 10, 1958, reshaped Western civilization, and (c) the novelist who observes that athletes in Florida suffer psychological problems because their state is shaped like a penis.

I CONSIDERED IT A PLUM TO cover the Texas Women's Open at River Crest Country Club in the fall of '48. The annual match play tournament brought to town the top lady golfers in the world—Babe Zaharias, Patty Berg, Betty Jameson, Betsy Rawls. That crowd.

Among other duties, I was now the golf writer for the *Press*. Possibly because I'd led the Paschal Panthers to a city high school golf championship, but more likely because nobody else on the staff cared about the sport.

I stumbled into two good stories that week. First, Babe narrowly avoided disqualification in her semifinal win over Helen Dettweiler. She found that she had too many clubs in her bag. She was horrified and tried to forfeit the match. But officials wouldn't have it. Babe was the tournament's biggest attraction. Innocent mistake, they ruled.

I got a quote from Helen Dettweiler that I should have put higher in the story, but I was too interested in similes at that age.

Helen had said, "I knew Babe was carrying too many clubs, but I didn't want to call it on her. We were even through 15, and I wanted to beat her straight up, on the golf course."

It turned out to be our own Polly Riley who beat Babe on the golf course. Polly didn't miss a fairway in the 36-hole final on River Crest's old-fashioned layout, where you can hit it out of bounds on 14 holes. Find the ball on the front lawn of a mansion. She didn't miss many putts either. She won 10 and nine, handing Babe the worst defeat of her career.

I worried that Walter Humphrey, our editor, always on the lookout for ways to promote the paper, would insist on a headline that said: "Press Employee Beats Babe." Fortunately, I escaped with a headline by Blackie that said: "Polly's Game Near Perfect."

But before Blackie wrote that head he suggested I do something with my lead. It read, "Miss Polly Riley found the River Crest greens as easy to read as Louisa May Alcott on Sunday, so today she's the Texas Women's Open champion."

Blackie circled the paragraph and said, "Is this for the *Fort Worth Press* or the Fort Worth Public Library?"

I hurriedly changed Louisa May Alcott to "the saga of Joe Boy and Spot," hoping there was a children's book by that title, and if there isn't, there should be. Blackie approved the change with a nod, and I went to breakfast at the White Way Café to drown myself in a plate of biscuits and gravy.

I covered the Texas Women's Open every October from '48 through '55, when it ceased to exist for financial reasons. Sponsors couldn't raise enough prize money to keep it on the LPGA Tour, which had been formed by a group of players in 1950.

Getting to know the Babe was an honor. She was friendly and entertaining. She could tell as many unprintable jokes as Sam Snead, and at times you had to remind yourself that you were in the presence of the greatest female athlete in history.

She had stock lines she dropped on you every year:

"The Babe's in town, who wants to be second?"
"How can I hit it so far? Boys, I just loosen my girdle and let her rip."
"You don't just swing at a golf ball, you gotta hit the damn thing."
"There's nothing like practice to help you think better under pressure."

And there was the line about her husband, George Zaharias, who'd been a pro wrestler known as "the Crying Greek from Cripple Creek" when they married in 1938. George became her manager, and as he grew wider through the years, Babe would say, "I thought I married a Greek god, but now I'm just married to a goddamn Greek."

Late one afternoon in 1951 I caught up with her on the River

Crest putting green before the tournament started. She was alone and chipping and putting when I approached her. She wore a white visor, a sweater, and knee-length skirt.

I was in my dual role as the golf writer for the *Press* and a member of the TCU golf team. My clubs were on a golf cart and I planned to sneak in a round under the guise of work. I reintroduced myself and impulsively asked if I could join her if she intended to play a practice round.

Babe said, "How much you got in your pocket?"

A little stunned, I said I supposed I could handle a $2 Nassau.

"Come on," she said. "Press when you get lonesome."

Off we went, the two of us, her telling jokes all the way around. We played 18 holes in two and a half hours. Her low hook off the tee went 275, 280, and outdistanced me. Ahead of her time, she was pounding it. In the mode of the era, I was still going for style. I played pretty good, shot a 75, four over. It helped me lose only $12—front, back, 18, and three presses. But Babe refused to take my money.

She said, "I don't mind robbing a college kid, but I can't rob a newspaperman. We need you guys."

She won the Texas Women's Open that year, and won it again the next year, making her a five-time winner. She'd won it three times as an amateur in '40, '45, and '46, when it was played at Colonial Country Club, a course she dearly loved.

It was in 1956, four years after her last triumph in Fort Worth, that she died of colon cancer, at the young age of forty-five.

What a pleasure it was for me to have known and spent time around that magnificent lady.

Chapter 9

Here Comes the World's Greatest
Sports Staff—in Our Own Minds

THAT WONDERFUL YEAR OF 1949 started off with Ben Hogan damn near getting killed in a car crash in West Texas, and ended with your hard-core Russian Commies developing their own A-bomb. Not a year you wanted to throw a lot of bouquets at.

Between those two uplifting events, Fort Worth chose the month of May to have itself a major-league flood. The Trinity River roared out of its banks after twenty-four hours of steady rain and engulfed the near-west side of town, rising up to the third floor of the Montgomery Ward building even though the Montgomery Ward building was bigger than Waco.

From there the flood went south and inundated Colonial Country Club's river-bottom golf course, turning it into an ocean. The tops of the tallest trees were barely visible.

My assignment in the paper's "natural disaster coverage" was to stand on the steps leading up to the pro shop from the 18th green and watch the floodwaters lap up to my loafers. I did this and reported that the Colonial National Invitation tournament scheduled for two weeks later—already a jewel on the PGA Tour—was going to be canceled. The course couldn't be restored to its bent-green elegance for six months or longer.

73

While I felt bad about Hogan and Colonial, I also felt bad about me. I'd suffered two double bogeys. Starting the year, my goal was to become Fort Worth's O. B. Keeler, the writer who covered Bobby Jones's career for the *Atlanta Journal*. Ben Hogan had become the game's dominant player, and he was mine.

I was ready. I knew golf, played the game reasonably well, and I'd been watching the game's stars play throughout my high school years.

I'd dashed around at tournaments in Fort Worth and Dallas following Ben Hogan, Byron Nelson, Sam Snead, and all the Jug McSpadens. I'd seen Snead win the Dallas Open at Dallas Country Club in '44, watched Byron win the Fort Worth Open at Glen Garden in '45, and followed Hogan winning both Colonial and then the Dallas Open at Brook Hollow in '46, and I followed Ben again when he won his second Colonial in '47.

To be honest, I was more awed by Byron's game at first. Tall and strong, when Byron wrapped his large bare hands around the grips and dipped into the shots, the golf clubs became bullwhips. He's still the fastest player I've ever seen. Curiously he didn't use a tee at times. He'd drop a ball between the markers, nudge it around with the club-head, and stripe it down the heart of the fairway. He made it look so easy.

I watched Byron on almost every hole when he won his record 18th tournament of '45 at Glen Garden in December, only four months after V-J Day—and we all remember what that meant.

It meant I was downtown that evening with everybody I knew, and thousands I didn't know, watching people fall about in revelry. It was a night when even ugly people could get laid.

I'm borrowing that line from a character in my novel *Rude Behavior*. The character was describing the '60s, that whimsical decade in which various portions of our society tried to take life to another level.

Some good news caught up with us in the late fall of '49. Pop Boone finally retired, taking the "Palaver" with him along with his fake bylines. He wrote under Jess A. Dam Lie on fishing, and under Adam Dubb when he wrote about golf. A damn dub, if I'm forced to translate.

Blackie officially took over as boss, and we all received raises. I leaped up to $34.50 a week. Blackie devoted the next three years to hiring original talents like Bud Shrake, Jerre Todd, and Gary Cartwright to join up with himself and myself to form the best sports staff in America—in our own minds.

Bud was the first addition. I recommended him as a replacement for Julian Read when Julian left to become a PR and advertising mogul. Bud's wit was known as far west as the TCU Drug on University Drive and as far east as the Pig Stand on the corner of Eighth Avenue and Park Place.

Blackie said, "What am I supposed to like about him?"

I said, "He's a natural writer, and he doesn't like sports that much."

When Bud came to the office for an interview Blackie asked him which sports he liked best.

"I'm torn between croquet and polo," Bud said.

That did it.

When the Dallas Texans came to Texas in 1952, it fell upon Bud to cover them. These were not the Dallas Texans (future Kansas City Chiefs) of Lamar Hunt, or the Dallas Cowboys of Clint Murchison Jr. They were the worst NFL team in history, the terrible New York Yanks, originally the Boston Yanks, brought to town by Giles Miller, a Dallas businessman.

Their big stars were the recycled Frank Tripucka and Buddy Young.

Texas wasn't ready for pro football, and proved it. The Texans played in a Cotton Bowl that held 75,000, but never drew more than 15,000. With five games left on their winless schedule, and Giles Miller's wallet looking like an elephant slept on it, the team was given back to the league.

I went to three games with Bud. The Cotton Bowl was close to empty. Only a pride of lions could be seen licking around on the bones of some Christians.

The situation gave Bud a line that Coach Jimmy Phelan dined out on the last half of the season. Bud suggested that instead of the Texans being ceremonially introduced before each home game, Phelan should send them up in the stands to shake hands personally with their twenty-seven fans.

The *Press* had its share of financial crunches. During the crunches Bud would be called upon to combine sportswriting with police reporting and rewrite duty on the city desk.

On the desk he lucked into a particularly engaging story. A deer escaped from the Fort Worth Zoo and was either captured by two policemen in a patrol car or run over by two policemen in a patrol car. At any rate, the deer wound up on a picnic table for the officers and their families. Bud wrote the story and put a historic headline on it: "Cops Eat Kids' Pet."

When Blackie grew tired of covering the Fort Worth Cats and wanted to devote full-time to his column, he asked if Bud or I wanted the baseball beat. Neither of us did, although the lure of train trips and writing over exotic datelines—Beaumont, Tulsa, Shreveport— was enticing.

We recommended our pal Jerre Todd, another product of Paschal High and TCU. Like us, Jerre looked for humor in everything life served up.

We assured Blackie that Todd was a born sportswriter, and he understood the emerald chessboard of baseball—he'd played on the 1950 state championship team at Paschal.

"Bring him around," Blackie said.

A week later we ushered Jerre up the stairs to the editorial floor. Todd looked the newsroom over. "Which one is he?" he asked. We pointed to Blackie in the sports department. Todd trotted across the city room, picked up speed, and did a hook slide into Blackie's feet.

Looking down at Todd, Blackie said:

"You're hired."

True story.

Those were the days when we'd bet on college football games, purely as an intellectual exercise, you understand. The local bookmakers were friends—Circus Face, Boston, Spot, Jawbreaker—as were their bagmen, Little Mike, Junior, Scooter, Puny the Stroller.

Sometimes we'd be asked by our friends among the homicide detectives to call in bets for them. One of them might say, "Twenty scoots each on Aubrin give the three and Climpson take the six and a half."

Our wagers turned Todd into our resident songwriter. Set to a familiar refrain, his prediction sheet song went:

Duke over Miami,
Pittsburgh to beat Penn State.
Oh, give me USC,
I love Purdue and three,
And the Sooners giving eight.

Another Todd song requires scene setting.

It's October 20, 1956, press box at Kyle Field, College Station. In a game interrupted by a violent tornado in the second quarter, Texas A&M has just nudged TCU 7–6 in a gigantic battle of undefeated teams. A heartbreaker for the Frogs and their fans. They'd not only suffered a crushing loss but felt the scum-level zebras had robbed TCU of two touchdowns. I did think All-America Jim Swink had scored twice from the one-yard line.

We were there in force. Blackie to handle the game story, me to do an analysis, Shrake to write a feature, Todd assigned the winner's dressing room, and Jim Hendricks, a part-timer and TCU student, assigned the losers' dressing room.

As we stood gathering our thoughts, the game over, Blackie looked at Jerre and Hendricks. "You two better get started to the dressing room."

Jim Hendricks said, "I can't go down there."

Blackie glared at him. "What did you say?"

Hendricks said, "Their hearts are broken. The Frogs will be crying. I can't face that scene."

Blackie said, "Get your ass down there to that dressing room, and I mean *right now!*"

"Oh, yeah?" said Hendricks with a snarl. "You didn't go to that school, *buddy!*"

We were stunned. In shock. We stared at each other. But after a moment, Todd broke into a grin, shuffled into a soft shoe, and, composing the melody and lyrics as he went along, he sang:

You didn't go to that school, buddy.
You never lived in Tom Brown Hall.
You ain't had no dealings with Chancellor Sadler,
You never went to the Howdy Week Ball.

Bud and I started laughing and joined in as Todd sang it again. Blackie stared at us, then *he* couldn't fight off a laugh, as the wounded Jim Hendricks wandered away.

Jim Hendricks survived and went on to graduate from TCU and make his way to New York to become a staff writer for *Aviation Week* and then *Medical Economics* magazine. Todd takes complete credit for shaping Jim's career.

By now, the *Press* was putting out a Sunday paper, and we'd gone to tabloid size, the back page awarded to sports. This made us more vibrant and gave Blackie license to expand the staff.

He made Andy Anderson our outdoor writer. Andy had come on board as a utility guy. Reporter, editor, slot man. This was in a period when, for some arcane reason, every paper in America suddenly felt the need for an outdoor writer.

Andy's departure into the duck blinds and fishing holes of the territory meant that we needed a full-time desk man. He turned up in the form of Charlie Modesette, a good-hearted fellow who came to us from Arizona. He was instantly named "Sick Charlie" by Todd when Jerre learned that Modesette had overcome Hodgkin's disease more than once.

Last on the expansion front was the arrival of Gary Cartwright. Gary was lured into our fold by Bud Shrake. They'd covered the police beat together when Cartwright was at the *Star-Telegram*. Bud's strenuous recommendation got Cartwright hired. He assured

Blackie that if typing was a circus act, Gary would be one of the Flying Punzars.

Puss Ervin, our grizzled but lovable bowling writer, gave Gary a nickname that would stick with him the rest of his life.

On Gary's first day at work, Puss glanced up from typing the results of the Tuesday night mixed couples competition at Bowlanes, and said, "Where'd the Jap come from?"

Gary did have a hint of an Oriental look, although his hometown of Arlington, Texas, was hardly a hotbed of ninja mercenaries.

Cartwright proved to be as brilliant a talent as ever forced the "Tomb of Mausolus" into the lead of a story on Breckenridge High's football team, and "the moon is a half slice of lemon" into the lead of a story on a Texas Tech–SMU football game.

He fit right in.

THE '50S GAVE US PLENTY TO write about where Southwest Conference football was concerned, and plenty to laugh about. For one thing, Abe Martin, the "Jacksboro philosopher," took over from Dutch Meyer as coach of the Horned Frogs.

Abe produced bowl teams, conference champions, and All-Americans, but mostly he livened up our sports page. It was impossible to come away from a visit with Abe without a quote that sold the story. Big games coming up to Abe could be a "spellin' bee," often a "sheep shearin'."

He said of his All-America tackle Bob Lilly, "He's just a big old green pea, but he'll stand in there for you like a picket fence."

Abe's description of his great running back Jim Swink: "Aw, he's just a little old rubber-legged outfit nobody can catch."

Bear Bryant arrived at Texas A&M to revive its fortunes about the same time Abe took over the Frogs. Bear, known as a defensive genius, introduced the word "pursuit" to the press.

Abe said, "Everybody's talking about pursuit, pursuit, pursuit. Shistol pot. That ain't nothin' but chase 'em and catch 'em."

Abe was an unemotional presence on the sideline in a game. He'd stand there in his lucky brown suit and crumpled hat, put his hand on a kid's shoulder before sending him into the game, and say, "Son, you go in there and get me a touchdown, I'll buy you a rubber dolly."

Hunter Enis, who quarterbacked TCU to a Southwest Conference championship in 1958, can't help grinning when he remembers Abe sending in plays from the sideline.

The player would arrive in the huddle, and Hunter would ask, "What did he say?"

The player would report, "He said get a first down."

Hunter achieved more success later in life. He and his partners in the Four Sevens oil company discovered natural gas in the Barnett Shale right there underneath the city of Fort Worth. To borrow from my Texas heritage, this made them richer than six feet up a bull's ass.

Jerre Todd should have copyrighted the Abe Martin anecdote that's still good banquet material. Jerre was on the sideline at the TCU-Rice game in '54 when Dicky Moegle, No. 47, a dazzling halfback, was leading the Owls to victory. Jerre stood near Abe when the coach waved to a player on the bench to come over. Excitedly, the kid trotted up.

Abe put his hand on the player's shoulder and said, "Tommy, No. 47 out there is killin' Billy on that sweep. I want you to go in there for Billy and stop that sweep for me."

The player hopped up and down, and said, "I'll try, Coach."

Abe said, "Sit down, Tommy. Billy's tryin'."

Moegle's name takes me back to the Cotton Bowl game between Rice and Alabama on January 1, 1954. I'm glad I can say I was there to witness one of college football's great oddities.

Rice was thrashing Alabama and Moegle was doing most of the thrashing when a screwball thing happened. Moegle tore off on another long run. He'd traveled about 50 yards when an Alabama player named Tommy Lewis dumbfounded the world by coming off the bench and tackling Moegle at the Crimson Tide's 45-yard line. The zebra awarded Moegle a 95-yard touchdown run.

After the game nearly every writer rushed to the Alabama dressing room to crowd around Tommy Lewis and hear him explain, "I was just too full of Alabama."

I rushed to Dicky Moegle in the Rice dressing room and came away with the best description of what happened. It was Moegle saying, "I saw the guy come off the bench, and I thought his helmet had rolled onto the field and he was coming to get it. I gave way a little to my left, but the next thing I knew, my ass was flat on the ground."

RIDING THE DESK ON VARIOUS AFTERNOONS, part of our job description, led to a couple of conversations I've committed to memory for the entertainment of friends. The voice on the other end is my own.

SECOND FAVORITE CALL:

"This the sports department like you said when you answered?"

"Yes, it is."

"I got a question about the city's swimming pools."

"What about them?"

"Do you know they're shut down right now? It's because of this infantile paralysis bullshit."

"Yes, sir. I understand they're taking precautions."

"But it ain't right."

"Why not?"

"In case you don't know it, Bubba, it's hotter than a sumbitch outside and I ain't no infant. I ought to be allowed to go swimming. I mean, yeah, it's okay to keep out the infants you don't want to get crippled or nothing, but it's not fair to a noninfant like me. You should put this in the paper."

"We appreciate you bringing it to our attention."

"You're goddamn right I did."

FAVORITE CALL:

"This the Fort *Whore* Press?"

"It's the Fort *Worth* Press, if that's who you're calling. This is the sports department."

"Sports, that's who I want. I've got a bone to pick with Blackie Sherrod. Is he there to talk to?"

"No, I'm sorry. He's not in."

"Well, tell him something for me. Tell him he ain't as smart as he thinks he is when he writes about my Arkansas Razorbacks. Tell him I'm a proud Razorback from Hot Springs except I live here now, and we ain't slabs of bacon."

"I'm sorry?"

"That's what he said Texas University turned us into Saturday. Slabs of bacon. He said it about college kids! And while I'm at it, I don't think 14 to 6 is that bad a score to get beat by, in case you want to write that down in your diary."

"Sir, I'm sure Mr. Sherrod was trying to be humorous. It was just a figure of speech."

"Like hell. It was slabs of bacon, is what it was."

BLACKIE WAS NEVER AN "I" GUY. He was rarely a "we" guy. He was more of a "this department" guy. At times he was a "said the man standing next to Darrell Royal" guy.

No one deplored the sight of "I" in journalistic print more than Blackie. There were too many ways around it.

Another hang-up for Blackie was length. When a game story ran too long with play-by-play, he called it a "snake."

I called it an "S." I am unable to say the five-letter word out loud in fear of nightmares. In Texas, if you'd bent down to find your golf ball in the rough, the rocks, a ditch, or a ravine as many times as I had and found a Copper H, a Water M, or an R S looking up at you, you might feel the same way. There's no such thing as a harmless "S."

I'd pave every desert and swamp in America. All creatures great and small, my ass.

Over time I changed the "S" into something else to describe the overlong play-by-play. I changed it in honor of the sportswriters of a long-ago era who relied on it for their second paragraph.

It goes: "Navy won the toss and elected to receive."

A good place to learn how not to write sports was in the pages of the old preseason football magazines, especially the *Illustrated Football Annual*, and later *Street and Smith's Football Yearbook*. Every section of the country had a poet to set the mood for the coming season.

The Deep South man:

"There's a photo finish shaping up in rootin' tootin' Dixie, and it's stuffed with the finest cotton, soaked in honeysuckle, and dripping with watermelon juice."

The man in the East:

"Up Navy! Up Pitt! Up Fordham! But look for Army's caissons to keep rolling along."

The Midwest man:

"The Golden Gopher sits high on the frozen tundra, and dares one and all to attack his breastworks."

The Far West man:

"From the Golden Gate Bridge to Hollywood Boulevard, they're shouting, 'Who'll stop the Trojans?'"

The Southwest man:

"Yippie-ti-yi-yee!"

WE WERE CURIOUS WHEN BLACKIE BROUGHT a cork bulletin board to the office and hung it on the wall. What was this for? We soon found out. He started thumbtacking stories on it that he deemed to be pretentious or precious. You didn't want to find yourself on the bulletin board.

The bulletin board earned a name. It was two words that came out of a lead in a *Star-Telegram* story on an autumn Saturday. The writer's name will be withheld here out of sympathy for his family.

The words bloomed in the writer's advance on the Arkansas-Baylor game he would be covering. He'd been seduced by the beauty that only nature could provide—yes, the subtle russet of the leaves in the Ozarks.

Subtle russet?

We howled. We danced around. We went to the bulletin board with it.

Those two words became the label for any piece that fell below our impeccable taste in literature.

Subtle Russet lives on for some of us.

Chapter 10

I Interrupt This Book to Speak of
Boyhood Heroes

THESE ARE GIDDY TIMES for the professional sports industries that occupy the hearts and pocketbooks of people living in the Metroplex today. Sweet word, Metroplex. For years now, that's how Fort Worth and Dallas media folk have referred to these sprawling suburbs, an area that used to be known as . . . well, Fort Worth and Dallas.

With this vibrant growth, which we call traffic around my house, has come a rash of pro teams that didn't exist when I grew up in Fort Worth, and Dallas was a thirty-mile trip on a two-lane road.

I appreciate how exciting it is for Metroplex residents to have Dallas Cowboys, Texas Rangers, Dallas Mavericks, and Dallas Stars in their midst, and even a Texas Motor Speedway for those who concede that auto racing is a sport and not a training ground for getting to Happy Hour.

All young boys have sports heroes. At least the ones who don't play with Suzy Homemaker ovens. In the Metroplex alone, they can plaster their bedroom walls with posters of . . .

Maurice (Bicuspid) LeBlanc of the Dallas Stars, whose smile alone is often mistaken for a tip on gold shares.

Gerd von Dunk of the Dallas Mavericks, whose armpits are soon to be replicated and available as book ends at Neiman Marcus.

Bulk Rash, 370-pound offensive tackle with the Dallas Cowboys, who would argue that Steroids is a town in Sweden.

Jesus Paso Doble of the Texas Rangers, who would like to hook up with one of the Desperate Housewives of Illegal Immigration.

Hank (The Humiliator) Rightfoot at the Speedway, whose lifelong ambition has been to die as he has lived—in a nine-car pileup on Turn Two.

That was humor just now. I made those people up.

I understand how the fans of pro sports might think my kid days were irrelevant. My heroes cavorted on the fields of Southwest Conference football, Texas high school football, and Texas League baseball.

In those days college football was to the press what the NFL is today, high school football was to the press what college football is today, and Texas League baseball was as close as you could come to the majors without hopping on a train to St. Louis.

Some of my heroes were admired from a distance. Like those of the Major League Baseball ilk. Major League Baseball dates back to the Battle of Hastings, and it dominated the nation's sports pages for centuries until twenty years ago, when the NFL dethroned it.

There were only sixteen major league teams in my youth as opposed to the forty or fifty of today. This made it easy for me to find the Wheaties boxes I wanted. There were these great photos of big leaguers on the sides of the Wheaties boxes.

When I'd go with my grandmother to buy groceries at the A&P, I'd rearrange the Wheaties boxes on the shelves, shuffle them around, examine the sides, look for a player I didn't have. This sometimes took a toll on the grocery clerks.

The look on a clerk's face told me he would be saying to himself, "Here comes the little brat who's gonna want me to climb up a ladder and see if I can find Ducky Medwick."

Jesse Owens was a big hero in the newsreels. He made every kid want to run faster. It was well known that Jesse Owens infuriated the Nazis at the Berlin Olympics by winning so many events.

Incidentally, I knew the Nazis were up to no good. Why didn't everybody? All it took was one look at their logo. The swastika virtually yelled out, "Here comes a shitload of trouble, people."

I should have written President Roosevelt about it.

FOUR OF MY BOYHOOD FOOTBALL HEROES—guys I watched perform more than once as a kid and as a high schooler—probably did more than any others to make the old Southwest Conference a memorable institution, and they had a great deal to do with my wanting to become a sportswriter.

The four were "Slingin' Sam" Baugh, Davey (Slingshot) O'Brien, "Dazzling Doak Walker, the Mustangs' Miracle Man," and Texas's Bobby Layne, "the Blond Bomber."

They're the Mount Rushmore of Texas football.

Aside from giving Texas writers an edge in the nicknaming game, all four were two-time All-Americans—Doak all three seasons. Two of them, Davey and Doak, won the Heisman Trophy. A third one should have. That was Baugh. Two of them led their teams to national championships, Sam and Davey at TCU. Three of them led their teams to world championships in the NFL. That was Baugh with the Redskins in '37 and '42, and Doak and Bobby together with the Detroit Lions in '52–'53. Layne did it for the Lions again in '57, although a late-season injury allowed Tobin Rote to finish the title run for him.

If there's a group anywhere with a more impressive résumé, it better take Godzilla to lift it.

They made me feel like I was living in the sports capital of the universe, and there was no question I was living in the sports capital of Texas, which was bigger than the universe anyway.

I TRUST YOU CAN IMAGINE HOW special it was for me to get to know these heroes after they'd hung up their game threads.

I first caught up with Sam Baugh in 1960, when he was the head coach of the New York Titans, who would become the New York Jets in the American Football League.

I'd flown to Gotham with Lamar Hunt and his Dallas Texans—the future Kansas City Chiefs—for their game against the Titans. The day before the game I spent time with Sam in his office in the decaying Polo Grounds in the Bronx.

I let Sam know I was a fellow Horned Frog, and wondered if people still asked him about the SMU game of 1935.

He said, "Ah, ever now and then a feller like you asks about it."

I said, "So how close were you to Bobby Wilson on that pass?"

Sam said, "Two things about it are a damn myth. People said if Jimmy Lawrence hadn't been hurt and on the bench, he wouldn't have let Wilson get behind him. Well, Hal McClure was there, and so was I. Bobby just made a great catch. Another thing. The play wasn't a surprise to us. SMU used it all season. People have forgotten what the rule was. A pass on fourth down that fell incomplete in the end zone was a touchback, same as a punt. I'm sure Bob Finley's pass would have landed in the end zone if Bobby hadn't caught it."

Before Sam went to the Washington Redskins, pro football was a game played by beer guts in baseball parks, to put it as nicely as possible. Baugh did his part to streamline it. In his rookie season of '37 he became the first quarterback to follow up winning a national championship in college—for TCU in '35—with winning an NFL championship in the pros.

I asked him if it was true that he took Dutch Meyer's passing game with him from TCU to the Redskins.

"Why, hell, yeah," he said. "The short passing game was Dutch's invention. When I got to the pros, everybody was runnin' the fullback up the tackle's ass. We used Dutch's offense and won with it."

I said, "Is it true you and some other guys got caught trying to kidnap the Baylor bear in Waco?"

"We were dumbass freshmen," he said. "They caught four of us, shaved our heads, and painted 'em green and gold. Pretty near embarrassing."

Did he always hate being called Sammy?

"Nobody called me Sammy but the damn newspapers. Sounds like a girl, don't it?"

Did he really develop his passing arm as a kid in Sweetwater throwing footballs through an automobile tire swinging from a tree limb?

Sam said, "Aw, shit, ever kid did that. There were plenty of old wore-out tires layin' around. The Depression saw to that."

I didn't ask, "What Depression?"

A university having an All-America quarterback followed by an All-America quarterback is as rare in college football as finding a football star without a honey on his arm. But it happened at TCU when Davey O'Brien took over from Sam Baugh.

Davey was only 5-7 and 150 pounds, but he brought even more glory to Fort Worth than Sam did. In the season of 1938, O'Brien won the Heisman Trophy and led the Frogs to an undefeated season and the national championship. He completed the fairy tale by beating Carnegie Tech, "the Beast of the East," in the Sugar Bowl by 15–7.

The *Star-Telegram's* leading writer, Bess Stephenson, told it this way on the front page:

NEW ORLEANS, Jan. 2—Strong men wept and women went hysterical. This was Monday afternoon when their TCU Horned Frogs were trailing Carnegie Tech 6–7 at halftime in the Sugar Bowl.

But Davey O'Brien made it all come out right for the thousands of Purple rooters who'd been waving pennants and ringing cowbells all week. He threw a 50-yard touchdown pass and kicked a field goal to put the game on ice, and the Fort Worth rooters let out a sigh of relief that sounded like a steamboat whistle.

It was a crime against God and Christianity—not to overlook me—that TCU, the nation's No. 1 team, was denied the Rose Bowl bid. I was set to go. Sister was going to take me on one of the special trains to Pasadena. But back-room politics intervened. No. 3 Duke was invited.

I was a crushed ten-year-old. Actually I was more of a pissed-off ten-year-old. All questions of right and wrong went up for grabs in my mind. Mimmie tried to comfort me. She said, "Look at it this way. TCU still has something to play for in the future."

It only took seventy-two years.

The wait made it especially enjoyable for me in 2011. June and I were invited to fly with friends round-trip to L.A. in a richer-than-six-feet-up-a-bull's-ass private jet. We spent three days rummaging around Beverly Hills, then watched Andy Dalton pass, run, and quarterback the undefeated Horned Frogs of Coach Gary Patterson to a thrilling 21–19 win over the Big 10's Wisconsin on a glorious afternoon in America's most famous stadium.

Life doesn't get much better than that for a college football silly.

But back to Davey. After two seasons with the Philadelphia Eagles, he tired of pro football, or I should say he tired of the Philadelphia Eagles not providing any pass protection. He quit the game and became an FBI agent. After serving ten years with the FBI, he retired and moved to Fort Worth to enter the oil business.

He'd show up at TCU workouts and sports luncheons and this was where we became friends. He was a good source on all things football.

The best thing Davey did was let me in on the fact that two new rules had been put in place before the 1934 season, and they changed football forever. The press ignored the changes for reasons that probably had something to do with dinner or cocktails.

One of the new rules was the elimination of a five-yard penalty for throwing more than one incomplete pass in a series of downs. But the big change was the rule that reduced the circumference of the ball by one inch, making it easier to throw.

Davey said, "Sam claims it never made any difference with him, but it did with me. I have to say it helped. It must have helped a lot of people. Teams started putting more stress on passing, and recruiting quarterbacks who could throw the ball."

History tells us that from the mid-1930s onward, the rule change didn't just usher in Sam and Davey, it gave the sport Dixie Howell at

Alabama, Ace Parker at Duke, Sid Luckman at Columbia, Cecil Isbell at Purdue, Paul Christman at Missouri, Billy Patterson at Baylor, and Jack Robbins and Dwight Sloan at Arkansas, "the Pitchin' Porkers."

You could say it was the start of ball games today that end 55–48.

DOAK WALKER AT SMU IS THE greatest college player I ever saw. He played both ways, and he was an all-around threat, right down to intercepting passes and placekicking. But it was his ball carrying you remember best. On his long runs, which were many, he seemed to glide, weave through traffic, and he made tacklers grab armfuls of air.

I happen to hold a lofty position, that of the official historian for the National College Football Hall of Fame, thus I am allowed to pontificate. So I say Doak was a latter-day Chic Harley, or Ohio State's Chic Harley was an early-day Doak Walker. They were handsome dudes, roughly the same size—around 5-10, 165—wore red jerseys and khaki pants, but they performed thirty years apart. Both were responsible for sayings. The Cotton Bowl is called "the House that Doak built," and it is said, "Chic Harley built Ohio Stadium as sure as there are bricks and mortar."

James Thurber was a student at Ohio State during Harley's career, and he once wrote, "If you never saw Chic Harley run with the football, I can't describe it for you. It wasn't like Red Grange or Tom Harmon or anyone else. It was a cross between music and cannon fire, and it brought your heart up under your ears."

The best I did for Doak was: "Poetry in motion. That's how the old sportswriters described the football immortals in their day. But if you applied the phrase to Doak Walker when he was at SMU, you'd have to say the only people who belonged in the backfield with him were Byron, Shelley, and Keats."

I was having dinner with Doak at a golf tournament in Florida for Heisman Trophy winners and I asked him who he considered the greatest player ever. I expected him to say Bobby Layne.

"Sam Baugh," he said.

I said, "You say Sam because you know I went to TCU."

"No, I saw him play when I was a kid," he said. "Baugh was the greatest passer and punter the game's ever known—and he was a hell of a defensive player, too."

I said, "I'm sure Bobby was the best who could party all night and still get it done on Sunday."

This moved Doak to tell his prized Bobby Layne story.

Once when they were vital to the success of the Detroit Lions in the early '50s, Layne gave Doak, his old high school teammate at Highland Park High in Dallas, $50,000 in $100 bills at the start of the season to hold on to for him. He told Doak never—*never under any circumstances*—to give him more than one thousand dollars on any given day.

But at 3 a.m. one morning Layne called Doak to say he urgently needed another thousand at this nightclub he was in.

Doak said, "Bobby, you told me never to give you more than a thousand dollars at a time. I'm not gonna bring it to you."

Layne said, "Doak, I've gotta pay the band and tip the bartenders and waitresses, and this is another damn day anyhow!"

BOBBY LAYNE USED TO SAY A man's goal in life was "to run out of cash and air at the same time."

He managed it by the age of fifty-nine. Far too soon, but he'd be the first to admit he earned it.

Bobby would come to New York for business or pleasure and sometimes call me at *SI* to meet him for a drink in the comfort of the big stand-around bar in Toots Shor's on 52nd Street.

One afternoon it came up that he'd spent part of his boyhood in Fort Worth. He was born in Santa Anna, Texas, out west near Brownwood, but the family moved to Fort Worth as he was reaching his teens.

He said, "We lived on Jessamine Street near Hemphill. I went to Daggett Junior High. I was set to go to Paschal, but my aunt and uncle in Dallas adopted me. That's how I wound up at Highland Park."

I said, "I remember seeing your name on the football in the Daggett library."

"What football?"

"A white football with red lettering on it. Daggett's colors. Your name's on there with the other players. Nobody but me knows Bobby Layne won the city junior high championship in 1938, the same season Davey O'Brien won the national championship for TCU in Fort Worth."

He said, "Now two people know it—you and me."

I found myself caught in an awkward situation on another day with Layne in Shor's.

Bobby arrived grumpy, to start with. He'd read that a panel of writers had proclaimed Otto Graham of the Cleveland Browns the greatest quarterback in NFL history.

"Otto Graham," Bobby said, sounding as if he'd swallowed a mouthful of Robitussin thinking it was Château Lafite.

"Otto was overrated?" I interpreted.

Layne said, "All I know is, we played six times and I won five."

"Nice stat," I said. "I might can use that someday."

"Ah, hell," he said. "It don't make a shit now."

Five minutes later the unmistakable voice of Howard Cosell was heard as he took up space on my left. Sweet Bobby was on my right.

Howard was a friend, I'm not ashamed to admit, no matter how many times he said, "This is the luckiest day of your life." He'd given my books and *SI* stories their share of pops on TV and radio.

Suddenly, after noticing Layne on my right, Howard went into one of his routines.

"Number 22," he said loudly. "The Blond Bomber fades back, surveys the field. Cloyce Box, No. 80, goes down the sideline. Jim Doran, No. 83, looks open on the right. Dorn Dibble, No. 87, crosses over the middle. But No. 22 looks deep and sees No. 37, the miracle man, Doak Walker, and—"

"Who the fuck *are* you?" Layne said, glaring at Howard. "My friend and I are trying to have a conversation here."

Cosell looked wounded.

"Hi, Howard," I said softly. "Talk to you later."

I said it as Howard dissolved into another group of customers.

Turning to Layne, I said, "You didn't recognize him? That's Howard Cosell. Don't you watch *Monday Night Football* . . . with Cosell, Meredith, and Gifford?"

"Not if I've got a card game," Bobby said.

Chapter 11

The Ben Hogan I Knew Probably Wasn't
the Ben Hogan You Knew

THE GHOST OF A MAN being eased off the passenger train on a stretcher at the railroad station in Fort Worth didn't look like he'd be able to play a hand of gin rummy again, much less a round of golf.

This was Ben Hogan on April 1, 1949, returning home after the Greyhound bus had put him in an El Paso hospital for two months to play the toughest course of his life—a double-fractured pelvis, fractured collarbone, broken left ankle, three cracked ribs, a near-fatal blood clot, and a severe circulation problem in his legs.

There to meet him were Marvin Leonard, his best friend, and a dozen other well-wishers. Leonard was the man who built Colonial and kept Ben on the tour financially when he was struggling. Present was a more civilized group of writers and photographers than you'd find today.

We were respectful and standoffish. No paparazzi swirling about. No reporters shouting in Ben's face.

"Hey, Ben! What's it like to be dead?"

"If you could hit the bus driver, what club would you use?"

I don't have to tell you that today's media has a lot to answer for.

Nobody saw much of Hogan for six months. He'd bought a home on Valley Ridge Drive in Westover Hills. If you'd grown up in a tiny frame house on East Allen Street on the south side of Fort Worth, a move to Westover Hills ranked up there with winning the National Open. Neighbors caught glimpses of him walking the winding roads in Westover trying to regain strength in his legs.

He didn't start hitting practice balls at Colonial until September. The country club didn't have as many golfing members then. It was easy for Ben to find secluded areas on the course to work at rebuilding his game.

On a day in November I found him on the putting green and worked up the nerve to introduce myself. I ran the only credits I had. On the golf team at TCU. Colonial was our home course, thanks to Mr. Leonard. I was the golf writer for the *Press*.

It made a difference to Hogan if you played the game. It meant you understood a little something of what he was about.

"I know your byline," Ben said.

He knew my byline?

I'm reminded of a time in another life when I joined my *SI* teammate Roy Blount Jr. in a cocktail-motivated routine about people who say, "I saw your book."

"You saw my book? What was it doing?"

"Oh, it was sitting right there."

"Was this in a bookstore or at a Texaco station?"

"A bookstore, I think . . . but there was furniture around."

"Nobody was bothering it, I hope. Like putting their hands on it? Flipping through the pages?"

"Not that I saw. Is this a book about a whale?"

"No. Kind of hard to find a whale in a book these days."

"I sure saw your book."

"Thanks. I'm glad nobody was touching it. I had a book die of pneumonia last year after somebody picked it up."

So Ben Hogan had seen my byline. Now he had a person to go with the name. This would be convenient.

What none of us could have guessed was that Hogan was preparing to enter the Los Angeles Open at Riviera Country Club in early

January, only eleven months after the Greyhound bus almost ended his life.

Ben started becoming the sports story of the year in 1950 by nearly winning that L.A. Open. He played amazingly well tee to green and posted what looked like the winning total of 280. Only one player was still on the course with a chance to catch him. It was his great friend and rival, Sam Snead. Sam needed to finish with birdies on the last two holes to tie.

When Ben heard that Sam had made a 15-foot birdie putt on 17, he moved to a window in the clubhouse to look down on the 18th green to watch Sam sink a 20-foot birdie for a 66 and the tie.

"I wish Sam had made three birdies instead of two," said Ben to the L.A. press. "I'm awfully tired."

What history overlooks—and what the movie *Follow the Sun* leaves out—is that it took eight days for Ben and Sam to engage in the 18-hole playoff. They couldn't play the following day. The course had been hammered with rain and was half covered in mud. Hundreds of cars parked on the Riviera polo field would remain stuck in mud for weeks after the tournament.

Ben and Sam went to Pebble Beach for the 54-hole Bing Crosby National Pro-Am when the L.A. Open playoff was postponed. They finally met a week later at Riviera on Wednesday, January 18, precisely thirteen days after the L.A. Open had begun on January 5.

They were even through the first seven holes. Then Snead birdied the eighth, and Ben blew a short putt for par at the ninth—he three-putted ten times in the tournament—and never caught up. Under sloppy conditions, Sam went on to win the playoff, 72 to 76.

I should have been at that L.A. Open for the start of the greatest comeback in sports history. But Blackie thought my time and the paper's money would be better spent if I covered TCU basketball in the Southwest Conference. At 6 cents a mile I could drive to Dallas, Waco, College Station, Austin, and Houston, stay in hot-pillow motels, and the whole season would be cheaper than one trip to L.A.

I was at the world premiere of *Follow the Sun* on the evening of March 23, 1951, at the Worth Theatre in downtown Fort Worth. Me and a date and Ben and Valerie, Ben's wife, and Glenn Ford and Dennis O'Keefe and Jimmy Demaret and many of Fort Worth's well-to-do citizens.

The movie was directed by Sidney Lanfield, a man known for *Hat Check Girl* and *Skirts Ahoy!* No doubt this qualified him to do a golf movie. Had he been there that evening, I would have asked him a serious question. Why hadn't he or someone in his wardrobe department found a white golf cap that wasn't too big for Glenn Ford's head?

PEOPLE LIKE TO SHRINK HISTORY. It's easier to digest. Hitler made everybody in Germany wear his logo and rearranged the map of Europe. But General Patton chased him into a Berlin bunker where the führer shot his bimbo, Eva Braun, and escaped to Argentina. Elsewhere, the Japs bombed Pearl Harbor, John Wayne invaded a dozen South Pacific islands, Gregory Peck cranked up the *Enola Gay*, and that was that.

Likewise, there are those who think Hogan's comeback started in Los Angeles in January and leaped five months to June, when he won the U.S. Open at Merion. It involved a little more than that.

He finished fourth in the Masters and third in the Colonial, and to everyone's astonishment he matched the world record for 72 holes with a 259 in the Greenbrier Invitational on Old White in White Sulphur Springs, beating runner-up Sam Snead by 10 strokes on Sam's home course.

Everybody knew where to find me on those spring afternoons. Out at Colonial. A college sophomore carrying the destiny of the TCU golf team on the shoulders of a terminal hook and betraying short irons.

When I wasn't gambling or engaging in Southwest Conference matches, I'd switch into my role of a sportswriter and watch Hogan hit balls. That's where I got to know him, and we formed a lifelong friendship.

I'd jump in a cart with my clubs on board and drive out to find him on the course. Pick a spot a safe distance away so as not to bother him. Soon he began to acknowledge my presence with a nod, so I moved within conversational distance of him. One afternoon I noticed him practicing a peculiar shot. Hitting a knock-down 3-iron about 175 yards, each shot landing at the feet of the shag boy.

When he took a break for a cigarette, I said, "Ben, if you don't mind me asking, what the hell is *that*?"

He said, "I need it at Merion."

Merion in Philadelphia was where he climaxed his comeback by winning the 1950 U.S. Open in the 18-hole playoff with Lloyd Mangrum and George Fazio. Which gives me an opportunity to solve the Case of the Stolen 1-iron at Merion. By Dashiell Hammett? Erle Stanley Gardner?

Start with the fact that it wasn't a 1-iron Hogan hit to the 72nd green, the shot that got him a tie in the Open, the club stolen overnight along with his golf shoes. Charming story about the collector who found the 1-iron years later, in the '80s, and donated it to the USGA museum, but Hogan hit that historic shot with a 2-iron, so it must have been the 2-iron that was stolen and has yet to be found.

Ben always said it was a 2-iron in his conversations with me. He said it was a 2-iron in his conversations with Herbert Warren Wind. It's a 2-iron in *Five Lessons*. Page 13. In later years Ben even once said it was a 3-iron. Fog of memory. Anyhow, his bag normally consisted of a driver, brassie, 4-wood, 2-iron through 9-iron, sand wedge, pitching wedge, putter.

I ask you to look again at Hy Peskin's famous photo in *Life* magazine of Ben finishing on the shot at Merion. That's a 1-iron? It looks more like a spatula from my kitchen.

That settled, I ask you to study Hogan's comeback record in 1950:

Los Angeles Open—2nd (lost playoff to Sam Snead).

Masters—tied 4th (behind Jimmy Demaret, Jim Ferrier, Sam Snead).

Colonial—tied 3rd (behind Sam Snead, Skip Alexander).

Greenbrier—won (by 10 strokes over Sam Snead, tied world record).

U.S. Open—won (in playoff over Lloyd Mangrum, George Fazio).

This is important. That record was achieved by a man who almost died, who was told he might never walk again, who took months to recover and rebuild his golf game. I remind you of it for a reason. When Tiger Woods suffered a handful of setbacks and made his so-called comeback, there were sportswriters everywhere who wrenched their backs trying to compare it to Hogan's. What nonsense.

Tiger's injuries consisted of a knee operation, a fire plug, a divorce, and an Achilles' heel. And his comebacks from the middle of 2008 through 2013, five years through eighteen majors, the only tournaments that mean more than money, did not produce a single win. Do-Da. The Big Empty.

In the midst of all that, I had my say about Tiger on the *Golf Digest* website. Here it is again:

NICE (NOT) KNOWING YOU

Friends have been asking me why I haven't written my take on "the Tiger Woods deal," so here it comes. First, let me just say that I'm still having trouble getting past the video games and Froot Loops.

That's if I'm to believe the report that Tiger was so distraught after his indoor athleticism became public—and turned into what some people call a Shakespearean tragedy—that he crawled into deep, lonely hiding and occupied his time playing video games and eating Froot Loops.

Maybe it is true, and that's why Tiger's agent, Mark Steinberg of IMG, said to the media at one point, "Give the kid a break."

Kid?

Tiger Woods was a month away from 34 years of age when his debutantes began turning up in the news. He was a grown man with a wife and two children. Well, we supposed he had a wife, but that was before we learned she was only an ornament.

Kid?

Kids flew B-17s in daylight bombing raids over Germany in World War II. Kids fought in Korea and Vietnam. Kids are serving today in Iraq and Afghanistan so Tiger Woods can live in a world where he can win 14 majors and match that number, the last time I counted, with 14 casting couches, most of them reserved for blondes.

Now excuse me a moment while I try to envision Ben Hogan, Arnold Palmer, and Jack Nicklaus playing video games and eating Froot Loops while they try to deal with a career problem.

Of course, Hogan, Palmer, and Nicklaus never set themselves up to become statues in Central Park.

They never pretended to be the All-American Daddy-Pop Father of the Year Who Also Wins Golf Tournaments.

They never sold themselves as the greatest Family Values brand ever, and conquered the marketplace with it, shamelessly scooping up hundreds of millions of dollars while saying, "My family will always come first."

They were never what Tiger allowed himself to become from the start: spoiled, pampered, hidden, guarded, orchestrated, and entitled.

I'll tell you what Hogan, Palmer, and Nicklaus were at their peak.

They were every bit as popular as Tiger, they endured similar demands on their time, but they handled it courteously, often with ease and enjoyment.

They were accessible, likable, knowable, conversant, as gracious in loss as they were in victory, and above all, amazingly helpful to those of us in the print lodge who covered them.

That was their brand. All the things Tiger never was.

As for Tiger's brand, boy, did that take a hit.

For all the Tiger idolaters out there, it must have been like finding out that ice cream sundaes give you gonorrhea.

Never in my knowledge of history has any famous personality—in sports, show biz, or politics—ever fallen so far so fast. Tiger Woods is graveyard dead, as the Southern expression goes.

Life as Tiger has known it is over. His reputation is ruined, possibly forever. His name that once meant mastery over competitive golf now invokes cringes, giggles, and all the internet jokes you want to pass along.

Sure he can come back and even win again, if he man's up, but if he does he will only be a hero to the "you-da-man" and "get-in-the-hole" crowd. And I can't imagine him coming back as a "humbled man." That wouldn't be the owner of a yacht insultingly named Privacy, the guy the press has slobbered over for these past 12 years.

I covered Tiger winning his 14 professional majors, but I can't say I know him. I knew the smile he put on for TV. I knew the orchestrated remarks he granted us in his press room interviews. I knew the air he punched when another outrageous putt went in the cup. That's it.

I once made an effort to get to know the old silicone collector. Tried to arrange dinners with him for a little Q&A, on or off the record, his choice. But the closest I ever got was this word from his agent: "We have nothing to gain."

Now it's too late.

I'm busy.

IT WOULD COME AS NO SURPRISE to any reporter that Ben Hogan, Jack Nicklaus, and Arnold Palmer were more important to me than Tiger Woods. The game of golf can speak for itself.

There was this afternoon at Colonial after Ben wound up practicing that he drove his cart over to mine, and said, "Let's go."

"Go?" I said foolishly.

"I think we can get in 18," he said.

Had Ben Hogan asked me to play golf with him? There was no one else around.

I said, "Uh . . . well . . . uh . . . sure . . . yeah."

We took both carts to move along quickly.

He hit every fairway, every green. He shot a three-under 67. His three birdie putts were under 10 feet. A dozen times I said, "Good shot." He ignored it.

I managed to make a bunch of pars, saving five or six of them with the trusted Tommy Armour putter. Got in with a 76.

The only comment Hogan made about my game was, "I wouldn't let that putter get away from me if I were you."

We had a drink in the old men's grill at Colonial, the room where one wall was lined with slot machines. The slots had yet to be outlawed.

I told Ben how much I enjoyed watching a great round of golf today.

"That wasn't even a good round of golf," he said.

What would you have responded? I could have done Kato, and said, "Not good round? You funny man, Green Hornet. Make joke."

But all I said was, "It wasn't?"

Ben said, "I didn't hit one shot that worked out the way I wanted. A good round of golf is when you hit three shots that turn out exactly like you plan. This means you're playing at the top of your game."

I must have played thirty or more rounds with him over the next ten years. I didn't keep count. Frequently just us. Other times we might come across two club members and Ben would invite them to join us. Several of the members were low handicap guys.

He never confessed his "secret" to me. He never even said, "The secret is in the dirt." That statement emerged in his elder statesman years.

But I think I know what the "secret" was. He overclubbed. Aside from the fact that he was continually striving for distance, he overclubbed for accuracy.

He once said to me, "When you *have* to get the ball on the green, you can do it more reliably if you overclub. It gives you better control. But you can't overclub every now and then. You have to do it consistently. You always overclub downwind. Keep it low, out of the wind."

This was the day Ben let me in on the fact that you need a heavy putter for fast greens. Controls speed better. I stroked a few putts with his "door knob," the center-shaft brass putter carved out of a door knob. It had been given to him by Ky Laffoon, one of his first friends on the tour. He used it to win every major. I was shocked to find that his "door knob" was no heavier than a parking meter.

There was never any serious wagering in the recreational rounds we played with Colonial members, but I do recall one specific day that made me nervous. The foursome consisted of Ben, Reub Berry, arguably the best amateur in the club, Carl Vandervoort, a former city champion, and me.

Ben threw up the balls to determine the partners for a $2 Nassau, automatic presses. Ben got Reub, Carl got me.

On the first tee as I was trying to remember how much money I had with me, Carl said, "Let's try not to look overconfident." Carl and I held our own on the front nine, and I staggered in every putt I looked at on the back. We partnered to shoot a five-under 30, and beat them out of $6.

I apologized to Hogan for the putts I sank.

Ben said, "Never apologize for winning."

Filed that one away.

He handed me a five and a one. I should have asked him to autograph the bills for framing, but I spent the money that night on a date.

TWO PERSONAL GOLF TALES. I relate them only because Ben Hogan has a cameo in each. In the dark ages of college golf everything in the Southwest Conference was match play except for the 72-hole individual conference championship.

On a spring day in May of '50 Texas came to town with a team led by Morris Williams Jr., an intimidating celebrity in Texas amateur circles. Our lusty circuit produced stars whose mere names struck fear into the hearts of opponents. In my era alone some of these names might be familiar to you—Don Cherry, Billy Maxwell, Earl Stewart Jr., Don January, Ernie Vossler, Joe Conrad, Wesley Ellis, and Morris Williams Jr. in Austin.

Morris was a slender guy, long enough off the tee and faultlessly straight with the irons. The only big match he ever lost was one up in the 36-hole final of the 1949 NCAA to North Carolina's Harvie Ward, who would become one of the finest amateurs in history.

That day it was my task to play Morris in the No. 1 singles match. The matches started on the back nine so we collegians could stay out of the way of Colonial's members going off on the front.

As we stood on the 10th tee, Morris whispered, "Is that who I think it is back there?"

It was.

Ben Hogan, sitting in a cart some distance away, had heard of Morris Williams Jr., a collegian who'd won the State Amateur, State Junior, and Texas PGA Open in the same year. He wanted to take a look at him.

"Want to meet him?" I said.

"No, I'm nervous enough," he said. "I've never played Colonial."

In that bygone era it was a tradition for TCU football players to come out and caddie for us lowly golfers in our matches. I thought this was a noble display of school spirit until I found out they only did it to receive passing grades in P.E.

My caddie that afternoon was Billy Moorman, an all-conference end from Odessa. As we walked down the 10th fairway, our opening hole, Billy said, "We gonna kick this T-sipper's ass today."

I said, "Speak for yourself. You don't know who he is, do you?"

"Naw, who is he?"

"I'll put it this way," I said. "If this was a football game, he'd be Bobby fucking Layne."

Although Morris had never seen Colonial, he was even par through 15 holes. I'd played out of my head and was also even par. We were all square in the match. It was my best round ever at Colonial.

Our 16th hole was Colonial's No. 7, then a narrow 400-yard par four with trees lining the fairway, a watery ditch in the left rough, trees in the right rough, and taller trees bending over the green.

If there was anything to add more pressure to the situation, it was the sight of Ben Hogan and Marvin Leonard in a cart. They showed up to watch us finish the match.

Morris put his drive in the heart of the seventh fairway, setting himself up for a 7-iron to the green. I tried to steer-job my tee shot but faded it into the rough behind a row of trees. Dead.

I was left with a 6-iron to the green. All I had to do with it was dig it out of the rough, put it through a tiny opening in the trees, and hit what I can best describe as a high-fade pull-hook. Then the ball would have to clear a clump of limbs as it floated down if it wanted to land on the green.

But that's what happened. It was the luckiest shot of my life. It somehow wound up six inches from the flag. A gimme birdie. "Gosh, Dan, great shot!" Morris called to me.

A less stable person might have been thinking, "I'm going one up on Morris Williams with two to play. I'm going to beat Morris Williams! I'll have to change my major. I'll have to turn pro and go on the tour."

It's a good thing I wasn't thinking any of that because of what happened next. Morris hit a 7-iron that landed on the front of the green, took one bounce, and slowly rolled into the cup for an eagle two.

Morris looked at me with an apologetic shrug. There was nothing for me to do but laugh.

When I glanced back at the cart where Hogan and Leonard were watching, Ben was shaking his head and turning the cart around to head for the clubhouse. He knew I was done. Stick a fork in me. Piss on the fire and call in the dogs, the hunt's over. Brought in crisp. All that.

Ben was right. I three-putted the next hole from 25 feet for a bogey and lost the match, two and one. But at least I'd been beaten by Morris Williams Jr., not Sam Sausage from Arkansas.

Unfortunately, there's a tragic footnote. Three years later Lieutenant Morris Williams Jr. of the U.S. Air Force, while stationed at Eglin

Air Base, was killed when his F-86 fighter malfunctioned during gunnery practice and fell from the skies over Florida.

A month earlier he had won the All–Air Force tournament. He was a year away from leaving the service and joining the PGA Tour, where he would have become part of the new breed that would dominate the game—Arnold Palmer, Gene Littler, Ken Venturi, Dow Finsterwald, Mike Souchak, Billy Casper—the guys who'd fight it out to see who was going to take over from Ben Hogan.

Morris might well have been the guy.

IN THE OTHER TALE, it might have been a crowning moment in a golf nut's life, but for me it was a nightmare. It was the day I played an exhibition round with Ben Hogan at Colonial in front of 3,000 paying customers.

Ben had been asked to play an exhibition at Colonial for the benefit of the United States Olympic Fund. The '56 Summer Olympics were coming up in Melbourne, Australia, in November.

He called me at the paper to say he wanted me in the foursome with him and his brother Royal Hogan, and Ray Gafford, a local pro at Ridglea Country Club.

I said, "There has to be somebody better than me, Ben."

He said, "No, you're who I want."

He didn't say why. Comedy relief was my first guess. On the other hand, it could have been my sterling performance in the annual Fort Worth City Championship. A month earlier at Rockwood muny, I joined Jerry Edwards, Ed Revercomb, and John O'Connell to win the city team title for Worth Hills. Same thing my dad had won at Katy Lake twenty-two years ago.

Then in the 72-hole stroke play competition for the individual city title, I birdied four of the last five holes in the final round to shoot a two-under 70 and became the leader in the clubhouse. But forty-five minutes later I was the runner-up in the clubhouse. A North Texas State college player, Harold Sexton, closed with an eagle and four birdies to beat me—and he didn't even live in the city.

Bud Shrake covered the tournament so I wouldn't have to write about myself. He attempted to put an embarrassing headline on the story: "Jenkins Low Resident in City Championship."

Fortunately Blackie killed it.

As for the exhibition, I didn't expect to work half a day at the office, and walk onto the first tee at Colonial without warming up and find so many fans lining the first fairway from tee to green, 565 yards away. I don't know how I hit a good drive on No. 1. Prayer may have helped. But next came the horror film. I cold-topped my 3-wood second. I cold-topped the 3-wood again. Then I cold-topped a 5-iron that skittered along the ground for 50 yards.

Dig a hole in the fairway and disappear, is what I wanted to do. It's what any sane person would have wanted to do.

But as I was headed to my ball, I realized Hogan was walking along beside me.

Ben said, "You can probably swing faster if you try hard enough."

It was the best golf tip anyone ever gave me in a moment of crisis.

I'd been swinging so fast, I must have looked like I was swatting a swarm of mosquitoes. I slowed it down, avoided any other catastrophes, and stole enough pars to get around in 77. Ben shot his usual 67.

After the round I had a drink with Ben and Marvin Leonard in the grill. We talked golf in general for a while, and then as I was exchanging a nod with someone in the room, I heard Ben saying, "He has length, you see—and he can *putt*." He was talking to Mr. Leonard but I realized he was talking about my golf game.

Now he turned to me. "Between the driver and the putter, your game can use some help."

I said, "You won't get an argument here."

With a serious look, he said, "If you will work with me three days a week for the next three months—and do everything I tell you to do—you can become good enough to compete in the National Amateur."

An offer of free lessons from *Ben Hogan*? That's what I was hearing?

Stumbling and stammering, I said, "Ben, that's . . . that's really . . . flattering . . . and I appreciate the offer . . . but I'm not that serious a golfer . . . I mean, I love the game . . . but all I want to be is a good sportswriter."

Ben looked at me like I'd committed treason. He held that cold stare on me for what seemed like a week. I wasn't sure whether to expect a knife wound or a bullet in the forehead.

Finally, he relaxed, sat back, and said, "Well . . . keep working at it."

Chapter 12

Ben Hogan, Part II, Now Appearing in a Chapter Near You

BEN HOGAN IS A CANDIDATE for the most intriguing figure in the history of golf, but where I was concerned he was the most important person in my life as a sportswriter, so I gather you won't mind if I go on about him awhile longer.

He was, among other things, the most meticulous person I've ever known.

To dine with him at Colonial or Shady Oaks was to observe a scientist staring into a microscope at dangerous amoeba. The first thing he did without fail was wipe off the silverware.

"You don't really know where it's been," he'd say.

One of his favorite dishes was navy bean soup with cornbread on the side. It's still offered every day at Shady Oaks, which was where Ben spent the rest of his years after Marvin Leonard opened his new club in 1959. Shady is smaller, quieter, more of a golf club than the family-oriented country club that Colonial has become. Colonial had been Ben's club throughout the '40s and '50s.

Ben's other favorites were scrambled eggs and bacon, a hamburger, and a club sandwich. But they had to be done perfectly.

Serve him steam-table eggs instead of eggs cracked individually and scrambled, and fat bacon—face a firing squad.

Serve him a frozen pattie for a hamburger—run for cover. Make it fresh ground sirloin.

The club sandwich would be dissected the moment it was placed in front of him. It would be sent back to the kitchen, and someone's life or job threatened, if the toast wasn't the ideal shade, if the bacon wasn't crispy-chewy, if the tomato had a knot in the center, if the lettuce was too limp, or if deli meat had been slipped into the sandwich instead of fresh roasted turkey or chicken breast.

It's no secret Ben was a private person, but he could surprise people by showing up at a debutante party or a charity ball. His choice of beverage was a Scotch and water in the '50s, but he switched to vodka martinis as an elder statesman, and more than one would be required.

Was he observant? Are the oceans wet? I found myself in his presence at a function in a private home one evening and listened to him comment on the molding, the hardware, and the light fixtures while I was looking for the waiter with the tray of drinks.

He studied rooms the way he studied a golf course. If it was a major, it's no myth that he'd walk it backwards before he played it to figure out the trouble he'd want to finesse when the championship started.

Unknown to most, he was an ardent fan of college football. We talked football as often as we talked golf. Like me, he'd grown up a fan of TCU, but in a previous era. His favorite players were two speedy halfbacks, Cy Leland and Red Oliver, in the early '30s. He'd wanted to play football in high school. He was fast, he said, but too small.

His penmanship was exquisite. It was another way in which he tried to make up for his lack of education. Street smart, he was. But he never finished Central (Paschal) High—just as Byron Nelson never finished Poly High on another side of town. According to Valerie, Ben always regretted never achieving a high school diploma.

His attire required the same amount of study as his food. His suits and slacks and blazers came from John L. Ashe, the finest men's store in Fort Worth in his day. He insisted his cashmere cardigans hang loosely. His golf shoes were made in London—with an extra spike in each sole to give him better traction. He never varied from his conservative colors—the grays, whites, navy blues, tans.

He took pains to see that his clothes, on or off the course, fit perfectly. Ben didn't just outplay his competitors, he outdressed them.

Tommy Bolt, one of Hogan's good friends in the game, fancied loud colors—red most often—and he would tease Hogan about wearing "dull old blues and grays," to which Ben once said, "Tommy, if I dressed like a fire plug, I couldn't play golf at all."

Another example of Hogan's closet sense of humor was his exchange with Dick Siderowf, the two-time British Amateur winner, one of America's top amateurs, when Dick played in his first Masters in 1970. Siderowf couldn't resist introducing himself to Hogan in the clubhouse after he played a practice round.

He said, "I was playing in front of you today, Mr. Hogan, and I'm not a long hitter, but even I reached 15 in two with a 3-iron. Your drive was past mine, but you laid up. How come?"

Ben said, "I didn't need a three."

THE NOTION THAT HOGAN DIDN'T ACQUIRE his repeating swing and controlled fade—suitable for winning U.S. Opens—until after the car crash in 1949 is hogwash.

He said in my hearing more than once, "I was a lot better golfer before the accident than I was afterward."

I reckon Ben won fifteen majors. In his time the Western Open and the North and South Open were bonus events, same as the U.S. Open, PGA, Masters, and British Open. The equipment companies matched the prize money if you won them.

When Hogan won the first of his three North and South Opens on Pinehurst No. 2, MacGregor equaled the $1,000 first prize. Valerie remembered it as "the richest I've ever felt in my life."

I have an easel and a pointer.

HOGAN IN MAJORS BEFORE THE ACCIDENT:
1940—won North and South Open

1941—runner-up, Western Open

1942—won U.S. "Wartime" Open, North and South Open, runner-up, Masters

1946—won PGA, Western Open, North and South Open, runner-up, Masters

1948—won U.S. Open, PGA, Western Open

HOGAN IN MAJORS AFTER THE ACCIDENT:

1950—won U.S. Open

1951—won Masters, U.S. Open

1953—won Masters, U.S. Open, British Open

1954—runner-up, Masters

1955—runner-up, Masters, runner-up, U.S. Open

1956—runner-up, U.S. Open

That's nine majors before the accident, six after.

The North and South dated back to 1902 but started losing its status after '46. The PGA of America decided it preferred money over history and charm. It declared the event "unofficial." Dick Tufts, a rigid New Englander and future USGA president who owned the Pinehurst resort, didn't take kindly to the PGA sticking a gun in his ribs.

Tufts said to PGA officials, "This tournament has been special to you people for fifty years." They apparently suffered instant memory loss.

The last North and South Open was held in 1951, Tommy Bolt won it, and Tufts said, "May the PGA drown in a vat of Boston clam chowder."

Something in that vein. Scratch one major.

Opinions differ as to when the Western Open lost its status as a major. It was a certified major from the days of Walter Hagen, Macdonald Smith, and Bobby Cruickshank through the days of Ben Hogan, Sam Snead, and Byron Nelson. It's a forgotten fact that a player received the same number of Ryder Cup points for winning the Western as he did for winning the U.S. Open and PGA. My theory is that the Western tumbled out of favor for good in 1956, when the Masters went on national TV and the Western didn't.

Scratch another major.

I spent a good bit of the '50s covering Ben Hogan. Usually it takes two to reminisce, but I'll go it alone. Some personal highlights:

IT WAS NO EXAGGERATION THAT OAKLAND Hills for the '51 Open looked more like a penitentiary than a golf course. The joke was that you had to walk sideways down the narrow fairways to keep the rough from snagging your trousers. Bunkers were everywhere, some in the middle of fairways. The greens were slicker than the top of Sam Snead's head.

Robert Trent Jones Sr. had been hired by the club to remodel the course and make it a ferocious test. During the week, Hogan said to the designer's wife, "If your husband had to play this course for a living, he'd be standing in a bread line."

Ben's three-under 67 in the last round, which overtook Jimmy Demaret, Bobby Locke, Paul Runyan, and Julius Boros, remains the greatest round anyone ever played on such a difficult course in the stress of a major's decisive last round. The average score of the field was 78.

Footnote to Ben's acceptance speech at the presentation ceremony. At the microphone for the public, he said, "I'm happy I could finally bring this course . . . this monster . . . to his knees."

In the locker room he called it something else.

I MAY HAVE WITNESSED THE LAST great shot the brassie hit in this life. The brassie has become as extinct as an honest politician. It was the 2-wood that today's golfers have never known because modern technology allows every arthritic, diabetic, tubercular, recovering heroin addict to drive the ball into the next area code.

The brassie was in Ben Hogan's hands on the 70th tee in the U.S.

Open at Oakmont in '53. Sam Snead was an hour behind Ben. They'd begun the final round one shot apart. I was among those who jogged back and forth from Ben's pairing to Sam's, and knew that Ben and Sam were all even at the moment.

The 16th hole, or 70th, was playing longer than 234 yards. There was a swirling breeze. Ben hit an intentionally high brassie. It held the line and the green, and left him with a 25-footer that he safely two-putted for a critical par.

"It was my best shot of the championship," Ben said. "That was a tough hole all week, and I was worried about it."

The par at 16 sent Ben to closing birdies at 17 and 18—a flaming three-three-three finish and a six-stroke victory over Snead.

CECIL TIMMS WAS THE SCOT WHO caddied for Hogan at Carnoustie in 1953, when Ben won the British Open and wrapped up the Triple Crown. Cecil moved to America for a while and dined out on the one time he helped Ben over those 72 holes of Carnoustie's somber linksland.

"Timmy" showed up at the Masters one spring as a spectator, and for the price of two pints at the outdoor bar on the Augusta National veranda, I heard Timmy's version firsthand.

Ben had played the 10th hole in the morning round with a driver and 4-iron. Now in the final round, his tee shot was in roughly the same spot, and he reached for the 4-iron again.

Timmy shocked Ben when he put his hand on top of Ben's, and said, "The wind's changed up there, sir. It's a 2-iron now."

Hogan gave his caddie the cold stare.

Timmy held firm.

Ben reluctantly took the 2-iron out of the bag and addressed the ball. But he stepped away, glared at Timmy again, and said, "If this goes *through the green*, I'm going to bury this club in your goddamn forehead."

With that, Timmy swore, Hogan took the hardest swing at a shot he'd taken all week, as if he were *trying* to hit the ball through the green just to prove the caddie wrong.

The shot wound up 10 feet above the pin. Ben sank the birdie putt and went on to his closing 68 and victory over Roberto De Vicenzo, Peter Thomson, Dai Rees, Tony Cerda, and the formidable American amateur Frank Stranahan.

"He didn't thank me," Timmy said. "I didn't expect him to. I was just doing my job."

I should have been at Carnoustie, and the curious thing is, I was on the continent anyhow. My mother had given me a trip to Europe for a college graduation present. I took a two-month leave of absence from the paper after Oakmont. Two good friends from high school and college went along for the education and fun of it all. They were the droll Bob Sweeney and the pretty and witty Carol Andrews.

We sailed out of New York on the *Queen Mary* the third week of June and sailed back to New York out of Southampton on the *Queen Elizabeth* in late August. In between we comparison-shopped the sidewalk cafés of London, Paris, Rome, Madrid, Venice, the Swiss Alps, the Riviera, and other postcard destinations. Bob Sweeney and I decided early on that if you'd seen one Madonna, you'd seen them all.

This was eight years after World War II, but Europe was still recovering. Parts of cities were in bombed-out ruins. England was still on rationing. One egg a day. Beef was nonexistent. But who cared? A Scotch and water was 34 cents, a cashmere sweater was $6.

It crossed my mind to go to Carnoustie. But I was in Venice on those dates, and, as it happened, I'd been taken hostage at a sidewalk café in St. Marks Square by a fetching young English babe—and I don't even remember her name. Except I know it wasn't Brett Ashley.

THE OLYMPIC CLUB, SAN FRANCISCO, 1955. Worst result in the history of sports. This was the time Ben Hogan lost that 18-hole playoff for the '55 U.S. Open to—Jack Fleck?

If Fleck was known to anyone other than the patrons of a driving range in Davenport, Iowa, nobody knew it. He hadn't won dook. But he lapsed into an "Open coma." The cup refused to get out of the way of his putts, and that will normally beat anyone, even Ben Hogan.

Ben was gracious in any defeat, but that time he was the most gracious I'd seen him. I knew why. His club company was only a year and a half old, and it was still in the red. The fact that Fleck was playing Hogan clubs was a nice publicity pop for the company.

After the playoff, Ben sat in the Olympic locker room as a dozen writers hovered around him. One of them said, "It was a tough loss, Ben. It would have been your fifth Open."

Staring at the floor, Ben softly said, "Sixth."

He counted the "Wartime" Open of '42 at Ridgemoor in Chicago. He put it in there with those he won at Riviera, Merion, Oakland Hills, and Oakmont. Me, too. Need you ask?

I'll argue this one more time in print. The 1942 Hale America National Open, as it was called, was broadcast nationally on the radio—I was listening—and drew a record number of 1,540 entries. There was local and sectional qualifying, like any other U.S. Open. It was contested under USGA rules. The prize money was the same as previous U.S. Opens. Ben was awarded a gold medal from the USGA that looks an awful lot like his other four.

That wasn't a U.S. Open?

If it were official, Ben's 10-under-par 62 in the second round would be the lowest single round in the Open, and his winning total of 271, which held off the challenges of Jimmy Demaret, Mike Turnesa, and Byron Nelson, would be a record.

There was an occasion in the late '60s when I asked Joseph C. Dey Jr., the executive director of the U.S. Golf Association—he reigned for thirty-four years—to make the case for why Ben isn't credited with a fifth U.S. Open.

Joe said, "Interlachen in Minneapolis was scheduled to hold the '42 Open, but the club withdrew after the war started. When Ridgemoor offered to hold a wartime version, we were delighted. The length and design of Ridgemoor were acceptable, but there was a manpower shortage. We couldn't prepare the course properly. I would love to give Ben a fifth Open. However, the lack of suitable course preparation at Ridgemoor prevents it from being official. But I do count it as a major for Ben."

Excuse me?

IT'S BEEN WRITTEN AND SPOKEN OVER the years that there was a rude and selfish side to Ben Hogan. He didn't suffer fools, it's true. If he didn't know you, or know something about you, he wasn't anxious to meet you.

He built a new home in Westover Hills with no guest bedroom in it. He loved dogs, but didn't want to care for one himself. He loved children, but he and Valerie never had any. They didn't think they could care for a child properly when Ben traveled so much on the tour—and wanted Valerie with him. Then it was too late.

Three incidents come to mind that touch on the subject of Hogan's, uh, shortness with people.

Ben's 69 tied him for the lead after the first round of the '59 U.S. Open at Winged Foot. A dozen of us surrounded him in the locker room. He sat on a couch, smoking, having a beverage, and answered questions cordially.

That was until Milton Gross, a nationally known sports columnist for the *New York Post*, came up with this one: "Ben, at what point today did you think you'd shoot a 69?"

Hogan stared at the columnist as if he were looking at a rodent, and said, "Milt, that's the stupidest damn question anybody has ever asked me."

We all fell about laughing. Everyone but Milt.

Mike Cochran, a bright light of the AP for many years when he was in charge of all things Fort Worth and West Texas, has a "Hogan moment" he likes to recall.

Although Ben was busy running his golf club company, he was still competitive in the Colonial tournament through 1967. He finished third in that tournament at the age of fifty-five.

After the second round, Ben came off the 18th green and headed up the steps to the pro shop, but found someone blocking his path.

"Hi, Ben," Mike said. "I'm Mike Cochran with the AP. I'd like to ask you a couple of questions."

Ben said, "*Move.*"

Mike moved.

Another incident involving a fellow writer. It didn't happen quite like this, but as Mark Twain or Liberty Valance said, "When the legend becomes the fact, print the legend."

Again at Colonial in the late '60s, Ben was leaving the locker room when he noticed that Sam Blair's badge identified him with the *Dallas Morning News.*

Ben said to Sam, "I'd like to talk to you about something when I'm finished today. Will you be around later?"

Sam said eagerly, "Yes, sir, I'll see you right here."

In the hours that passed, Sam's mind had its way with him. Hogan was going to ask him to write his autobiography. It would be a bestseller. It would be a movie. Sam would sign a two-book deal. He would be offered a three-picture deal. He would buy a villa on the French Riviera and leave the newspaper grind behind him forever.

When Hogan returned, Sam made himself easy to find.

Ben said, "Now you're with the *Dallas Morning News*?"

"Yes, I am."

Ben said, "Do me a favor. Have your people over there tell the delivery boy to stop throwing the damn paper in Mrs. Hogan's flower bed."

BEN WAS A SHY MAN. Many of us believe his shyness was often mistaken for rudeness. Byron Nelson agreed. Byron and Ben had known each other since they were thirteen. They had each achieved success, but Byron revealed that he had never been invited to Ben's home.

"He was the hardest-working golfer that ever lived," Byron said. "It's a funny thing, but even when I was beating him on the golf course he would tell people I was a good player but I'd be better if I practiced more."

It had been my suspicion that Byron's early success was a driving force in Ben's career. Nelson won the Masters and the U.S. Open and eight other events on the tour before Ben got out of the box.

But it may have started with the confusion surrounding the legendary caddie tournament at Glen Garden in 1927, when they were fifteen years old. First, where would a poor kid get a set of clubs? Ben's came from spending part of his caddie fees at Grant's Five and Ten downtown, where an old club could be bought out of a barrel for a dollar. He slowly assembled a set of "eight or nine clubs, a mix of steel and hickory," he remembered, adding that his first goal in life was to have a full set of steel-shafted clubs, steel having become the "new thing" in golf in the mid-'20s.

About the caddie tournament. Both kids believed it was a nine-hole medal play match. They tied with 39s when Byron sank a long putt on the last green. They went to sudden death, and Ben's par four over Byron's double-bogey six gave Ben the title—he believed. But two club members rushed up to insist they had to go the full nine holes. They played on, Byron made up the two shots, then sank a 20-foot putt on the last green—again—to win by one, scoring a 41 to Ben's 42.

Maybe you couldn't blame Hogan for sensing a conspiracy. Byron was the club's "favorite kid," polite, more likable. Eight more holes had given Nelson the chance to win. Then the aftermath.

A year later Byron, the favorite kid, was given a junior membership in Glen Garden. And Ben, who had quit caddying, was told by the country club that he could no longer practice in the caddie yard. He was forced to move full-time to Katy Lake, the public course with sand greens, to work on his game. He turned pro at eighteen, two years ahead of Nelson.

I once got up the courage to ask Ben if Byron's early success had been a force in his life, the hometown thing and all?

"Why, hell no," Ben said. "I wasn't surprised Byron did well. He was a natural athlete, a damn fine golfer. Valerie and Louise were very good friends. Byron and I had known each other since we were kids, but we were nothing alike."

Indeed not. Ben smoked, Byron didn't. Ben enjoyed a cocktail,

Byron never did. Ben cussed, Byron didn't. Ben gambled on the course, Byron didn't. Ben's other favorite sport was football, Byron's was baseball. Ben's golf perfection came hard, Byron's came easy.

Ben surprised me the day I asked about Byron's early success having an influence on him.

He said, "If anyone gave me more incentive to succeed, it was Ralph Guldahl. Ralph was from Dallas. We were the same age. I didn't think he could play a lick. He had this fast, floppy swing. But in 1933, when we were both twenty-one, he finished second by a stroke in the National Open at North Shore in Chicago—he should have won it—and there I was, the club pro at Nolan River Country Club in Cleburne, Texas."

Jimmy Demaret liked to tease Hogan about Guldahl. Jimmy would say, "Ralph Guldahl was the greatest player in the world from '36 through '39. In those four years he won two National Opens in a row, three Western Opens in a row, and the Masters. But Ben says if he had Ralph Guldahl's golf swing, he'd be ashamed to take it out of town."

One of the best-kept secrets in golf, although not from me, was that Ben Hogan and Sam Snead, known for their intense rivalry, were much better friends than Ben Hogan and Byron Nelson.

Before Ben passed away in '97, he left Valerie a list of people he wanted to serve as his honorary bearers. Jim Murray and I were the only two writers included. We were extremely honored.

Other bearers were golf executives, business associates, and some of his Fort Worth friends—Tex Moncrief, George Beggs, Gene Smyers, and Dee Kelly among them. Six golfers were included—Sam Snead, Tommy Bolt, Ken Venturi, Herman Keiser, Shelley Mayfield, and Mike Wright, the Shady Oaks pro.

At the end of the funeral ceremony, Sam Snead bent over and kissed Valerie on the cheek, and tearfully said, "I feel like I've lost a brother."

Byron Nelson's omission as a bearer wasn't lost on anyone. But the true nature of their relationship, like Luca Brasi, sleeps with the fishes.

———

TODAY'S MULTIMILLIONAIRE PROS WHO BOTHER TO write thank-you notes are a rare breed. If a note comes from one of them it will have been sent by a secretary saying the hero would have written it himself but he didn't have any stationery in his Orlando apartment.

Not so in a kinder, gentler day. I'll share one of three notes Hogan wrote to me. It was in response to a column I'd written about him shooting a remarkable 69 in gale-force winds to capture his fifth Colonial.

May 7, 1959

Dear Dan,

I want to drop you this note to thank you so very much for the wonderful article you wrote about me day before yesterday. I not only thank you for that one but others you have written during the past years.

The one day before yesterday, however, was such an outstanding one that I felt I had to write and thank you. Here's hoping some day I shall have the opportunity to return your favors. With all good wishes and kindest personal regards, I am

Gratefully,
Ben

My first book, *The Best 18 Golf Holes in America*, was published in 1966, and Ben graciously wrote the foreword—for free. I'll close this chapter with a condensed version of it, not because of what his words say about me, but because of what they say about him.

BY BEN HOGAN

Regardless of how successful a touring pro becomes, a sad thing about his life, I think, is how little he is able to see and enjoy the places he visits and what a small amount he ever learns about all the superb courses and clubs at which he plays. His life is consumed with getting from one town to another, with dedicating himself to the serious practice he needs for good scoring and, finally, with the competition itself. This, at least, is how it always was for me. Tournaments consisted of long hours on the practice tee, the competitive rounds, and a constant preoccupation with my game. Golf is the most unconquerable of games, and to play it well consistently demands tremendous sacrifices.

This book has enabled me to discover a multitude of fascinating things about places I have visited many, many times but never really came to know; about courses that were known to me only as adversaries. It's for anyone who takes his golf seriously, who knows the feel of a well-hit 5-iron, and warms to certain names—Merion, Augusta, Oakmont—though he may know no more about them than his television set has displayed.

Most of the holes Dan has selected are familiar to me. I have played fourteen of them. I do not know any writer who could have undertaken the task supported by more ability, knowledge or interest in golf. I have known Dan for twenty years as a fellow Texan, a fellow resident of Fort Worth, and as a very able golfer, but most often as a working golf writer. I could not count the times I have spotted him at the Masters, the U.S. Open, or elsewhere, striding along the gallery ropes, chatting with my wife, Valerie, or choosing a correct moment to offer a word of encouragement. He has written many kind words about me, and I am truly grateful. But having lost a lot more tournaments than I ever won, I would argue that no one could be as good as he has frequently made me seem. I wish I could have been that good.

That was the only Ben Hogan I knew.

Chapter 13

As Arnold and Jack and the
Majors Go Marching By

IT'S A LITTLE EMBARRASSING FOR ME—me the history junkie, the keeper of memories—to confess that I hadn't heard the term "major championship" to describe golf's leading tournaments until a day in 1954 in Augusta, Georgia. I was covering the Masters for the fourth year in a row, a romance with the dogwood that's gone on for sixty-three consecutive years. That's forty-six more than Grantland Rice covered—thanks for asking.

When I lump those years together, they become a maze of pimento cheese sandwiches, egg salad sandwiches, and country ham and red-eye gravy for breakfast upstairs in the main clubhouse, where I've often dined overlooking the veranda and wished I'd been there in the '30s, when the wraparound balcony served as the press room.

I've covered the Masters through six tournament chairmen, from Clifford Roberts, who was always helpful to me—my relationship with Ben Hogan didn't hurt anything—on up to Billy Payne, who has already proved he ranks up there with Cliff in leadership. And I've watched the press center evolve from a green tent kept open at one end to catch the breezes, to the Quonset hut, to the present auditorium, or amphitheater, or whatever it is.

It was Herbert Warren Wind who introduced me to the word

"majors." When Herb spoke I listened. He was to golf writing and golf history what the Sistine Chapel is to ceilings, or to put it another way, what fried food is to Texans.

"A golfer's true greatness," Herb said on the Augusta National veranda that day, "must always be measured by the number of major championships he wins."

Herb had befriended me, a young writer from Fort Worth covering Ben Hogan. This was the spring after Hogan had scored the Triple Crown, winning the Masters, U.S. Open, and the British Open in the same year, actually over a span of four months.

The word "major" made sense to me, but in the '50s the pros were still referring to the big ones as bonus tournaments or national championships. There are purists in our trade who love to point out that Bobby Jones's thirteen "majors" are all national championships—his four U.S Opens, five U.S. Amateurs, three British Opens, and one British Amateur. They were the championships of the U.S. Golf Association and the Royal & Ancient, golf's two ruling bodies. This makes them extra special.

When the press ordained the Masters a major, which was five minutes after Gene Sarazen made that double eagle in 1935, the club companies placed it among the bonus tournaments. Winning a bonus tournament or national championship not only meant matching prize money, but larger paydays for exhibitions, clinics, outings, and magazine ads.

Ben Hogan enjoys the smooth taste of a Chesterfield.

Sam Snead says there's nothing like a cold Coca-Cola after a hot round of golf.

Herb Wind was a man in a checkered golf cap, tweed suit, shirt and tie, and shooting stick, a Yale man who studied at Cambridge in England. He was sociable, painfully polite, and could tell fascinating tales of literary folk and popular athletes he'd known, and could cut a figure down to size in his own debonair way.

Herb made me laugh the day I asked him about Robert Sweeny, a romantic figure who'd won the 1937 British Amateur and was runner-up to Arnold Palmer in the 1954 U.S. Amateur. He'd moved in social circles from Long Island to Palm Beach. The word was that Sweeny had volunteered and flown Spitfires in the Eagle Squadron of the RAF when World War II broke out.

Herb said, "Yes, well, it's sometimes easier to do that sort of thing than pay your bills."

There was the day Herb and I were checking in for our press credentials at Royal Birkdale for the '71 British Open. We found ourselves receiving a lecture from the proper Englishman George Sims, who for many years was in charge of the press for the R&A.

After handing us our badges and armbands, George said, "You will *not* walk to the left of No. 1. You *must* stay to the right of No. 4. Crossing the seventh is *not* allowed. Please do *not* attempt to circle behind the 10th. It is *imperative* that you keep right of the 14th, and by *all* means have your badge and armband visible at all times."

Herb smiled and said, "Thank you, George. Now if you will hand me my copy of *The Pilgrim's Progress* I'll be on my way."

Aside from his profiles in *The New Yorker*, Herb was known for his book *The Story of American Golf*, published in 1948 and updated twice since. It's still the finest history ever written on the game. By 1957 he would become even better known for writing *Ben Hogan's Five Lessons: The Modern Fundamentals of Golf*.

When Herb's *Five Lessons* came out, the book introduced the world to two strange words: "pronate" and "supinate." Herb wrote that Ben "pronated" in his swing when, at impact, his forearms and hands were in the perfect position and his left foot was slightly opened in his stance.

Personally, I'd have bet one kidney that Ben Hogan—like me—had never heard the words "pronate" and "supinate," much less used them in conversation.

I said to Herb, who was a member at a quaint private golf club on Long Island, "You people at Sands Point may pronate and supinate, but if we tried it at Goat Hills in Fort Worth, our tee shots would wind up in somebody's front yard across the street, which may or may not be out of bounds, depending on the rules of the day."

Herb had been a fixture at *The New Yorker* for seven years, but he was soon to be the first golf writer for a new publication called *Sports Illustrated*. That relationship lasted only four years. Herb returned to *The New Yorker* where he was more comfortable with leisurely deadlines and no space restrictions.

He may have been paid his highest compliment by Herb Graffis, an old Chicago sportswriter turned golf industry promoter. In a group of writers who were discussing the most talented in their trade, Graffis said, "Let's face it. Herb Wind can write better than all of us put together with a bucket of whitewash and a paintbrush stuck up his ass."

In any case, Herbert Warren Wind gets full credit for establishing the notion that pro golf's biggest events should be known as "majors."

However, it took Arnold Palmer to sell it.

I WAS STILL AT THE *PRESS* in 1960 when I covered Palmer winning his second Masters with birdies on the last two holes to defeat the unlucky Ken Venturi. That was when Palmer became the "Whoo, ha, go get 'em, Arnie" that the public would begin to worship as if he were Lassie.

In his press conference after winning that Masters, Arnold talked about his desire to win "majors," and tossed out the possibility of a modern Grand Slam. He was thinking about entering the British Open in July at St. Andrews. Only a handful of Americans had won it, he reminded us, adding that it said something about the British Open title when greats like Bobby Jones, Walter Hagen, Gene Sarazen, Sam Snead, and Ben Hogan had gone over and tried to win it—and did.

Will Grimsley of the AP was in the audience that afternoon and saw Arnold's comments as a magazine piece. So it was that one week before the U.S. Open in June, out came an article in *The Saturday Evening Post* by Arnold Palmer as told to Will Grimsley with a headline shouting, "I WANT THAT GRAND SLAM." Interestingly, the word "major" never appears in the piece. But there is a reference to golf's "Big Four."

Any mention of Arnold Palmer is prohibited by law without Cherry

Hills attached to it. The last day of the 1960 U.S. Open at Cherry Hills in Denver has been immortalized and replayed so many times in print and on TV, I feel like I've only heard about it instead of being there.

Right down to the end on that bright afternoon of June 18 it produced a clash of eras involving three of the greatest names golf would know. A thirty-year-old Palmer, the current king, a forty-eight-year-old Ben Hogan, the past king, and a twenty-year-old Jack Nicklaus, the future king.

It remains to this moment the most incredible last day of a major I ever covered.

Since I was there, I can verify what took place in the Cherry Hills locker room between 18s on "Open Saturday."

My golf writing pal Bob Drum and I had gone in the locker room for lunch. At that point in history the "working press" was welcome in the locker room to chat, dine, hang out. This was because the players needed us print people to help spread their fame, make them richer. They no longer do. They have TV.

We'd scooped hamburgers and ice tea off the buffet and were sitting on a bench near an exit when Arnold Palmer came by on the way to his fourth round. He was not to be mistaken for a threat. He'd shot 72-71-72 and was seven strokes and 14 players behind. Nobody had ever come back to win from that far behind in a U.S. Open with only 18 to play.

"There's two guys working hard," Arnold said. Latrobe humor.

Bob Drum had been covering Palmer since he was a junior golfer in western Pennsylvania. They were good buddies. Partly through my friendship with Drum, I'd come to know Arnold fairly well.

"Go on, boy, get out of here," Drum said. "Go make your usual six birdies and shoot 73."

A reference to Palmer's aggressive style. Arnold's spiraling popularity was partly due to him thinking he could drive the ball through tree trunks, hit irons out of quicksand, hitch up his trousers, take a drag on a cigarette, and sink a 30-foot putt. But too frequently his boldness scared up as many bogeys as birdies.

"That first hole bugs me," Arnold said. "I ought to be able to drive the green. I've come close."

The first hole at Cherry Hills was a downhill 346-yard par four, but protecting the green was a ditch and a big patch of USGA cabbage. Length was needed to reach the green, but a lucky bounce wouldn't hurt.

Palmer had double bogeyed the hole in the first round, birdied it in the second, but bogied it that morning.

"What good will it do you?" Drum said.

"I can get a birdie or an eagle," said Arnold.

"Great," Drum said. "You'll tie for 28th."

Arnold said, "If I start with a birdie I might get it going for a 65. A 65 would give me 280. Doesn't 280 always win the Open?"

"Yeah, when Hogan shoots it," I said.

Palmer laughed and went out the door.

What happened over the next thirty minutes came in a series of verbal reports. Maybe I ought to mention that TV was covering only the last four holes then.

Now in the Cherry Hills locker room a guy poked his head in the door and said, "Arnie drove the first green! He two-putted for a birdie!"

Bob Drum grinned. "I'll be damned."

Time passed.

Then a USGA committeeman came in and said, "Arnold chipped in for a birdie at two."

Drum and I laughed.

More time passed.

Another USGA committeeman came in with a walkie-talkie, and a big grin. He called out, "Arnold almost holed it for an eagle at the third. He got the birdie. He's three under."

Drum and I looked at each other. Should we? Naw. He'll make a bogey any minute.

A moment later we heard that Mike Souchak had driven into the ditch at No. 1 and made a double bogey. We shrugged. Had the leader opened the door? Lot of golf left.

Now an excited Cherry Hills member entered and hollered, "Arnie holed a 20-footer for birdie at the fourth! He's four under through four!"

Drum said, "That son of a bitch!"

I said, "Yeah."

We tore out of the locker room door and set a sportswriters' record for the 3,000-yard run to catch Palmer at No. 5.

It was the fastest I'd moved since I ran after Foot the Free in the Goat Hills parking lot to collect the eight bucks I'd won from him before he slipped away—and wouldn't remember it later.

It was the fastest Robert Francis Xavier Drum of the *Pittsburgh Press* had moved since World War II, when he was Sergeant Drum of the U.S. Army. "You are aptly named," said his commander. "Big, loud, and empty." This was in '43, when Drum was chasing Rommel out of North Africa and capturing the Wadi Zim Zim.

We arrived at No. 5 in time to see Palmer miss a birdie putt. But he sank a 20-foot birdie at the sixth and stiffed a 7-iron at the seventh and went to six under through his first seven holes. In front of him and behind him, the field was feeling shock waves.

Arnold impulsively went for the flag at the 233-yard eighth hole but found a bunker and bogeyed. But he got back on track and parred the ninth. He was out in a five-under 30.

We pushed up against the ropes at the 10th tee. Palmer saw us as he arrived and came over to the ropes.

"Fancy seeing you here," he said with a grin. "Who's winning the Open?"

"Everybody!" Drum said, loud enough for two fans to glare at him.

Over the last hour the lead had been held or shared by Arnold Palmer, Ben Hogan, Jack Nicklaus, Mike Souchak, Julius Boros, Ted Kroll, Dutch Harrison, Jack Fleck, Jerry Barber, and Dow Finsterwald. It was a demolition derby out there.

On the 10th tee Arnold said, "Damn, I wanted that 29."

"The 30 ain't bad," I said. "Some of 'em are starting to back off. One or two more birdies might get it."

Arnold relieved me of my Coca-Cola, fresh from a concession stand, and my pack of Winstons.

"Keep 'em," said Drum, a nonsmoker. "He has eight more packs in his pockets."

I did have two more. You can't have too many on deadline.

Arnold kept the Coke and Winstons. My contribution to what would be his dramatic victory.

He birdied the 11th hole and parred the others on the back nine for his fantastic 65 and winning total of 280 that caused him to throw his red visor in the air. He needed a little help, though, like any Open winner.

Every player in contention faltered on the closing holes one way or another, mostly on the greens. Drum and I drifted back and forth between groups to absorb it all.

Nicklaus, the beefy crew-cut amateur, had eagled the seventh and birdied the ninth and parred 10, 11, and 12, and stood over a 10-foot birdie putt at 13 that would put him two ahead. But he stroked it two feet past the cup, missed it coming back, and wound up three-putting. In fact, he three-putted three of the last six greens. And just when my mind was writing a story about an amateur winning the U.S. Open for the first time since Johnny Goodman in 1933.

Now it was crunch time for Hogan. He had hit every green in regulation—34 in a row. He looked flawless. A young Hogan. When he holed a 20-foot birdie at 14, he pulled into a tie with Palmer. He had a chance to seize the lead with a 10-foot birdie at 16, but it curled out.

A Hogan-Palmer playoff was looking like a mortal lock, but here came Cherry Hills' 518-yard par-five 17th hole. Ben placed his drive and second shot in perfect position, and with Palmer back on the tee watching, Hogan faced a 70-yard pitch, the pin down front just beyond the pond.

Two pars to the house would give Ben 280. A birdie and par would put him in at 279. Either way, the pressure would be on Palmer.

Drum and I were inside the ropes, no more than 30 yards away from Hogan as he addressed the pitch shot, and my mind was writing a story about Ben winning his fifth "official" Open, his sixth overall.

Mere seconds before Hogan hit the pitch, I whispered to Drum, "I'll tell you one thing. He *will* be over the water."

Yeah, right.

Ben hit the pitch fat. Just a tiny bit fat. I could hear it. The ball struck the embankment and rolled back in the water.

A sad scene followed. Ben removed a shoe, rolled up a pants leg, and splashed it out. But he missed the 15-foot putt for par. Then for the first time I ever saw him do it, he lost his composure. He went for an extra-long tee ball at the 468-yard uphill 18th, but his foot slipped and he hooked the drive into the lake. He suffered a triple bogey seven.

He would finish tied for ninth, four back. A younger Ben Hogan would have played to clinch a par at the last hole to keep the pressure on Arnold.

In the locker room later, Ben said, "Palmer was having a good round. I thought I needed to finish four-four to beat him. I thought I hit a good shot at 17 . . . a good shot." He knew better. I'm sure of it.

A cigarette and a drink later, Ben said, "Hell, don't feel sorry for me. I played 36 holes today with a kid who could have won this Open by 10 shots if he'd known what he was doing."

A kid named Jack Nicklaus.

On deadline and into my last pack of Winstons, I wrote:

DENVER, Colo.—So it had come down to this. The 60th National Open golf championship had arrived at the moment when one immortal had to give it to another—from Ben Hogan to Arnold Palmer, with drenched wishes.

It came down to the 71st hole of a gasping last day here at Cherry Hills Country Club, down to a portrait of an aging Ben Hogan with a pants leg rolled up, standing in a watery grave, an ineffectual instrument of destiny in his helpless hands. Hogan had plainly lost the Open when he hit a pitch shot into the pond guarding the next to last hole. Now he had to wade in and make what he could of it and get out of the way.

Arnold Palmer had been lucky they let him inside the ropes for the first three rounds, but in the fourth he scored the most incredible knockout in golf history. He won this Open with a stunning six-under 65 over the final 18, elbowing his way through a convention of contenders like a Shriner who'd lost his fez. They fell all around him.

ON THE *FORT WORTH PRESS* BUDGET, there was only one way I could make it to St. Andrews for the British Open. Have Amelia Earhart turn up alive in Fort Worth and fly me to Scotland.

It was just as well I wasn't there. Palmer battled all the way with Roberto De Vicenzo, Gary Player, Peter Thomson, and Kel Nagle. Roberto led the first two rounds, but Kel Nagle, who was little known outside Australia, led after 54 holes by four strokes over Palmer. This set the stage for another Augusta–Cherry Hills charge by Palmer.

Out ahead of the Australian, Arnold shot a four-under 68 to reach the clubhouse with a 279 and the look of a winner. The Slam was alive. Nobody could have figured that Nagle would do something out-rageous like birdie the last two holes for a 71 and beat Palmer by a stroke.

I followed the action on the UP wire machine in the office at the *Press*. Had I been at St. Andrews, I'm afraid I would have been unable to stop my Olivetti from writing: "Meet Kel Nagle. Here's a man who really knows how to screw up a good story."

SPORTSWRITERS LOVE A DYNASTY. A dynasty sells. Something else they love is the sheer fun of seeing a dynasty crash and burn. That sells, too. In golf there has never been a greater dynasty than Jack Nicklaus, who tricked us. He never crashed and burned.

Jack would need a U-Haul to carry around his impressive records. His eighteen pro majors breaks down into six Masters, five PGAs, four U.S. Opens, and three British Opens. He was runner-up in nine-teen majors, and by one stroke in eight of them. Finished in the top five in a total of fifty-five majors.

Let the fawns of Tiger Woods chew on all that for a while.

Most of those records will stand until golf is played on top of Mt. Everest, or English is spoken in New Orleans. Interesting stat: if

Lee Trevino and Tom Watson had never picked up a golf club, Jack would have eight more majors. He was second to each of them four times.

Nicklaus may not have been the greatest shotmaker who ever played the game. He grants this was Hogan. But Jack was the first to combine astonishing length with accuracy from the tee—and he did it using persimmon, which is not a town in France. And he was the first to hit high long irons and hold them on the greens.

He was unquestionably the greatest winner. Nobody hit more crucial shots or sank more crucial putts in majors, and do it over a longer period of time than anyone ever. How about twenty years?

All athletes want to win, or claim they want to win, but I contend the greatest were those who utterly despised the thought of losing.

They come in all decades and all sizes. Ben Hogan was one. Sugar Ray Robinson another. Sam Baugh and Doak Walker on the football field. Sandy Koufax on the mound. Joe DiMaggio in the outfield and at the plate. Michael Jordan on the hardwood. Carl Lewis on the track. Michael Phelps in the pool. Martina Navratilova on the court. Too many to list, but so few when measured against the millions who've competed.

I once asked Jack if this mind-set applied to him.

He said, "I only know I was blessed with a God-given talent, and it would have been a shame to waste it."

It was my duty and pleasure to cover sixteen of Jack's eighteen victories in the majors, and sixteen of his nineteen second-place finishes in the majors. His winning of majors, his repetitious challenging to win majors, and his seventy-three tour victories brought with it a saying in the press rooms.

"Jack Nicklaus comma," we muttered to each other when Nicklaus's name would go up on the leaderboard. Sometimes we weren't joking.

Another thing set him apart for me personally. He was the best interview of any athlete I ever covered in any sport.

I'd seek out Jack before a major got under way. He'd tell me everything I wanted to know about the current state of his game, the key things to know about the golf course, and what 72-hole score it might take to win. When it ended, his analysis of why he won or lost would go on as long as you wished. Jack wasn't short on opinions about all things pertaining to humans, which brings up a Johnny Miller remark: "Nobody has ever heard Jack Nicklaus say 'I don't know' about any-thing."

It isn't always true that behind every great golfer there's a great wife. But I thought it was true in Jack's case. Barbara Nicklaus was the successor to Valerie Hogan as the champion golf wife. Attractive, sweet, gracious, generous, thoughtful . . . that was Barbara. It was easy to see why the wives of the other players of the era nicknamed her Wonder Woman.

I've given considerable thought to the secret of Jack's dominance. It evidently wasn't a handicap that his small hands forced him to use the interlocking grip instead of the standard Vardon. And it evidently wasn't a handicap that he was color-blind. Green to him looked sort of gray, as best he could describe it.

It was his mental attitude. And nothing sums that up better than a single quote. He once said to me: "I've never missed a putt in my mind."

But maybe Australian Bruce Crampton said it best. Crampton was runner-up to Jack four times in majors, and finally came to a conclu-sion: "We all suffer from human deficiencies," Bruce said. "Jack just suffers from fewer of them."

THIS JUST IN. Jack's 65 in the '86 Masters reminds me that I've been privileged to cover five of the greatest last rounds ever played in the long history of golf. Rounds that shook the earth, brought the greats from behind to win a major. The others were Hogan's 67 at Oakland Hills in the '51 U.S. Open, Arnold's 65 at Cherry Hills in the '60 U.S. Open, Johnny Miller's 63 at Oakmont in the '73 U.S. Open, and, just recently, Phil Mickelson's otherworldly 66 in the 2013 British Open on torturous, baffling Muirfield.

No jokes were needed. Those stories told themselves.

Chapter 14

Behind the Scenes in the Wonderful World of Golf

HAVING SPENT MUCH OF MY LIFE around tournament golf, I could tell you about so many crisp 5-irons I've seen played out of awkward divots and so many fabulous 4-woods I've seen hit out of cuppy lies, your head would spin around like Linda Blair's in *The Exorcist*. But I'm too nice a guy to do that to you.

What I will do is share some enthralling moments in journalism that occurred beyond the fairways and greens, moments that you couldn't dislodge from my memory with a 5-iron or a 4-wood.

IT WAS THE NIGHT BEFORE THE last round of the Masters in 1959, the one where Art Wall came out of nowhere to win it with a 66. Bob Drum and I were having cocktails in the lobby of the mammoth Bon Air Hotel, once a gathering place for contestants and Calcutta pool participants. Art was standing alone in a corner.

We went over to visit with him. Golf talk. Pleasant. But an older Southern gentleman, notably overserved, barged into our circle. He said, "Ain't you Art Wall?"

Art confessed that he was, in fact, Art Wall.

The man said, "Ain't you the old boy who's supposed to have made all them hole-in-ones?"

Art said, "Yes, sir. I've made thirty-four so far."

The Southern gentleman gaped at him. "Bubba, who you tryin' to kid? *Bobby* didn't make but three!"

I had my lead.

THE YEAR WAS 1962. It was the first of two engaging incidents involving this bureau at Colonial tournaments.

It happened that George Low was on the scene. "America's Guest." The putting wizard. A man known as someone who followed the PGA tour to make a living on wagers. He was a good source of information.

George cornered me outside the pro shop before Colonial's final round on Sunday. He planted $1,000 in $100 bills in my hand, saying he wanted to bet it on Arnold Palmer, the tournament leader, against any other player of someone's choice on today's round. He was certain I could find a gentleman with such sporting blood, this being my hometown. I did know people of that persuasion. I went down to the shade trees behind the ninth green and found Bill (Circus Face) Jerdan and J. B. (Jawbreaker) King in their straw hats and sport coats. Circus Face said, "I'm just relaxin'. I don't know nothin' about golf—except it's real slow."

Jawbreaker said, "I'll pick somebody," and studied the pairings sheet in his hand. A moment later he crammed $1,000 cash into my palm, saying, "I believe I'll take old Ted Kroll."

"Ted Kroll?" I almost yelled. "Ted Kroll against *Arnold Palmer?*"

"You want some of it?" Jawbreaker asked.

"No thanks," I said. "I'll just spend the next four hours trying not to get mugged." The two grand in bills in my pocket felt like a grapefruit.

I reported to George that he had to beat Ted Kroll today. He looked pleased. But four hours later he didn't look pleased. On a severely windy afternoon, Arnold shot a woeful 76 and Ted Kroll, having finished two hours earlier, had come in with a 75.

"Get my ass out of Texas," George said.

As I handed Jawbreaker the $2,000 in cash, and was much relieved to be rid of it, he said, "Wonder how come I picked old Ted Kroll?"

I said, "If I had to guess, I'd say you knew the forecast was for high winds this afternoon. Palmer was teeing off last, and Ted Kroll would be going out early under easier conditions."

J.B. said, "Aw, hell, I ain't that smart . . . am I?"

IN THE SPRING OF '65, again at Colonial, I had assured my *SI* bosses that the Colonial tournament would be a good story because it was "the Masters of the Southwest."

I made that up, but it was true. Great course. "Hogan's Alley." Strong field. Huge galleries. When I returned to Fort Worth I discovered that the jacked-up mini and the headlights halter top had found their way to the tournament. The young ladies wearing them seemed to be doing the Shake or the Locomotion, even as they stood still. They had everything going for them but a sign around their necks that said: IF YOU DON'T BELIEVE HE LOVES ME, JUST ASK HIS WIFE.

This was convenient. Heavy rains arrived on the weekend and all but ruined the tournament. Rain plus George Knudson and Bruce Crampton. What I was left to write was the rain, Colonial history, Knudson, Crampton, and the jacked-up minis.

I included guys in the clubhouse who held up numbers to the windows, scoring the young ladies like Olympic dives. One creative gentleman brought a poster board with a message on it to display at a proper moment. The message said: "TELL THE ONE IN BLUE TO TURN AROUND."

It worked out nicely that I had such subjects to deal with since the downpours on Sunday and Monday forced the final round to be played on Tuesday. That was well past *Sports Illustrated*'s deadline.

Crampton won after Knudson led for five days, but my piece

couldn't tell you that. My piece had to be in by Monday afternoon. So it ended with, "But after all that, it didn't much matter who won."

Back in the office in New York an editor changed the kicker line to, "But that's the way it is with the Colonial. Come hail or high water, it gives the pros an event to remember."

That "hail or high water" thing just wouldn't turn him loose. But either way, it was the only story I ever wrote without a result in it.

FILE UNDER EXOTIC. It was the trip June and I took to Morocco in 1970. I went to do a piece about Claude Harmon and his golf pupil, King Hassan II. "Where a Golf Nut Is King" would be the headline.

We hit Marrakesh, Casablanca, Rabat, and Fez. We wandered about in the midst of casbahs, Saharan dancers, hash cookies, Berbers, camels, veiled women, Yvonne de Carlo, Peter Lorre. We were royally treated by the helpful Abdessian Jaidi, Moroccan general consul in New York.

Monsieur Jaidi arranged a dinner party for us and Claude Harmon at the home of the king's private architect. It was there that Claude made a toast that wound up belonging to Big Ed Bookman in *Semi-Tough*.

Claude seized everyone's attention, and said, "You come into this world naked and bare. . . . You go out of this world you know not where. . . . But if you're a thoroughbred here, you're a thoroughbred there."

Monsieur Jaidi attempted to translate the toast to the Arab guests among us. "No, you are not horse," he said. "Yes, naked the person, but horse is honorable. Yes, you leave the world, but horse . . ."

The morning I watched the king play golf, it was on his private nine-hole course inside the palace walls in Fez. Pheasants waddled along the fairways. I was nervous. How should I greet the king?

Claude said, "He's a king, but he's an intelligent man. He speaks English. You stick out your hand and you look him in the eye."

I did exactly that. I stuck out my hand to King Hassan II, I looked him in the eye, and I said, "Good majess, your morningsty."

————

IN THE DULL, commonplace occurrences of day-to-day living, there are dinner party exchanges you can't forget. One of them was in the Gray Fox restaurant in Pinehurst in 1971. I was covering a short-lived golf tournament, the Liggett & Myers U.S. Match Play Championship.

There were two tables of us, side by side. June was with me and we were sitting with Jack Whitaker and other CBS folk. At the next table among the others was Bill Brendle, the network's sports PR guy.

A week earlier I'd lunched with Brendle in Shor's and he complained that his wife, Frances, had sold his Nazi sword in a garage sale. Now I was telling Whitaker about it. Jack said with surprise, "Bill was in the war? I've known him twenty years and he's never mentioned it." With that, Jack hollered at the table, "Billy, what outfit were you in?"

Brendle called back, "Fifth Infantry. The Red Diamonds."

Jack said, "Second Armored."

Back at our table, Whitaker said, "I'll be damned. We were both in Patton's Third Army and I *now* find out about it. We saw some action in a couple of siege towns, but we missed Metz. Metz was the worst. The German 88s were up there. The Americans were stalled down below."

Jack hollered at Brendle again.

"Billy! Were you at Metz?"

Brendle hollered back.

"I fucking *took* Metz!"

THE NIGHT OF THE FIRST U.S. Open at Pebble Beach in 1972, June and I were having dinner at a French joint in Carmel with two longtime Texas pals, Dave Marr, the 1965 PGA champion who was entering a new career as a TV commentator, and Don Cherry, a top amateur golfer who'd left Wichita Falls to become a Walker Cup player and "the singing golfer."

After Cherry entertained us with tales of his colorful personal

life—"I married a Miss America, a Miss Universe, and a *Mistake*"—
the conversation moved on to Jack Nicklaus's slim lead in the Open
and whether he'd hold off the challenges of Arnold Palmer, Lee Trevino, and Bruce Crampton.

I was prepared for anybody to win but Crampton, the Australian.
He was a good player but walked around with the look of a pout-
ing brat. I knew many pros on the tour found him to be rude and
unfriendly.

Turning to Marr, I said, "I may have to write Crampton tomorrow
night. Tell me three things he's done to you guys to make you dislike
him."

It took only a second for Dave to respond. He said: "Get born . . .
come to America . . . stay."

THE 1975 U.S. OPEN AT MEDINAH on the outskirts of Chicago—that
place where the clubhouse looks like the Babylon Marriott—made
you wonder if God had invented golf and misery in the same week. It
was hot, it was humid, and Lou Graham won after Jack Nicklaus, Tom
Watson, Ben Crenshaw, Frank Beard, Hale Irwin, Bob Murphy, and
John Mahaffey helped give it to him.

Nicklaus was tied for the lead with three holes to play, but bogeyed
all three, totally out of character. Crenshaw was leading on the 71st
tee but hit it in the water. Beard could have won if he'd only shot a
poor old 76, but he shot a poor old 78. Watson could have won if he'd
only shot a two-over 73 on Sunday, but he shot a six-over 77. All of the
others had their own morbid tales to tell.

When Mahaffey and Graham tied to force the 18-hole playoff on
Monday, the groans in the press tent could be heard in Racine, Wisconsin. First, the press was unhappy there'd be a playoff at all, and
second, there weren't a lot of Jack Nicklauses in it.

I was on a tough deadline Monday after Lou Graham beat
Mahaffey 71 to 73, and the local workers had apparently taken the
day off. There was no food or drink anywhere. Even the water cooler
had been removed from the press tent. Unions.

I was sweating, thirsty, hungry, and irritable but pounding the keys to meet the deadline when I heard a voice behind me, the soft Southern voice of a young lady.

The voice said, "Be nice, Dan. He's really a good guy."

I looked around to find Patsy Graham, Lou's wife.

I fell about laughing. She saved the week for me.

THE '83 U.S. OPEN AT OAKMONT was a mess. Two violent storms interrupted play on Friday and Sunday. Lightning struck trees and Larry Nelson struck Tom Watson and Seve Ballesteros with his putter on Monday.

But the thing I remember best was going to meet Dave Marr for lunch in the players' lounge of the clubhouse. I got there early and saw only one player, J. C. Snead. He was stretched out on a couch.

I didn't know J.C., only his reputation for being gruff and unhelpful to his pro-am partners. I'd made sport of him in print.

I was in the lounge a matter of seconds before a volunteer in a tournament blazer grabbed my arm. "You're not allowed in here. This is for players only."

I said, "You take a week's vacation to do this shit, don't you?"

The volunteer said, "I'm just following the rules, sir."

"He's with me!" J.C. spoke up to the guy.

The volunteer released me, saying, "If a player invites you, it's okay."

I took a seat on the couch next to J. C. Snead. But before I could thank him, he said, "You still think I'm an asshole?"

A friendship was born.

IT WAS JARRING. It was sentimental. It was historic. It was the '86 Masters. Jack Nicklaus, at the age of forty-six, fired a 65 to come from four strokes and nine players back to win his sixth green jacket and 18th major.

Nicklaus caught and passed Australia's Greg Norman, Spain's Seve Ballesteros, South Africa's Nick Price, Germany's Bernhard Langer, and Japan's Tommy Nakajima, not to overlook Tom Watson and Tom Kite of the USA.

I was by then on deadline for *Golf Digest*, swiftly typing that if you wanted to put golf back on the front pages where it hadn't been since Ben Hogan's Triple Crown, you let Jack Nicklaus go out on the Augusta National in the last round and kill more foreigners than a general named Eisenhower.

That's when something occurred that I don't remember, but Walt Bingham does. Walt is a good friend and was once my editor in the *Sports Illustrated* days.

Walt recalls a young writer sitting next to me taking it upon himself to say, "Wow. Have you ever seen a story like this? So big you can't write it?"

"No," I said, without looking up, continuing to type.

I hope the incident is true.

If you aren't aware that no story can ever be bigger than your deadline, you've chosen the wrong profession.

THE FOLLY OF POLITICAL CORRECTNESS became a little too personal for me when I started to tweet at the majors for *Golf Digest*. I quickly learned to tweet gingerly. This is because I discovered there were long lines of people in our midst who live in Victimhood and hope to be insulted, affronted, disparaged, or even physically injured by a mere joke.

In today's celebrity culture in which I work, I realize that Britney Spears has at least two million more followers than I do, and I know that somewhere there's a serial rapist whose likeness has been on TV who has 27 million more followers than Britney Spears. I can live with that.

To most people, a tweet goes along the lines of, "I'm leaving the canned goods aisle now and heading for the bakery."

But I have to endure the attacks of commenters and bloggers if I happen to tweet something in 140 characters that makes people laugh or maybe even think.

What can happen is that an attempt at humor can turn a male blogger or commenter into Vladimir Lenin on four cups of Colombian dark roast, and turn female bloggers and commenters into Magda Goebbels on amphetamines.

I have even watched a bunch of youthful sportswriters—my own people—become moralistic on an issue. And by the way, if there's anything sillier than a moralistic sportswriter, it can only be one of our left-wing, moonbat university professors—whose numbers are legion, regrettably—hiding behind "academic freedom" to spout Marxist garbage at impressionable students.

Ah, nostalgia. There were no word police around when Arnold Palmer lent his name to a chain of cleaners and I quoted Dave Marr saying, "If I'm looking for a cleaners, I'll go to Chen Ching-po."

And there were no word police around when Taiwan's T. C. Chen blew the U.S. Open at Oakland Hills in '85. After leading for three rounds, Chen coughed up a quadruple bogey eight on Sunday, and I couldn't keep from writing how it was only a reminder that most things made in Taiwan seldom last more than three days.

It's unfortunate today that I can't glance up at the scoreboard at an LPGA tournament, read all those Oriental names at the top—Shin, Jeong, Kang, Kim, Sung—and borrow from my late colleague Furman Bisher to say in all good humor that it sounds like pots and pans being tossed down a staircase.

But I've learned to laugh off bloggers and commenters the way I laugh off airport security guards these days—the ones who try to keep my belt and golf cap from blowing up Delta 1482 to Atlanta.

Folks, I take a backseat to no one—I mean, *nobody*—in my contempt for political correctness. It's censorship. It's an assault on humor. It's an assault on free speech. If carried to an extreme, it's a plot to destroy America.

Thought up by nitwits in the teaching industry and those silly geese in the Modern Language Association, it has sadly been latched on to by the editors of our nation's newspapers. They live in fear that a joke might offend an Islamic terrorist, and the Islamic terrorist might write an angry Letter to the Editor, and then where would we be?

TOP, LEFT: Catherine Louise O'Hern Jenkins—my mother.

TOP, RIGHT: Dear old dad—Bud Jenkins, his ownself.

LEFT: Aunt Loes (Sister) before leaving for Hollywood and her job at Paramount in the wardrobe department.

BOTTOM: Mimmie and Pap. Is he a U.S. deputy marshal out of central casting or what? But just a granddad to me.

"If that little kid back there behind us in a striped shirt grows up to be a golf writer, this game is in *BIG* trouble!"

TOP: From a tough lie at Goat Hills to the TCU golf team—with no change in the swing.

MIDDLE: Day before 1941 U.S. Open at Colonial. That's me in the striped shirt following the foursome of Tommy Armour, Gene Sarazen, Lawson Little, and Byron Nelson.

BOTTOM: Posing with Ben Hogan in '53 after a round of golf. That's his "door-knob" putter I'm holding.

TOP: With Ben at what must be a National Open in the late '50s, since I seem to be wearing my gold USGA press badge.

MIDDLE: World's greatest sports staff in 1955, posing for a *Fort Worth Press* Christmas card. Standing left to right, Jerre Todd, Blackie Sherrod, His Ownself. Seated: Andy Anderson, Bud Shrake.

BOTTOM: Hanging out at TCU football workout with my guru and grandfather, Blackie Sherrod.

TOP: Senior writer at work on the *Sports Illustrated* floor of the old Time-Life Building. We dressed better in the early '60s. Office with windows was huge.

MIDDLE: In the company of immortals. Two of football's greatest players, Doak Walker and Bobby Layne. Honored to call them friends.

BOTTOM: Aftermath of a "Poll Bowl." These Irish fans evidentially didn't like my piece on the 1966 Notre Dame–Michigan State game.

112201 11/22/66 NOTRE DAME, INDIANA .. Irate students of the University of Notre Dame burn all copys of SPORTS ILLUSTRATED because of what they say is adverse copy about the Notre Dame footba team and head Coach Ara Paraseghian... UNITED PRESS INTERNATIONAL   JEM/jem

TOP: Doing an instruction article with Arnold Palmer in Latrobe. The only instruction article I ever wrote, or read.

MIDDLE: Two of my favorite saloon owners: Toots Shor and Danny (P. J. Clarke's) Lavezzo.

BOTTOM: A cigarette to calm the nerves before teeing off with my partner Johnny Miller and Jack Nicklaus in the World Cup Pro-Am in Marbella, Spain, 1973.

TOP: Here are a couple of gentlemen, Ben and Byron, who'll play you, and they'll use persimmon.

MIDDLE: Freezing writer with America's first men's medalists in Olympic ski racing, Billy Kidd and Jimmie Heuga, in Innsbruck, Austria, 1964.

BOTTOM: Playing speed golf with Prez Bush 41 at Holly Hills Country Club in Maryland, 1990.

Be it known that

Dan Jenkins

was an invited guest
of
President George Bush
on board the
Presidential Retreat, Camp David

June 23, 1990

PRESIDENT OF THE UNITED STATES

TOP, LEFT: Just offering proof, is all.

TOP, RIGHT: On the movie set near the "honey wagon."

LEFT: Humble sportswriter's display cases in World Golf Hall of Fame.

BOTTOM: Humble sportswriter accepts induction into the World Golf Hall of Fame in 2012, St. Augustine, Florida.

TOP: Daughter beats Dad on deadline at 2012 U.S. Open, drops by to gloat. Only happened this once.

MIDDLE: With Marty Jenkins and Danny Jenkins, two ferocious ends on the McBurney High Highlanders of '79.

BOTTOM: Prettiest lady in the room at "21" in the early Gotham days—and she's with me.

Astoundingly, the word "foreigner" is now frowned upon. This means that if Gary Player became the first foreigner to win the Masters, as he did back in 1961, my piece would have had to begin:

"South Africa's Gary Player today became the first passport-challenged golfer to win the Masters."

But while the word "foreigner" now lives in danger, the word police have wrapped their arms around "European." I'm stunned by this. I've been traveling to Europe for sixty years and become friends with Englishmen, Frenchmen, Germans, Spaniards, Italians, Swiss, even a Belgian, but I've never met a European.

A gentleman has never come up to me on Jermyn Street, the Via Veneto, the Bahnhofstrasse, or even on the links of St. Andrews, and said, "Hello, I am a proud European. You are a proud North American, yes?"

Not yet, Gunther.

Still and all, I feel good about the United States of America, the greatest nation in human history. Our people have proved they can survive any evil, overcome any threat to our freedom—maybe even PC.

There are hopeful signs. I have a gray-haired friend who has finally rid himself of the ponytail he's been wearing since 1968. I now come across more and more people who hate carrot cake. I've seen a woman in a red car actually use her turn signal.

Sometime soon we're going to be asked to fight off an attempt to invade us, and we shall respond testily, not only with the word "unacceptable" but quite possibly even with our Army, Navy, Marines, and Air Force.

Taking advantage of our political correctness, some pissant country that leads the league in dirt will be poised at our border. It will be led by a ruler who looks like Hugo Chávez in a gilded quilt with a peacock on his head.

The invaders will be lured into thinking we're weak because 315 million Americans have suddenly collapsed by being offended by something.

Chapter 15

We Wanted to Get Out from
Under the Soot, Is All

HISTORIANS OF SPORTS JOURNALISM, a small group but one that still outnumbers Norwegian comedians, have recorded that the world's greatest sports staff—in their own minds, that old gang of mine—began breaking up in the late '50s.

Blackie Sherrod, who had put us together, couldn't resist an offer to revamp the sports department of the *Dallas Times Herald*, and he took Bud Shrake with him as his ace writer and intrepid explorer of Big D nightlife.

I inherited the job as sports editor of the *Press* and managed to keep the ship afloat for three years, thanks to the efforts of Jerre Todd, Gary Cartwright, Andy Anderson, "Sick Charlie" Modesette, and Puss Ervin.

Jerre Todd was the next to go. He left to start his own PR and advertising firm. It became wildly successful. Starting with a group of bowling proprietors for clients, he grew to represent the Colonial golf tournament, banks, oil companies, car dealers, and beauty pageants. But there was a reason he left the newspaper business in the first place, a reason that struck at the financial heart of journalism itself.

"I wanted a color TV," he said. Still says it. Gets laughs.

It would be remiss of me not to speak of the time that Jerre and I shared an apartment with a package of bologna.

We were both single then, dating the Too Tight and Too Cheap. Friends came from miles around to check on the package of bologna, the only thing in the frig—we ate every meal out. They wanted to see how much the bologna had swollen since the last visit. When it reached the size of a football, Jerre spiraled it into an outdoor garbage can.

But better times lay directly ahead for us.

June and I found ourselves unattached, available for dinner dates, the fires were relit, and we married.

This didn't detract my friends from coming up with songs, dances, and snappy patter to celebrate June changing my life.

At social gatherings Jerre Todd relished performing his version of "June in January."

It's June, not Joan you'll marry
The word's all around.
She puts a spring in your heart,
With never a frown.
Your columns are pure white blossoms
*   June wears like a gown.*
And there's one more reason to smile—
Joan's moved out of town.

Bud Shrake and Jap Cartwright's big number was a takeoff on "Surrey with the Fringe on Top."

Gips and jerks and chumps scooter-roon-o
Jenkie's going out with his June, oh
Always going out with his June, oh,
When his column's in.
Hand in hand they stroll at their leisure
He'll do almost anything to please her.

He's got the Frogs and Owls in a teaser
And they both should win.
Oh, they'll have a cottage on Mulberry Lane . . .

I believe I've stated elsewhere that nothing was sacred in our crowd.

We bought a two-story house on Sunset Terrace, a shady street only a block long, on the edge of downtown. It dated back to the turn of the century when the neighborhood was known as Society Hill. The tag no longer belonged, but that didn't ruin the charm.

We found the house sitting empty, tracked down the owner, who was living in Connecticut and was eager to sell it. It was our wedding gift to each other.

We were doing okay as young people go. I was the sports editor of a daily newspaper, and June was the fashion coordinator of the Fair Store downtown—Fort Worth's Neiman Marcus. The former TCU Homecoming Queen had once been a fashion model at the Fair in her college days.

Our next-door neighbor on Sunset Terrace was Mrs. Watt Reynolds of the Reynolds Cattle Company, a ranching family that occupies 100 years of West Texas history. Behind her large red-brick home were the remnants of what must have been a carriage house and stables.

I learned from Mrs. Reynolds that I wasn't the first writer to sit on her front porch.

She said, "Edna Ferber sat right where you are today. We couldn't have been nicer to her. We helped her in so many ways, telling her about ranch life and cattle breeding, then she went off and wrote that awful book."

That awful book was *Giant*.

It spawned the movie starring Elizabeth Taylor, Rock Hudson, and James Dean, a film that New York critics considered an accurate depiction of Texas, and intelligent Texans considered a farce.

The biggest news of 1960 for the couple living on Sunset Terrace, not Mulberry Lane, was the birth of their twins, Sally and Marty.

The waiting room at Harris Hospital in those wee hours of the morning was occupied by friends from high school, college, and journalism, who came and went. Two stayed till the end—Marty McAllister and Pat Driskill, the former Pattie Ann O'Dell, my first ex-wife.

It was a Paschal thing.

The most wonderful words I'd ever hear spoken came from a smiling nurse named Mary, who stuck her head in the waiting room and said: "Girl at 3:57, boy at 4:04. Everybody's doing great."

And I would never forget the first hazy words that June Jenkins, radiant mother, said when I went to her bedside. Smiling faintly, she murmured: "Chocolate sundae."

SALLY, MARTY, AND DANNY ENJOY HEARING how they could have been born in the Cotton Bowl.

Their mother was sitting on the photo deck of the Cotton Bowl two weeks before the twins were born. I was covering Darrell Royal's Texas Longhorns whipping Bud Wilkinson's Oklahoma Sooners, but was poised to rush June to the hospital if the twins kicked in.

The following year of '61 June was again seated on the Cotton Bowl photo deck with Danny Jenkins while I covered the Longhorns defeating the Sooners again. Danny was born twelve days later.

All three of our kids have done nothing but make us laugh and marvel at their varied talents and make us proud to have arranged their birth.

If you read, you may know what Sally's been up to in the journalism and literary world, like writing best-selling books and prize-winning newspaper columns. Marty once looked so much like me swinging a golf club, our friends shook with laughter. He has defied family genes and knows how to take things apart and rebuild them, from Range Rovers to electrical things to the economy—and like me, he only eats brown and white. Danny is married to the alluring Paulina, they have a delightful son, Noah, and Danny operates a travel and tourist business in Costa Rica. Having spent many summers growing up and living in Hawaii, Danny demands that an ocean be near at all times.

While June and I were doing our thing, Jerre Todd was discovering Melba Jordan, the sweetest and most beautiful redhead in the history of Dallas and suburbs. They married and have their own family of comedians, led by their sons Brooks and Britt.

The two couples, Jenkinses and Todds, would remain closer than family for the rest of this book and into eternal bliss.

Melba Todd would be disappointed if I didn't include a word about the ladies we honor in our Hall of Fame of Waitresses.

There was long tall Agnes, whose nickname was Mansfield, at the White Way Café, a breakfast joint near the *Press*. None of us could forget the morning Cowboy Hardly, a *Press* photographer, asked for cream gravy on his cantaloupe.

Mansfield said, "I'll do it, but I don't see nobody in here who's gonna watch you eat it."

The Todds and Jenkinses were dining at a fish camp one night on the Intracoastal Canal in Ponte Vedra, Florida, and after we'd finished the fried catfish, June asked our waitress, Paula Jean, for a cappuccino.

Paula Jean said, "A whut?"

June described a cappuccino.

Paula Jean said, "Hon, that ain't got here yet."

And there was Donna at the Brass Rail in downtown Dallas. The four of us spent many evenings in Dallas in the early '60s. Bud and Blackie were there, and we'd reassemble.

Donna seemed to be our waitress at the Brass Rail every time we dined there. Without fail, I would always order the plate of navy beans, ham bits, and rice. It was impossible to resist.

The evening we were back in the Brass Rail after the twins were born, we informed the waitress of the happy event.

Donna said, "What'd you name 'em? Ham Bits and Navies?"

ANYONE WHO BOTHERED TO LOOK AROUND the sportswriting landscape of Fort Worth and Dallas might have noticed that most of the staff of the *Fort Worth Press* was now part of the staff of the *Dallas Times Herald*.

Gary Cartwright had moved to Dallas in the dead of night. Blackie hired him to help cover the pro football wars between Clint Murchison's Dallas Cowboys and Lamar Hunt's Dallas Texans.

It was there that Gary would hone his talents into their finest pitch, and in '65 he would write his classic lead on a Dallas-Cleveland game in which Don Meredith's late-hour interception sealed the Cowboys doom and resulted in a wrenching 23–17 loss. Jap wrote: "Outlined against a gray November sky, the Four Horsemen rode again Sunday. You know them—Pestilence, Famine, Death, and Meredith."

Of course there was one more to leave Fort Worth, and I got the call from Blackie in the early fall of '61.

He said, "You ready to tear yourself away from the isosceles triangle copy paper?"

I said, "What do you have in mind?"

He said, "Executive sports editor. Run the staff. Write the second column. Cover golf and all the football you want to."

I said, "Would this be for fun? I have a wife and three children now."

Blackie said, "Double what you're making now, and we furnish pencils."

"Deal," I said. It was escaping the isosceles triangle copy paper that did it.

A word about the world's greatest sports staff in our own minds. Four of us—me, Bud, Jap, and Blackie—would have the audacity over the years to write and have published a total of fifty-four books. Both novels and nonfiction. Some of them best-sellers, some of them better than best-sellers, according to Jap.

This may not be the winner among sports staffs, but it's my entry in the derby.

Chapter 16

So There We Were, Living and Working
in Big D—My, Oh, Yes

MY TIME IN DALLAS, FOURTEEN MONTHS, was a combination of hard work, professional satisfaction, much frivolity, and eating chili and rice at Shanghai Jimmy's.

Moving from the *Press* to the *Times Herald* was a bigger shock than I'd imagined. The *Herald* was a locally owned paper dating back to 1888. It was in a modern building downtown. Big local readership. The typewriters were new, the copy paper rectangular, desks spacious, chairs comfortable, snack bar handy, a sprawling, big-time city room filled with busy people.

Bud Shrake and I passed each other like two shoppers in a department store. I was arriving at the *Herald* as he was going six blocks away to the *Dallas Morning News*, there to write the lead sports column and compete with Blackie Sherrod. Dallas readers were fortunate.

Here's Blackie on Rocky Marciano knocking out Jersey Joe Walcott:

Walcott went slowly to the floor, head down, as a Hindu on a prayer rug. His knees touched, and then his brow, and there he remained, like an upended slice of cantaloupe.

And here's Shrake handling a legendary game on a tough deadline:

BATON ROUGE—On a Halloween night that exploded with heroism, a booming Ole Miss punt came down out of the sky and into the arms of a muddy, nakedly dramatic figure, and it was finally time for Billy Cannon to win another game for LSU.

We lived in a modern apartment in a complex close to downtown Dallas. Blackie was a resident there, as was Don Klosterman, who was then with the Texans. The complex was owned by Lamar Hunt, who offered us a break on the rent but our journalistic integrity demanded we refuse it.

Lamar was the youngest of all pro football owners, roughly the same age as myself, and we struck up a friendship. He was close to the biggest sports fan I've known. He attended every sports event in town. I played in a member-guest golf tournament as his partner at Dallas Country Club. He went so far as to like soccer. He was known to invite former SMU athletes over to his house to "shoot some baskets."

Lamar was a very wealthy young man, but he didn't live like it or act like it. This was despite the famous remark of his father, H. L. Hunt, the old wildcatter who'd built the family fortune in oil. When a reporter asked his daddy how long Lamar could support a pro football team that was costing him $1 million a year, H.L. supposedly said, "About 150 years."

I'll not soon forget the evening Lamar came over to our apartment and asked me to come outside to see his new car. "Watch this," he said, proudly showing me this miracle of push-button windows.

I said, "I hate to tell you, Lamar, but everybody on our sports staff has a car that does this."

About the chili and rice. A carton of it brought you a step closer to heaven. Shanghai Jimmy himself was a wiry little man, an old retired Navy vet whose career was printed on the menu. "Ran the Yangtze River out of Shanghai on the USS *Panay* in '28 and '29 . . ."

The place was a hole in the wall within walking distance of the

Herald, but to us it was a shrine. The Double No. 9 quart-size carton was the thing to order. Jimmy would put in a scoop of rice, pat of margarine, scoop of his secret chili, another scoop of rice, another pat of margarine, a final big scoop of secret chili. Shredded cheese, chopped onions, and celery available for those who wished to enhance the taste.

Shanghai Jimmy's was the scene of the Great Chili-Rice Eat-Off of 1962, an event promoted by Blackie and our good Cleburne pal, Jack Proctor, fellow journalist.

It matched the *Times Herald* against the *Cleburne Times-Review.* Cleburne was thirty miles south of Fort Worth and the model for the fictional town of Claybelle, Texas, in *Fast Copy*, a newspaper novel set in the '30s that I had to get out of my system.

Jack Proctor was a throwback to the old Dallas newspaper wars of the '30s, when there were four dailies in town. Jack worked for the *Dispatch* and went up against crime reporters from the *Morning News, Times Herald*, and *Journal.* He still wore loud checkered sport coats and snap-brim hats that would do honor to Front Page Farrell.

Jack worked in the days when a reporter made up a story if he couldn't find one. He once wrote a story about an enjoyable dinner with Clyde Barrow and Bonnie Parker at the Stockyards Hotel in Fort Worth, one of their hideouts. A suite is named for them there today. Jack wrote a heartwarming piece about the celebrated bank robbers.

The trouble was, the editor of the *Dispatch* found out that Jack's dinner with Clyde and Bonnie had taken place at the same time that the couple was killing a Fort Worth motorcycle policeman on Fort Worth's Jacksboro Highway.

Jack enlarged our vocabularies. I may have been the most infected, for I still sometimes refer to a whore lady, book author, tooth dentist, tootat, food cook, stickup-gangster, money banker, and wife-women. Jack married seven wife-women.

There had been a lot of lip between the two sides in the weeks leading up to the Chili-Rice Eat-Off. Lip was what we called trash talk then. In a final rules discussion it was decided that it would be less confusing if each team selected one tiger to represent it in a battle of who could eat the most cartons of Double No. 9.

Blackie chose the strapping Pete Fisher, a UP photographer whose office was in the *Times Herald* building. Proctor countered with Bad Hair Bentley, a portly "Yellow Pages salesman."

Jack bragged that Bad Hair was known as the top knife and fork man in Johnson County. His nickname derived from the fact that under a certain light, his hair resembled a mat of squashed red grapes.

Bud Shrake, now of the *Dallas Morning News*, was chosen as the impartial judge as we gathered in Shanghai Jimmy's that afternoon.

After a half hour of socializing, Jimmy lifted his scoop, Pete and Bad Hair were poised with their cartons and spoons, and at the drop of Proctor's ballpoint pen the contest was on.

Pete's and Bad Hair's first two Double No. 9s went down easily enough. The third slowed their pace, and the fourth was an all-out struggle. When they were barely into their fifth, they both surrendered.

That's when Jerre Todd, an observer, pointed out that Bud Shrake had already finished his own fifth carton of Double No. 9 and was enjoying a cigarette and a bottle of Pearl.

The impartial judge had idly outeaten the two tigers.

IF YOU STUMBLED ACROSS THE GOLF novel *Dead Solid Perfect* when it came out in 1974 and read far enough to find a fictitious Texas high school football team used in a gambling scam, I hereby confess that the Corbett Comets were born on the sports pages of the *Times Herald* twelve years before the novel came out.

Corbett was conceived out of idleness by the trio of myself, Jap Cartwright, and Dick Hitt, the newspaper's Herb Caan. Dick wrote a popular column that may have peaked in popularity when he started a game in which readers made contributions. These were the dog days of SMU football and readers chimed in with the following results:

"Heinz 57, SMU 0"... "Loop 820, SMU 0"... "Suite 205, SMU 0"... "Channel 5, SMU 0"... "Social Security 461-87-0394, SMU 0."

The fictitious Corbett Comets were led by the twin running backs

Dicky Don and Ricky Ron Tooler. They were coached by the lovable Shug Noble. Each week in a one-paragraph short buried among the high school results was that Corbett had trampled another hapless rival by 62–0 or worse.

Corbett's colors were a proud blend of bruise black and welt blue. Among their victims were the Groover Gobblers, the Consolidated Standard Staplers, South Taggertt's Bean Receivers, and O. R. Kent's Steaming Okra.

Coach Shug Noble was occasionally given a quote. Something in the range of: "Our pine knots showed up howlin' mad tonight, ready to hitchee like them orphans do, and I'm happy they done it like they did."

Blackie never noticed the stories. In fact, he never knew it was going on until the team banquet at the end of Corbett's undefeated season, where we presented him with a bruise black and welt blue Corbett bumper sticker. The team banquet was held at Gordo's—it had the best pizza and chicken-fried steak sandwiches in Dallas.

In later years Blackie insisted he knew it was going on but he didn't want to do anything to hinder staff morale.

I COVERED GOLF'S FOUR MAJORS FOR the first time in '62 while I was working in Dallas. The Masters and U.S. Open had been on my schedule for ten years, but Blackie agreed to add the British Open and PGA if it wouldn't bankrupt the paper.

It was a good year to cover the majors. There wasn't a lurker among the winners. I got Palmer, Nicklaus, Palmer, and Player in that order.

The big moment at the Masters came when Palmer stiffed his shot at the 12th hole in the playoff on his way to beating Gary Player and Dow Finsterwald. Celebrating the shot, the scoreboard keeper showed no favoritism whatever as he put up a message in huge red letters that said: GO ARNIE.

Arnold may have played the best golf of his life at Oakmont in the U.S. Open, but he lost on the greens to Jack Nicklaus. Arnold three-putted 11 greens over the regulation 72 holes. Nicklaus three-putted once. Then Jack overwhelmed Palmer in the playoff, 71 to 74. It was a stunning sight to watch Jack outdrive Arnold by 50 to 80 yards off the tee.

Palmer recovered and lapped everybody at Troon on the west coast of Scotland in his third—and my first—British Open. He'd won at Birkdale the year before, but this was a superior performance. Arnold had been reinventing the British Open by his presence, and the fans showered him with the kind of love and affection that hadn't been seen, I was told, since Ben Hogan at Carnoustie.

I was inspired to write the following for the *Times Herald*:

TROON, Scotland—Arnold Palmer's Grand Slam slumbers in a shallow grave back in Pittsburgh, but you might as well try to tell 20,000 British subjects that the Queen is Tuesday Weld.

On that first visit to the linkslands of Great Britain I got to know members of the British golf writing fraternity, in particular the stars— Henry Longhurst of the *Sunday Times,* Peter Ryde of *The Times* of London, Pat Ward-Thomas of *The Guardian,* and Leonard Crawley of the *Daily Telegraph*. This was before the late Peter Dobereiner came on the scene at *The Guardian* and *The Observer*, and outwrote them all.

It was also before Henry Longhurst became known on American television for saying, "Ah, yes, there you have it."

It's part of British broadcasting lore that Henry, while announcing for the BBC during an Open at Royal Lytham & St. Annes was asked through his headset by the director to fill a moment of air time during a lull, and he did so with, "Well, here comes the old 4:35 from Black-pool to Lytham. Let's see if we can read the numbers on the engine. Ah, yes. Five, two, six . . . seven, nine, four . . ."

Peter Ryde, a tall, elegant gent, Oxford-educated, replaced the retiring Bernard Darwin on *The Times* in 1953, Darwin having been the world's first golf writer—he started in Vardon's day. Peter claimed he was given Darwin's job because he happened to stroll through the city room one day with a bag of clubs strapped over his middle-handicap shoulder.

Pat Ward-Thomas was a flight lieutenant during World War II whose Wellington was shot down over Holland. It resulted in his spending the rest of the war in Stalag Luft 3. That may have sharpened his acid wit.

I'd said to Pat at Troon that I intended to be at the first tee when Wednesday's opening round started at 7 a.m.

"What on earth for?" he asked.

This was when very few Americans entered the championship—only Arnold and four or five others of any prominence.

"I want to see the ceremony," I said.

Pat looked confused. "What ceremony?"

I said, "Like at any big sports event. At our Open they announce the first pairing, and some official says, 'Gentlemen, play away.' At the Kentucky Derby they sing 'My Old Kentucky Home' as the horses come on the track. At the Indy 500 they sing 'Back Home in Indiana,' and an official says, 'Gentlemen, start your engines.' Something must happen here."

Pat thought about it for a moment. "No," he said. "I believe the starter simply makes sure the tee markers are in the proper place, then tells the Nigerian to hit it."

As he stood watching an American pro take an inordinate amount of time over a putt, Pat once remarked: "Doesn't he realize my life is ebbing away?"

Leonard Crawley was a large man who looked larger in his tweeds and plus-fours. His mustache seemed capable of nesting a flock of wrens. He was the most capable golfer of all the British writers. Four times a Walker Cup player in his younger days.

We became friends when I helped him out on a story.

Troon's 11th hole, "The Railway," was the most dangerous on the golf course. It was long and tight with moguls for a fairway, bordered on the right by the railway and on the left by heather and scrub.

Ben Crenshaw said of Troon's 11th what he'd said of the Road

Hole at St. Andrews—"The reason it's a great par four is because it's a par five." What Arnold did at Troon's 11th was hit a magnificent 2-iron second shot of 220 yards off a hanging lie. The shot hugged the railroad boundary—"the brave side"—drew into the green, and came to rest close enough for him to sink a four-foot putt for an eagle three under the prevailing conditions. It was the defining moment in the championship.

I left Palmer with his lead, which would result in a six-stroke victory, and when I arrived in the press tent I ran into Leonard Crawley, who stood at the bank of telephones with a receiver in his hand.

"Dan," he said. "You were at the 11th, of course. What did Palmer hit to the green?"

I described Arnold's 2-iron shot. Leonard nodded and put the phone back to his ear. Walking away, I smiled as I heard him saying, "Palmer's second to Troon's 11th from a difficult lie was without a doubt the greatest 2-iron I have ever seen played."

Leonard has been credited by journalists on both sides of the Atlantic for having written the greatest lead on any golf story in the history of golf stories. This one: "Despite the abominable handling of the press luggage at the Geneva airport, the Swiss Open got off to a rather decent start yesterday."

TWO OTHER TRIPS TOPPED OFF MY Dallas residency. One was the longest week of my life when I dropped in on the Dallas Cowboys at their training camp in Northfield, Minnesota.

How many columns could a man write about Jesse James and the Younger brothers and their failed bank robbery of 1876? How many columns could a man write about the town that produces Malt-O-Meal?

I did write more than one column on Don Meredith. We sat around in his dorm room at St. Olaf College when he wasn't practicing. He revealed how he chose SMU over TCU. Coach Abe Martin at TCU said, "Don, at TCU you can keep on wearin' your T-shirts and Levi's and be comfortable." Don said he'd been wearing T-shirts and

Levi's his whole life. At SMU they were wearing beltless slacks and tassel loafers. Thought he'd try that.

We listened to music and he introduced me to his new favorite country artist. This was 1962, mind you, but the artist was Willie Nelson. Dandy was always ahead of his time.

The other trip was to Houston a couple of days before Christmas for what would be the world's longest football game. It was the AFL championship game between the Houston Oilers and Dallas Texans. The site was Jeppesen Stadium, a small arena with trees around it. It was used by the University of Houston for home games, and it said everything about the struggles of the new league. There was an overflow crowd of 37,000.

On a gray, windy day the game went into a second overtime and was finally won 20–17 by Lamar Hunt's Texans when a former TCU All-America fullback, Jack Spikes, broke loose on a run for 19 yards to set up the winning 25-yard field goal by Tommy Brooker. Spikes, who led all the ballcarriers in rushing, was voted the game's MVP.

I don't think any of us in the press box felt like we were covering something historic, like the first pro football game to go four quarters and two overtime periods. Considering the stadium and surroundings, it felt more like we were covering a state high school championship game between Dumas and Nederland.

Chapter 17

Zeroing In on the Yankees, the Bigs,

the Show, the Apple

WHEN THE FIRST ISSUE OF *Sports Illustrated* came out in mid-August of 1954—Eddie Mathews of the Braves on the cover, in case you weren't born yet—I thought it was the greatest idea since Ranch Style beans.

I well remember how it became my goal to work there someday, and this attitude held a grip on me even after the magazine's weekly covers began to display bird dogs, fly casters, sailboats, lady archers, and trotting horses.

If there was any doubt in my mind that I wanted to work in New York City, it was removed in the winter of '58 when *SI* brought me up there to "intern" for two weeks, as the magazine did other "stringers" from around the country now and then.

They put me up in the Algonquin Hotel on 44th Street, which was a four-block walk to the original Time-Life Building at One Rock Plaza in the heart of Rockefeller Center on 48th Street.

This was one year before the company moved into the new skyscraper at 50th and Sixth Avenue. They gave me an office on the fourth floor, where *SI* editorial was located. It was by the windows that looked down on the ice skating rink and over at the entrance to the RCA Building.

My first day when the perks started coming I wondered if anybody around there worked for a living. The man distributing newspapers came at ten and dropped me off copies of the *Herald Tribune*, *Times*, *Daily News*, *Post*, *Mirror*, *World-Telegram*, and *Journal-American*. This was before our thoughtful labor unions killed all but three of them.

Next came the coffee and Danish wagon being pushed along the aisles in case I hadn't eaten breakfast. Rolls, bagels, croissants—anything?

Now came the shoeshine man.

Then it was time for lunch.

They didn't give me much to do. I think they just wanted to see if I liked Scotch and didn't walk splay-footed.

I was single and the experience couldn't have been more seductive if I'd been a screenwriter called to Hollywood for two weeks and given a suite at the Chateau Marmont with Gina Lollobrigida for a roommate.

I was twenty-six and a sports editor and writing a daily column with my picture in it back home, and I could have been happy with that the rest of my life, but the Manhattan visit made me more restless and ambitious than ever.

I returned home more determined to keep pestering *SI* with items and story ideas so that one day I'd be called up to the Yankees.

Over the next three years I sold the magazine numerous items for the "Scorecard" section, which was then called "Events & Discoveries." They paid $250 for an enlightening item. Things started looking brighter when they gave me story assignments.

They sent me to New Orleans to cover the Sugar Bowl basketball tournament, which for some reason was important that year.

They called me in a panic and had me track down Homero Blancas and write a piece after he shot that world-record 55 in an amateur golf tournament in Longview, Texas. I can't remember how I tracked Homero down for a phone interview, but I did.

Time magazine, the parent of *SI*, sent me north of Fort Worth to do a piece on somebody named "Big Daddy" Don Garlits, the future king of drag racing. You could fill up a shot glass with everything I knew about drag racing. It looked to me like a guy climbed into a Roman candle, went 1,000 miles an hour for 100 yards, then jumped out before it blew up Denton, Texas.

Then they assigned me to cover the world championship rodeo finals in Los Angeles. I was a Texan, right? All Texans know about rodeo, right? I'd been going to Fort Worth's annual indoor rodeo since I was a kid, but what I knew about rodeo equaled what I knew about drag racing. I'd been on one horse in my life. That was in junior high, and I quickly discovered that I didn't like sitting up there so high.

But I knew a man to ask about rodeo in L.A. He was Casey Tibbs, the six-time world champion saddle bronc rider. He gave me a quick course in what to look for in every event—saddle bronc, bareback, calf roping, steer wrestling, bull riding—and a quote that made my story.

Tibbs said of the young guy who won the saddle bronc title, the classic cowboy event, "That boy Kenny McLean rides a buckin' horse the way it ought to get rode."

SI loved that quote. Guys up East.

In the spring of '62 I did a presumptuous thing. A query came saying the magazine was working on a story about the trials and tribulations of putting. Talk to some golf pros and ask them these questions. Need file soonest.

Well, I'd been talking to pros about golf my whole life and had a stockpile of material, but instead of sending the reportage to New York, I wrote the story myself. All 3,000 words of it.

Two or three days later I received a call from Ray Cave, who was the golf editor, saying I'd hit a home run. They were running the story as a bonus piece under the headline, "Lockwrist and Cage Cases." I'd be getting a nice check. The check was four-figures, breathtaking for a newspaper guy.

To grab the reader I poured every dance step I'd learned from Fred and Ginger in the lead, and with Cave's cosmetic touches, it came out:

The devoted golfer is an anguished soul who has learned a lot about putting just as an avalanche victim has learned a lot about snow. He knows he has used putters with straight shafts, curved shafts, shiny shafts, dull shafts, glass shafts, oak shafts, and Great Uncle Clyde's World War I saber, which he found in the attic. Attached to these shafts have been putter heads made of large lumps of lead ("weight makes the ball roll true," salesmen explain) and slivers of aluminum ("lightness makes the ball roll true," salesmen explain) as well as every other substance harder than a marshmallow. He knows he has tried forty-one different stances, inspired by everyone from the club pro to Fred Astaire in *Flying Down to Rio*, and as many different strokes. Still, he knows he is hopelessly trapped. He can't putt, and he never will, and the only thing left for him to do is bury his head in the dirt and live the rest of his life like a radish.

Ray Cave had become my cheerleader on the staff, had lobbied to get me hired. He said the putter story clinched it.

I was sitting at my desk in the *Dallas Times Herald* sports department near the end of November when the phone call came from New York.

"Dan, this is André Laguerre. I'm calling to ask if you would be interested in joining *Sports Illustrated* in New York as a staff writer?"

I didn't ask about salary.

I didn't ask about medical benefits.

I didn't ask about vacation time.

I didn't say, "What is my career path?"

I wouldn't have said it even if some moronic professor had invented it by then.

I didn't say I'd have to check with my wife. I knew June would be as excited about it as I was.

What I said was, "André, let me think about it for two seconds . . . I'd be delighted."

André replied, "As are we. Well, this didn't take long, did it? I'll have someone get in touch with you about the move and other details. We'll look for you sometime after the first of the year."

I'll never forget that afternoon. I was alone in the sports department. After hanging up the phone, I sat there for a moment, stared at nothing, and thought about the big change that had just come over our lives.

I believe I may have started singing, "We'll have Manhattan . . ."

Yeah, I think I did.

Chapter 18

"Life Is Just One Texas-OU Game After Another with Fun in Between"

IT WAS AT A DINNER PARTY in Dallas in the early '6os that an attractive young society babe made the above statement. I knew it would find its way into a book someday. Now it has.

At this moment it serves to remind me that I did football in the '6os while the hippie scum made love, not war.

Most of my time was spent dealing with such gentlemen as Darrell Royal, John McKay, Bear Bryant, Woody Hayes, Duffy Daugherty, and Ara Parseghian, while America's drowsy flower children were rolling joints with Prince Valiant and Pocahontas.

What did I miss? Not much. At parties I seldom met anyone who had a last name. I did meet assorted great Americans and wonderful human beings who ate all the food in the house, and tried to eat the brown loafers off my feet, mistaking them for burritos, before they curled up on the carpet to watch a Bela Lugosi movie.

When inconveniently erect, their entire vocabulary consisted of, "Wow . . . like, really," and, "Is there any ice cream?"

I met others who swallowed capsules and dashed into crowded restaurants to interrupt everyone's conversation.

I watched acid put people flat on their backs so they could relive 400 years of the Ottoman Empire, or steal Charlton Heston's chariot and race through the streets of Constantinople while Maria Ouspen-skaya waved a sword and chased them on her Harley.

What I did miss in the '60s was seeing a president of an American university grow a spine. I'd like to have seen Bear Bryant in charge of a campus under siege from a group of "student revolutionaries." Bear would have greeted them with, "Guess what? You people don't go to school here anymore."

It might have saved us from becoming overpopulated with real vampires and zombies.

I MUST DEVOTE A FEW MOMENTS to André Laguerre, the man who gave me college football to cover when I arrived at *SI*.

To those of us who admired him, he was our Harold Ross–Max Perkins–H. L. Mencken. A legendary editor, but with what I would argue was a more impressive résumé.

Born in England to a French diplomat father and an English mother, André spent his boyhood in France, England, Syria, and the United States. He rejected Oxford to become a freelance journalist, writing for both English and French language publications.

At the age of twenty-three and with a press credential from *Paris-Soir*, a French daily, he covered the 1938 Munich agreement at which Neville Chamberlain gave Czechoslovakia to Hitler.

André enlisted in the French army as a corporal when World War II started. He fought beside the British in a couple of battles in 1940, and accompanied the British forces when they were ordered to retreat to Dunkirk. He was one of the last of the 340,000 men to be evacuated to England in that miraculous exercise. He was badly wounded in the neck and shoulder when his evacuation ship was sunk by a mine. He somehow survived in the sea until he was rescued by a British destroyer. He never joked about that part—too many men were drowning around him.

His war could have ended there, but he recovered and enlisted in the Free French Forces, and soon wound up as General Charles de Gaulle's chief press attaché. He traveled with de Gaulle to North

Africa in '43, where the general visited the French troops, and to Washington, D.C., in '44 for confabs with FDR.

After the war Laguerre stayed on with de Gaulle until he took a job as a writer for *Time* in the Paris bureau. He became a standout reporter covering the continent and socializing with the elite personalities of Paris. One person in the mix was the existentialist Albert Camus.

In the Hoy Yuen bar one night after work at *SI*—the Hoy preceded the Ho Ho as the staff hangout—I asked André what Albert Camus was like.

Puffing on his cigar, André said, "A rather interesting chap—if you liked talking about Albert Camus."

By '51 André was the Time-Life bureau chief in both Paris and London, and his commanding presence had made him a favorite of Henry Luce. It was in '56 that Luce offered André the choice of running one of his magazines in New York.

"Are any of them in trouble?" André asked.

"*Sports Illustrated*," said Luce. In those early years *SI* was indeed hemorrhaging money.

"I'll take that one," said André, who came in '56 as the assistant ME under managing editor Sid James, a *Life* grad. André took charge in 1960, James moving to publisher.

André never laughed raucously at anything. If entertained by something, it was sort of a bemused chuckle. One occasion when he almost went beyond that was in the Ho Ho, and I'd just returned from Europe on an assignment, and had stopped over in Paris. André asked where I'd stayed in Paris. I said I spent two nights in the Napoleon Suite in the Hotel Crillon.

Chuckling, André said, "Of course you did, dear chap."

I had actually shared the suite with Bill Creasy, a CBS producer and Gotham friend. We'd done it on a whim—and our combined expense accounts.

That was the trip where Creasy and I flew home upstairs in first-class on a TWA 747. Just three passengers up there, the two of us and a dog. A well-mannered King Charles Spaniel, the victim of a divorce. We gave him his own tin of beluga.

Those were the days when air travel was a delightful experience—as opposed to today's flying pig pens.

Another time in the Ho. It was the night after Bud Shrake and I had been introduced to Frank Sinatra in Shor's. Toots introduced us. He knew Frank considered himself a photographer. Bud and a vat of J&B combined to tell Sinatra they would get him a press pass to shoot the Floyd Patterson–Eddie Machen fight in Stockholm that Bud was going to cover.

Now in the Ho over one more grand majestic final, Bud said to André, "I've hired a photographer to cover the fight with me."

André asked who that might be.

"Frank Sinatra," Bud said.

That time, André's response went past bemusement.

André's last encounter with Clare Boothe Luce, he admitted, forced more than a chuckle from him. The wife of Henry Luce, she was one of the most talented women of modern times. Magazine writer, editor, playwright, war correspondent, U.S. congresswoman, U.S. ambassador.

Clare Booth Luce had written a series of articles on skin diving—her latest interest—for *SI* in 1958. André had been Clare's editor on the piece, evidently a mischievous one in Clare's view.

As Laguerre told it, when they accidentally met in a hallway after the editing process, her only words to him were: "Well, André, still the pixie, I see."

In his fourteen years as the ME, André lifted *Sports Illustrated* from a circulation of 900,000 to 2.5 million, and transformed it from a fashion–fishing–sailing–dog show–travel journal into a writer's magazine that covered pro and college sports energetically.

The first wave of writers who flowered at the magazine under André included Roy Terrell, Tex Maule, Jack Olsen, Bob Creamer, Herb Wind, Alfred Wright, and Gil Rogin. I'll modestly insert myself into the second wave with Frank Deford, Bud Shrake, Roy Blount Jr.,

John Underwood, George Plimpton, Mark Kram, Ron Fimrite, and Bill Johnson.

André also presided over a Murderer's Row of photographers—Neil Leifer, Walter Iooss Jr., John Zimmerman, Marv Newman, Mark Kaufman, Heinz Kluetmeier, and Johnny Iacono, to name a few.

Nathalie Laguerre, André's wife and the mother of their two daughters, was a charming lady that June and I knew through dinner parties at their Fifth Avenue apartment. She was actually Princess Nathalie Alexandria Kotchoubey de Beauharnais, a descendant of Catherine the Great.

After I'd earned my stripes as a productive writer—doing twenty-five to thirty pieces a year—André told me the three most welcome things I would ever hear from a boss. He said at different times, "You can't get too much hate mail to suit me—it means you're doing your job," "You can't spend too much of our money entertaining if you're getting good material for it," and "If you don't like the way some of our editors are handling your work, come see me and we'll fix it."

Don't tell me he wasn't a great man.

WHEN I ARRIVED FOR WORK ON the twentieth floor of the new Time-Life Building it was the second week of January 1963. I reported to André in his office in my oxford gray Brooks Brothers suit, my white button-down Brooks Brothers shirt, and my red and blue striped Brooks Brothers tie, assuming this was still the uniform.

André said, "What would you like to cover?"

I said, "Whatever you need me to. But as long as you're asking, college football and golf. They're what I know the most about. If you don't like football and golf growing up in Texas, they drown you at an early age."

He gave me college football and said I could help Al Wright with golf and take it over from him in a couple of years. He put me in an office on the east side of the floor where I could gaze down on Radio

City Music Hall. If "New York, New York" had been composed by then, I would have hummed it on the way home.

Except I didn't have a home yet.

We had driven to New York in my faithful Olds 88. June had made a bed in the backseat for our three dumplings—ages two, two, and one—while I supplied us with enough thermoses of coffee and cartons of cigarettes to see us through the Battle of Stalingrad. We'd loaded as many suitcases as possible into the car, put our furniture in storage, and crept through a blizzard near Cleveland, and why we went that way is still a mystery.

We'd survived a bunch of going-away parties with friends in Fort Worth and Dallas. Most of our friends seemed to think we were moving to another planet and would never be seen again.

Blackie had hired me for the only two jobs I'd ever had, and I didn't know what to expect when I told him I'd accepted the *SI* gig. I said I regretted leaving him and the paper, and meant it, but I told him I was looking forward to the challenges of New York.

He responded with what I think . . . maybe . . . possibly . . . was a compliment.

He said, "You won't have a problem. Right or wrong, you're the most confident writer I've ever known."

After three days on the road we arrived in Westchester County, where June's older sister and brother-in-law, Pat and Bob Young, had agreed to put us up until we could find and buy a house. Fortunately, their home in Hastings-on-Hudson was a large one. They had four youngsters of their own—Missy, Julie, Stephen, and Christopher.

The former Pat Burrage was a beautiful, curvy blonde who had moved to Manhattan with two Texas girlfriends during the war to seek her fame and fortune. While studying at the Art Students League of New York, Pat became a John Robert Powers model by accident. She had gone with one of her girlfriends to an interview with Powers at his agency. Pat was hired but the girlfriend wasn't.

Pat won the Miss Rheingold contest—a big deal in New York in the '40s. Her likeness was plastered on city buses. From there she enjoyed a long career of fondling cereal boxes and smiling at kitchen appliances on billboards and in magazine ads and in TV commercials.

Pat's description of her modeling career: "I spent twenty years either bending over a hot stove or leaning against a cold refrigerator."

Bob was a handsome dude. Tyrone Power's long-lost twin brother. He was an account executive at Benton & Bowles, and frequently had to visit Cincinnati to stroke the good people at Procter & Gamble.

We bought a house in Briarcliff Manor in Westchester County, and for a year and a half I lived the wretched life of a commuter while June lived the wretched life of a commuter's wife.

I'd catch the train at the Ossining station, not far from Sing Sing prison, and it would take me to Grand Central Station, which left me with a cab ride or a hike to the Time-Life Building. Three hours out of my life on a workday just to get to the office and back. When I wasn't doing that, I was out of town on assignments.

After six months of commuting to the city and air travel, June said, "We can't live like this."

I said, "No, we can't. I'll be dead or insane by the time I'm thirty-five." So it was that before I discovered there was anything in the village of Briarcliff Manor other than the grocery and deli, June was looking for an apartment for us in Manhattan. She found one in the fall of '64 that we could practically the same thing as afford.

It was on the Upper East Side and we would spend the next thirty years as happy dwellers of Manhattan, which is where I learned that private school tuitions made you type faster.

For nine years we rented, but in 1972 the novel *Semi-Tough* bought us the sixteenth-floor penthouse on Park Avenue that June had found. It came with a huge terrace, three smaller terraces, views in every direction, three working fireplaces, six bedrooms, a master bedroom with a fireplace and terrace—all that good stuff.

I wasn't sure we were good enough people to deserve that apartment, but June and I and the kids braved it for twenty years. Then one day a Wall Street child star made us an offer we couldn't refuse—forty times what we paid for it. June had been a good little shopper.

That made it easier to return to earth, and into a much smaller apartment on what I called "Park Street."

The novel bought us something else, the oceanfront house on Hanalei Bay on the island of Kauai. We spent winter weeks and summer months in Hawaii for twelve years. I wrote parts of three novels there and we enjoyed a constant flow of guests from back home. Otherwise, June played tennis, did beach time, and doctored the lawn while our kids made lasting friendships with some of the Hawaiian kids.

It was a special time in one of the most beautiful places in the world. I could be pulled away from the typewriter for sunset picnics on the lava rocks around a tidal pool, and for hiking the magical trails of the Na Pali coast to be mesmerized by waterfalls and blue grottoes.

We sold the house when the kids were out of college. It was a long commute, Hawaii, and my own view was that even paradise could become tiresome for those who didn't surf or grow weed.

We bought a second home in Ponte Vedra Beach, Florida, headquarters of the PGA Tour, and I enjoyed looking at another ocean for seven years. My golf game was also reborn there. Of course, the problem with golf in Florida, I discovered, was that a hook or slice that missed the fairway was in danger of bouncing off the shin of a real estate agent.

Chapter 19

When Covering Saturday's
America Was Ice Cream

MY FIRST HIGH-PROFILE ASSIGNMENT AT *SI* was covering a big, loud, galloping story—the Wally Butts–Bear Bryant–*Saturday Evening Post* scandal. "The Story of a College Football Fix," screamed the headline.

I had nothing against Benjamin Franklin or Norman Rockwell to make me want to doom *The Saturday Evening Post* after 250 years of its homespun existence, of publishing stories by Jack London, Rudyard Kipling, Ring Lardner, F. Scott Fitzgerald, and other known quantities.

All I did in a series of pieces was defend college football from the naive, the arrogant, and the plain stupid.

The *Post* story was based on the word of an Atlanta insurance man who claimed to have accidentally overheard a phone call between Georgia's Wally Butts and Alabama's Bear Bryant in which Butts, formerly the successful football coach at Georgia and now the athletic director, gave away Georgia's game secrets to Bear nine days before the Georgia-Alabama game of September 22, 1962. *Nine days?* Butts immediately filed a $10 million libel suit against the Curtis Publishing Company, parent of the *Post*. And Bear followed suit.

The scandal caused me to spend so many weekends in Atlanta that spring and summer I felt like hiring out as a greeter in Aunt Fanny's Cabin, a restaurant in the city where you were guaranteed that nothing fernlike would plop down next to your Southern fried chicken.

To those who knew anything about college football, the story was absurd. That Bear Bryant and his Alabama team of '62, with Joe Namath at quarterback and Lee Roy Jordan at linebacker, would need any help defeating that particularly pitiful Georgia football team was laughable. Alabama won 35–0.

The insurance man's notes were judged harmless "coach speak" by every coach I interviewed—from Darrell Royal at Texas to John McKay at USC, from Johnny Vaught at Ole Miss to Bud Wilkinson at Oklahoma.

They agreed that most coaches are good friends off the field of battle, and that fans don't realize this. Coaches often talk on the phone about rules changes, X's and O's, officiating crews, recruiting. They'll kid around. And they found nothing in the notes that would have helped Bear Bryant's team in any area against Georgia.

In the weeks leading up to the Butts trial in Atlanta, the air in Georgia and Alabama was filled with rumors, counter-rumors, accusations, boasts, speculations, and gossip. I wrote that not since the Scopes trial in 1925—when two irascible orators, Clarence Darrow and William Jennings Bryan, argued the theory of man's ascent from the ape on the courthouse lawn in Dayton, Tennessee—had the South been as emotionally aroused over an issue.

Once the South had heard the Bible interpreted for the world to judge. Now it was primed for a heated debate on another sacred institution of the South—college football.

The opinion of the college coaches happened to be shared by every judge from Atlanta through the U.S. Supreme Court. The judges ruled that the *Post* "rushed to judgment" and that the notes didn't come close to proving a "football fix." Butts was awarded a record $3 million in punitive damages, but the amount was eventually reduced to $460,000. Bryant settled out of court with Curtis Publishing for $300,000 after taxes.

The legal fees the magazine spent for publishing the story and stubbornly standing behind it through all the legal processes would have fed the Balkans for a decade. Unfortunately, it was sizable enough to put *The Saturday Evening Post* out of business.

I could only feel bad about Jack London, Rudyard Kipling, Ring Lardner, and F. Scott Fitzgerald.

ANOTHER BREAK CAME MY WAY THAT first year. As the new college football caretaker, it became my chore—curse, privilege, honor—to predict who would win the national championship, and pick the nation's Top Twenty. All that for *SI*'s preseason college football issue of 1963.

The magazine hadn't done a preseason forecast in three years. The first two forecasters, Herman Hickman and Red Grange, had brought name value to the project, but nothing but embarrassment in their selections.

But what did Herman Hickman and Red Grange know about prognostication? They'd only played the game.

Impulsive as it was on my part, I convinced André to rethink our college football coverage. In the past it had focused on Yale-Harvard, Army-Navy, and tailgate parties. But there was this thing called the race for No. 1, I said, and it should guide our coverage. André liked the idea of races, even when it didn't involve thoroughbreds.

That season the majority of the forecasters—the wire service predictors, the experts in the football mags, the syndicated doctors of mathematical rankings—were going with USC, the defending national champion, or Ole Miss, Alabama, Oklahoma.

I wanted to be different but have a dog in the fight and picked Texas. Darrell Royal's Longhorns had flirted with No. 1 in '59, '61, and '62, would play vicious defense—a Royal trademark—and would be led by a multitalented senior quarterback, Duke Carlisle, a kid with the name of a riverboat gambler.

Over the past half dozen years Darrell had become a choice subject, one of the most accommodating coaches, and a friend.

Darrell had long since become known for his Royalisms.

Of his vicious linebacker, Tommy Nobis, the coach said, "He's just one of those pigs who likes to jump in the slop."

To his recruiters, he said, "Don't bring me any of those big old linemen whose legs touch all the way to their knees."

Regarding his determination to build his teams around a strong defense, he'd say, "Like the old gal said at the barn dance, 'I'm gonna dance with the one that brung me.'"

When I called to tell him I was picking Texas No. 1, he said, "Have you looked at our schedule?"

"Of course," I said.

"That's good to hear," he said. "I was afraid you'd lost your eyesight. You know we play Oklahoma and Arkansas back to back, and on the road."

"I know that," I said, "and you don't have to tell me Baylor, Rice, SMU, and TCU will all be stronger."

Darrell said, "Everybody we play, their eyes will be rolled up into BBs, and they'll come at us like very angry people."

I said, "Coach, you just described how *your* team plays—that's why I'm picking you No. 1."

Objective journalism, as it applied to me, went Dixie in that season of '63. I have to admit I've never rooted so hard for one particular team, before or since, as I did for those Longhorns. You might could add that I was rooting for my magazine prediction.

There were worrisome moments that would do justice to a movie where the hero is down to scant seconds trying to locate the nuclear device and disarm it before it blows up the curvaceous leading lady, not to mention the rest of the world.

The scariest moment came in the Longhorns' eighth game, against Baylor in Austin. Texas was 7–0, still holding on to No. 1, and Baylor was 5–1, and its fans were bragging about their passing combo of Don Trull to Lawrence Elkins, and waving green socks in the air.

I'd created the green socks thing, and now felt terrible about it. I'd quoted Darrell in a previous story saying Baylor had no football history to be proud of, and their fans were the kind of people who wore green socks.

Texas pushed across a touchdown on the ground in the third quarter, but a 7–0 lead didn't strike anyone as secure with Trull pitching and Elkins catching and the Texas defense working overtime.

I'm happy I didn't have any serious medical problems in the game's last two minutes. That's when the Bears drove 78 yards down to the Longhorns' 19-yard line with 29 seconds left. For a good reason, as it turned out, and for one of the few times all season, Royal had put Duke Carlisle in at safety, the quarterback being the best and most instinctive athlete on the team.

So it was that when Trull fired the pass to a wide-open Elkins in the end zone with those 29 seconds left, it was Duke Carlisle who came racing over from 10 or 12 yards away to cut in front of Elkins and make a leaping interception. Greatest interception in UT football history.

A sweating Jones Ramsey, Texas's much liked sports information director, had been standing next to me during Baylor's desperate drive, and about five seconds after Carlisle's interception—and my sigh of relief—Jones said, "Like Darrell says. Three things can happen when you throw a pass, and two of 'em are bad."

Afterward, at Darrell's usual postgame party for the press in a suite at the Villa Capri Motel—plenty of food and drink available—I said to him, "Coach, those green socks almost did you in. It was stupid of me to use the damn quote. I had no idea it would make Baylor turn lunatic."

Darrell said, "Aw, you were just doing your job. It was stupid of me to say it."

Sometime during the evening a writer said to Royal, "When you come right down to it, Coach, today was a pretty ugly win."

"Yeah," said Darrell, "but Ol' Ugly is better than Ol' Nuthin'."

THE SEASON BELONGED AS MUCH TO Navy's Roger Staubach as it did to the Longhorns. He was the most exciting player in the land. Roger the Dodger. Passer, scrambler, escape artist. Alert Heisman voters.

Staubach was obvious cover material, so I went to Annapolis to do him in mid-November. But when I met Wayne Hardin, Navy's agate-eyed coach, I found out the job wasn't going to be easy. I learned I wasn't there to interview a college athlete, I was there to interview Rita Hayworth.

Hardin said, "More people would like to see Roger Staubach right now than any celebrity in the world. If we opened the doors, do you know how many writers and photographers would show up at our practice? It would be close to five thousand."

From there I went to Durham, North Carolina, and watched Roger lead Navy over a good Duke team 38–25. Then came an interlude outside the Navy dressing room.

A group of us, writers and photographers, waited an hour, one hour, for the dressing room door to open. Eventually, out came Budd Thalman, Navy's steadfast sports information director, who said if we stood back, stayed calm, and kept a safe distance, he would produce "Rog."

Staubach appeared in his dress blues with the white cap under his arm. He was followed by Hardin, who lit a cigar. Hardin and Thalman stood on either side of Roger like presidential bodyguards.

"Fine game, Roger," somebody said.

"Thanks."

"Duke was pretty good."

"Sure was."

"Were you worried when the score got close?"

"Sure was."

"Guess you're looking forward to Army?"

"Beat Army," Budd Thalman said.

"Guess you take a lot of razzing from the team about the publicity."

"Sure do."

"Why were both of your knees taped during the game?"

"New-style uniform," Hardin cut in. "Well, Rog, you're keeping forty-three other boys waiting on the bus. Let's go."

A photographer moved in about three feet from Staubach, crouched, and aimed up at him for a portrait. Thalman pressed his hand against the photographer's shoulder, smiled, wiggled his finger like a teacher telling a child he's being naughty, and said, "Too close."

I wanted to blurt out, "Watch him! He's going to try to rape Rita Hayworth!" But I only laughed.

I wrote the cover piece, which was flattering to the quarterback, as it deserved to be, then something happened on Friday, November 22, 1963, that created havoc around the magazine, as it did everywhere else in the world. The assassination of President Kennedy.

Three days later, on a Sunday evening—closing night for the issue—I was summoned to the "color room" to see André. On the big screen was the proposed cover of Staubach, a painting of him in his dress blues and white cap. A firm-jawed, gray-haired gentleman was sitting next to André. I was introduced to Henry Luce.

I listened as André told Luce that every magazine in the world was going to put Kennedy on the cover, but *SI* intended to be different. He said he'd like to keep Staubach, a Navy man like JFK, on our cover, and added, "Dan, our college football writer, has written a good story on the Navy lad."

I'd heard one thing about Henry Luce. He asked rapid questions and expected straight answers from his people. He turned to me.

"Is Navy going to beat Army next week?"

"Yes," I said. "No doubt about it."

Then he asked, "Is Staubach going to win the Heisman Trophy?"

"Absolutely," I said.

Luce slapped André on the knee, stood up, and said, "Go with it." And walked out.

THE ARMY-NAVY GAME IN FRONT OF the usual 100,000 in Philadelphia's Municipal Stadium on December 7—the Blue & Gold against the Black & Gold—turned out to be an unwanted spine-tingler where this reporter was concerned.

Roger Staubach had an unforgettable battle with Army's Rollie Stichweh, but Navy survived, 21–15, stopping a desperate Army drive on their two-yard line at the finish.

This was the same Army-Navy game that's gained a certain fame over the years owing to a member of our tribe. In our midst was a sportswriter from out west known for consuming spirits during contests. The game was over and a group of us were replaying it over the food and drink that was provided in the press box. The fellow from out west overheard us as we spoke of the exciting plays performed by Staubach and Stichweh.

Having listened to part of it, the writer slipped away and went to a telephone and called his office long distance. There were ear-witnesses.

The person on the desk back at the paper asked if the writer would like to fix anything before his story went to press.

The writer said, "Yeah, one thing. Change all the Armys to Navy and all the Navys to Army."

I wasn't hoisted on the shoulders of staff members and carried down the *SI* halls until Texas defeated Navy 28–6 in the Cotton Bowl and wrapped up the national championship, thus making me a genius.

But Roger deserves the last laugh, exemplary fellow that he is. After leaving Annapolis and serving four years in the Navy, including a year of service in Vietnam, he took up pro football and led the Dallas Cowboys to their first two Super Bowl victories in 1971 and 1977.

His success continued after he left the pro game. He remained in Dallas and started the Staubach Company, a commercial real estate business that grew to be worth over $600 million. Sometime around 2007, when he was still the CEO of his company, I was asked to do an evening of sports talk with him in Fort Worth before an audience at Colonial Country Club.

We relived some of the moments I've mentioned, and toward the end of the evening I remembered another thing from the past. When he was deciding where to go to college to play football, he had received only two offers. One from Navy and the other from Purdue.

I reminded him of it, and said, "Roger, have you ever thought about what would have happened if you had gone to Purdue instead of the Naval Academy?"

He said, "You would never have heard of Bob Griese."

Chapter 20

It Matters Not Who Wins or Loses
but How You Write the Game

AS A LIFELONG FAN of college football, one who stubbornly refuses to see a doctor about it, I can't believe I didn't come up with the term "Poll Bowl." It describes the event perfectly. The term was sitting right there to be had, but I missed it.

Apparently I was too content to be covering a Big Game, a Pigskin Classic, a Battle of Undefeateds, a Game of the Year, a Game of the Decade, a Game of the Century.

Poll Bowls go back as far as Walter Camp, although they didn't have that name, and they'll keep popping up despite a phony, money-grabbing postseason playoff to decide who's No. 1. Teams in the play-off will be decided by a "blue-ribbon selection panel." Some deserving team will invariably be left out, but you can't have everything. I can hear the words of a panelist now: "Yes, I understand Notre Dame is four and eight, but let's not forget the Irish are a very good draw on TV."

Pat me on the head and send me off to the support group, but I'll continue to believe it was a better world when voters and doctors of numbers tried to settle things. We've known seasons that ended with two, three, four, five teams claiming the national championship, but so what? The arguments were fun, and we had nothing to lose but more bumper stickers.

I first heard a game called a Poll Bowl on a Saturday in October of 1967 in the press box at Notre Dame, when No. 1 Southern Cal had come to South Bend to play the No. 5 Irish.

I heard it from Roger Valdiserri, Notre Dame's sports publicity director, prince of a fellow and a pro at his job. I don't know if Roger thought it up or borrowed it from somebody, but he said it and I've been running with it ever since.

That same day Roger gave me another line for my story. O. J. Simpson was having a headline afternoon against the Irish, leading the Trojans to a 24–7 win—getting himself discovered nationally—when Roger slipped up behind me on the press row.

He said, "O.J. doesn't stand for Orange Juice. It stands for, 'Oh, Jesus, there he goes again.'"

AS PRESIDENT MUFFLEY SAID ON THE phone to Premier Kisov regarding General Jack Ripper in *Dr. Strangelove*, call me funny in the head, just a little funny in the head, but I like deadlines. I liked deadlines on Poll Bowls. A deadline meant it was my turn on stage.

Never file too long. An editor might trim the wrong thing. Never file too short. An editor might insert something he'd take for fact that he heard from one of the talking heads on TV.

File as soon as possible after the game. That way you have to trust your first impressions. They're usually the most reliable.

Some of the best sportswriters I've known secretly enjoyed deadlines, but chose to act as if they didn't.

I'd watch Blackie Sherrod fret over the typewriter, both in a press box and in the office, then finish up, relax, and say, "It's easy if you have no pride." Nobody had more.

Red Smith said there was nothing to writing. "All you do is sit down at a typewriter and open a vein."

But he liked performing. I occasionally sat next to him on press row.

Jim Murray liked to distinguish between day and night deadlines.

"If it's a day game, I take a stab at making sense," he'd say. "If it's a night game, I write Sanskrit. Night baseball was the end of literature as we know it."

People who were friends with John Lardner said he could spend an hour searching for the right word in a paragraph, but once he found the word, the rest came easily.

In my years of caretaking college football for *SI*—from '63 through '72—I was somewhere at a game every week and on the average two of them were Poll Bowls.

Four of those games live on. Famous football games do this.

One was the Notre Dame–Michigan State game on November 19, 1966, in East Lansing, Michigan. It had a six-week buildup. For me personally it resulted in a group of literary-minded Notre Dame students burning 1,500 copies of *Sports Illustrated* after my story on the game came out. I also received an endearing fan letter from a Notre Dame student, which said: "Go straight to HELL! You lousy son of a bitch."

All I'd done was write:

Old Notre Dame will tie overall. Sing it out, guys. That is not exactly what the victory march says, of course, but that is how the big game ends every time you replay it. And that is how millions of cranky college football fans will remember it. For 58 minutes in overwrought East Lansing the brutes of Michigan State and Notre Dame pounded each other into enough mistakes to fill Bubba Smith's uniform, but the 10–10 tie that destiny seemed to be demanding had a strange, noble quality to it. Then it didn't have that anymore. All it had was this enormous emptiness for which the Irish will be forever blamed.

In the last two minutes the Irish chose to burn the clock. Instead of trying to win with passes and a possible field goal, they settled for the tie, no doubt knowing that Notre Dame, being Notre Dame, would out-poll the Spartans in the AP and UP rankings and be declared the national champion.

They tied one for the Gipper.

A HOLLYWOOD-STYLE POLL BOWL presented itself a year later. This was the matchup on November 18, 1967, between No. 1 UCLA with Gary Beban and No. 2 USC with O. J. Simpson. It unfolded before 90,000 screaming basket cases in the Los Angeles Coliseum.

USC coach John McKay, like Darrell Royal, was one fun guy to deal with. Witty and helpful. I have fond memories of joining him for breakfast in his suite at the Ambassador Hotel in L.A. on the mornings after Trojan games I'd cover. He'd explain what I saw and what I hadn't seen. We both liked creamed chipped beef on toast—don't spread it around.

McKay treated the UCLA game in '67 like any other big one. He'd keep his team loose, saying, "Remember this. Whatever happens Saturday, eight hundred million Chinese won't give a shit."

At a press conference the day before the game a writer accused McKay of overworking O. J. Simpson. O.J. had been carrying the ball 35, 40 times in a game. Didn't this tire him out?

John said, "The ball's not that heavy. I'll tell him when he's tired."

On deadline I didn't worry about how many people in Hollywood could read, I was busy running away with myself.

In that college football game for the championship of Earth, Saturn, Pluto, and Los Angeles, UCLA's Gary Beban had a rib cage that looked like an abstract painting, and USC's O. J. Simpson had a bandaged foot that looked like it belonged in a museum of natural history. But they kept getting up from knockout blows and doing these heroic things, so guess what? In the end, the difference in one of the biggest games since the ears of helmets stopped flapping was that a guy with a name like a Russian poet—Zenon Andrusyshyn—couldn't place-kick the ball over a guy with a name like the president of the Van

Nuys Jaycees—Bill Hayhoe—and that was the ball game. After
O.J. put the Trojans ahead with a 64-yard touchdown run,
Zenon would try to side-boot a field goal or an extra point for
UCLA, and Hayhoe, who is 6-8, would raise up and bat it away.
The last time Hayhoe did it, he tipped the leather just enough
to make the Bruins fail on a conversion, and USC got away
with a 21–20 victory in a spectacle that will be remembered for
ages, or at least as long as German-born, Ukrainian, Canadian-
bred soccer-style kickers play the game.

In the Trojan dressing room, McKay said, "We knew he kicked the
ball low, so we put the tallest guy we had in there on defense and told
him just get to the line of scrimmage and hold up his arms. I call that
brilliant coaching."

TEXAS AND ARKANSAS AND THEIR COACHES, Darrell Royal and
Frank Broyles, had been playing each other in Poll Bowls for ten
years, but nothing like the one on December 6, 1969.

After a season-long buildup, the No. 1 Longhorns and No. 2
Razorbacks met with undefeated records in a game that sportswriters
branded "the Big Shootout." President Richard Nixon came down to
watch it and present a trophy to the winner.

All week long in Texas the people said Hogs ain't nuthin'
but groceries, and on Saturday in Fayetteville, Arkansas,
their No. 1 Longhorns were going to eat—to quote the
most horrendous pun ever conceived by a Lone Star wit—
"Hog meat with Worster-Speyrer sauce." That's not exactly
what the Longhorns dined on up there in the thundering zoo
of the Ozark hills. Texas experienced one hell of a time winning
the national championship 15–14 over a fired-up Arkansas
team that for three quarters made the Longhorns look like
No. 117.

Despite the dramatic finish, the Big Shootout was a Big Dud. Texas, a team averaging 44 points a Saturday, committed six turnovers in the game's first three quarters. This made it convenient for Arkansas to take a 14-0 lead into the last quarter.

Only through the miracles of James (Slick) Street, the Texas quarterback, did the best team prevail. In that last quarter Street scrambled 42 yards for a touchdown, slid through tackle for a two-point conversion, and later fired the gambling 44-yard pass on fourth down to Randy Peschel, his tight end, the play that set up the winning touchdown. Darrell had called the play on the sideline, and later explained, "Sometimes you just have to suck it up and pick a number."

Royal knew his team and fans were taking the Razorbacks too lightly. I was roaming the practice field with him the day before the game. He said, "Our people don't understand there's no such person as King Kong, and if you think there is, you can get ready to wipe your bloody nose."

Then he put on his game face, and said, "Arkansas. What's the state good for? All they do is sell jams and jellies by the side of the road."

James Street had already caught my fancy—he was one of the best college athletes I ever covered. Over two seasons he never lost a game as the Longhorns' starter. Earlier in the '69 season I was in Austin doing prep for the OU game coming up. I was in the dressing room waiting for a moment with Royal. The team was filing out for their workout as I stood studying the season's slogan on a sign posted over the door.

All coaches have slogans posted over the door. This stuff: PLAY LIKE A CHAMPION TODAY . . . SHOW ME A GOOD LOSER AND I'LL SHOW YOU A LOSER . . . PRIDE IS YOUR GREATEST ASSET.

That season Darrell's slogan was:

WHAT I GAVE I KEPT.

WHAT I KEPT I LOST.

I may have been scratching my head as I looked at the sign when James Street walked by. He playfully slapped me on the arm, laughed, and said, "When you figure out what that shit means, let me know."

THE GRACE KELLY OF POLL BOWLS was played in Norman, Oklahoma, on November 25, 1971. Nebraska and Oklahoma lived up to their notices, and even though the Cornhuskers slipped by the Sooners 35–31 with a late, desperate drive, OU also deserved a standing ovation at the finish.

Dave Kindred, a colleague who was then with the *Louisville Courier-Journal*, wrote the best news lead. "They don't have to do it anymore. They've played the perfect football game."

My *SI* effort said the same thing, but it took more words:

In the land of the pickup truck and cream gravy for breakfast, down where the wind blows through the walls of a diner and into the grieving lyrics of a country song—down there in dirt-kicking Big Eight country—they played a football game that produced heroes all over the field and will be discussed by self-styled gridiron intellectuals everywhere. The game was for everybody, of course. For all those who'd been waiting weeks for Nebraska and Oklahoma to meet, for the visiting guys with big stomachs and bigger Stetsons, for the luscious coeds who danced through the Norman afternoons drinking daiquiris out of paper cups, and for the cerebral types who will keep wondering whether it was the greatest collegiate football game ever played. Under the agonizing conditions, it may well have been.

In essence, the game was won for Nebraska with a pearl of a punt return in the game's first three minutes. Everything else keeps balancing out. The two teams swapped touchdowns from scrimmage, four for four, and OU added a field goal. But always there lingered the one thing they hadn't traded—the sudden, shocking, twisting, whirling 72-yard punt return by Nebraska's Johnny Rodgers.

Johnny Rodgers returned to Lincoln a year later and I can't let him depart from this chapter without dredging up something I wrote about him from the press box in Boulder, Colorado, on a Saturday in November.

If the typesetters aren't careful, Nebraska's Johnny Rodgers may leap right out of this sentence, and like the hummingbird he is, go flitting through ads, photographs, along the margins of the pages, in and out of other stories, and out the back cover if that's what it takes to beat somebody. For three seasons, Rodgers has been the super gnat of college football, and—well, there he goes again, darting from the Contents page into the kidneys of the Colorado Buffaloes on another surreal punt return.

Rodgers won the Heisman Trophy in 1972, and took the trouble to thank me in his acceptance speech for the things I'd written about him, becoming one of the few athletes who ever thanked a sportswriter in public for anything.

NOBODY COACHED IN MORE POLL BOWLS than Paul (Bear) Bryant. He was an imposing presence to anyone who was ever around him. His Alabama teams lived in Poll Bowls throughout the '60s and '70s, but I first got to know him when he came to College Station to revive Texas A&M football in the '50s.

Bear oozed leadership and was a bit of a showman, too. When he arrived on the A&M campus, the Aggies staged a bonfire to welcome him. Bryant stepped up on the platform, took off his coat, slammed it on the floor, grabbed the mike, and said, "I'm ready to fight 'em right now!"

If fist bumps had been in fashion, 2,000 A&M cadets would have broken their knuckles on each other.

Bear brought the ritual of entertaining writers to the Southwest Conference. He'd invite small groups of us from around the state to his home for drinks, snacks, off-the-record chitchat.

In his first year at one of those gatherings, Bear said, "I guess you people know I could own every one of you with a bottle of whiskey and a hooker."

Somebody said, "Coach Bryant, that may have been true of a previous generation, but—"

Bear stopped him. "Aw, I'm just messin' with you. I know all of you are upstanding gentlemen or I wouldn't have you in my home."

Bryant's star recruit at Aggieland was John David Crow, a big, bruising ballcarrier. John David was an All-America halfback and Heisman Trophy winner in 1957, when he almost led A&M to the national championship. Crow carried the Aggies to an 8–0 record and No. 1 before they lost their last two games to Rice and Texas in close upsets by a total of three points.

John David Crow deserved the Heisman that season, but Bear had to help sell him to voters. Most Heisman winners need a salesman.

When a Houston writer said to Bryant, "Coach, John David only gained 562 yards from scrimmage. That's not many yards for a Heisman candidate."

Bear said, "That don't count the people he knocked down."

In a season long after Bear was at Alabama, lore has it that three of his players came to his office on behalf of Linnie Patrick, a highly recruited running back. Linnie wanted to wear a headband, and they were there to plead his case. Linnie had seen other black players wearing headbands on TV. Bryant, as you might guess, had a rule against headbands.

One of the group said, "Coach, Linnie says it will instill pride in him. He says it's part of his heritage."

Bryant said, "I have no problem with that."

And looked down at the paperwork on his desk.

The players thanked him for making it so easy, and slowly shuffled away to leave. But as they reached the door, they heard Bear's voice.

Bear said, "Tell Linnie he can wear a headband—or his helmet."

I had to admire Bear's flare for showbiz. Sitting in his Tuscaloosa office on a morning in the late '60s, I heard him talk about how much he liked "hitters" on his teams.

"See that helmet over there," he said, nodding at a white helmet on an end table. "That was Lee Roy Jordan's helmet. He was the best hitter we've had around here." I glanced at it.

Bear said, "Take a close look. It's got the color of every team we played on it when we won the national championship in '61."

I walked over and examined the helmet. I noted a smudge of orange for Tennessee, a smudge of blue for Auburn, a smudge of maroon for Mississippi State, a smudge of yellow for Georgia Tech. Other smudges.

I wasn't a cub reporter. I knew teams polished their helmets before every game.

"Nice work, Coach," I said. "Who's your artist?"

"Smart-ass sportswriters," he grinned. "It works on recruits."

IT WASN'T A POLL BOWL, but the Tennessee-Georgia game that opened the season of 1968 was a Big Event—it introduced the world to artificial turf. Tennessee won the interior decorating award that day.

I was there to write about it, and Walter Iooss Jr. was there to shoot it. The real excitement occurred before the kickoff.

We were down on the sideline. I wanted to test the carpet with my shoes. Walter was organizing his cameras when this uniformed policeman approached. He had the belly, the drawl. He was right out of central casting.

"Your foot touched that line, boy," the officer said to Walter.

Startled, Walter said, "What?"

"Your foot touched that sideline."

I suppose I should mention that Walter's hair might have been too long for the officer's taste.

"We work for *Sports Illustrated*," I said, hoping the name would mean something. It didn't.

"I don't believe I was talking to *you*," the officer said.

"Just trying to help out," I said, smiling.

He said, "I'll let you know when the helpin'-out time comes."

"I'll be careful," Walter said, fooling with his equipment.

"I'm gonna be watchin' you, boy."

"Yes, sir."

"See these notches, boy?"

The officer showed Walter his night stick. There were several notches on it.

"I see those," Walter said.

"Know what them notches is for?"

"No, sir."

"Them notches is for hippies."

"Really?"

"Ever time I hit me a hippie, I put a notch in my stick."

"I can see that," Walter said.

"You want to be one of them notches, boy?"

"No, sir, I don't."

"You watch your foot, then. Don't put your foot on that line. You put your foot on that line again, you gonna be a notch."

I'm happy to report that Walter didn't become a notch.

But I'm reminded of a line a character says in *Limo*, a novel about TV and Hollywood that Bud Shrake and I wrote together: "It's not all bluebirds and lemonade in the big league."

Chapter 21

When Every Street Was a Boulevard
in Old New York

WE TOOK MANHATTAN. But only Midtown and the Upper East Side. I, myself, tried never to go to the West Side, except to see if any bodies had bubbled up to the surface in the Hudson.

June woke up with a smile every day in Manhattan. It didn't take long for us to learn the shortcuts. Where to go, where not to go, when not to go. Just because New York got the good movies five weeks ahead of Chicago or any other city didn't mean you had to stand in line. The 4:30 on Tuesday or Wednesday afternoons worked well for us.

Nobody had to teach me the "international slide." I was fully aware that it didn't matter if you knew the name of the rope guy at "21." What mattered was if he knew *your* name.

You never made eye contact with anyone on the sidewalks. It was best to assume that everybody was Son of Sam. But there was quaintness to be appreciated.

Like the black dude one day on Fifth Avenue. He came bopping along and singing with a radio held up to his ear. But on closer examination, it wasn't a radio—it was a chocolate donut.

I learned from our friend Nick Pileggi that when dining in certain restaurants in Little Italy we might find ourselves sitting near a member of one of the Five Families. So it would be in the best interest of everybody concerned if I didn't tap the guy on the arm, and say, "Great hit last week, Guido—loved the concrete shoes. I hear the fusilli's good here."

We were quick to observe that New Yorkers had something to do and were busy doing it. And they had no patience for people who had nothing to do, or nothing to do but shop. Most of our New York friends were busy doing something and were originally, like us, from somewhere else anyhow.

One of the good things about our life in Manhattan was not having to buy cars for the kids when they reached high school. A nice savings.

Sally's junior high and high school was Spence, a private girls school. Her years there helped her dominate the pinball and car racing machines in Candy Kitchen, an ice cream–candy shop near the school.

But her Spence education undoubtedly helped her get into Stanford for the best $10 million I ever spent. I may have exaggerated the tuition.

Sally's mom and dad agree with her that the most important person in her life in grade school at P.S. 6 was a teacher named Elinor Buckley. She taught Sally to read in the second and third grades. By the end of the third grade, Sally was reading at a sixth grade level, testing off the charts, and by the sixth grade she was plundering my bookshelves at home, looking for another Dostoyevsky.

But the best thing Elinor Buckley did was keep teaching in the fall of '68, when the dog-ass teachers union screwed the children and went on its scandalous two-month strike. Miss Buckley asked a group of parents like us to chip in, and she rented a small room in the basement of a church and taught her kids throughout the strike.

"I owe Elinor Buckley my career," Sally has said. "I was practically illiterate in the second grade, but she saved me. There were days in the strike when only three or four of us showed up at the church, and we would just play Hangman, but it helped with our spelling and vocabulary. I'll never forget the day I was the only one to show up.

It was pouring-down rain. But instead of sending me home, she took me to the Whitney Museum. She should have been paid more than the mayor."

We say Elinor Buckley deserves a statue in Central Park. The city could lose one of the Simón Bolívars to make room.

Marty and Danny went to McBurney, a private coed school. It helped them get into the University of Arizona and TCU. They went to McBurney because they wanted to play football, and McBurney fielded a high school team. They each played end, and while I didn't see as many games as I'd wished due to my *SI* travels, I did see them catch passes and tackle people up at Riverdale and at some stadium out on Long Island—and I liked hearing them holler at their teammates from the sideline, "*Hurt* somebody!"

If there was a serious downside to raising our kids in Manhattan, it was "Suicide Hill." We didn't appreciate the dangers of it until the statute of limitations was over, and the subject came up at a Thanksgiving dinner.

Suicide Hill was near our first apartment at 25 East 86th. It was the block of 87th Street between Madison and Park. It became a sidewalk slalom course for our own skateboarders and other kids.

The skateboarder was challenged to go as fast as possible down the hill while dodging dogwalkers, elderly ladies, pizza deliverers, third generation Lindbergh baby kidnappers, trash barrels, and sidewalk grates, yet be nimble enough to make the right-hand turn at the corner of 87th and Park, or grab a lamppost, to avoid flying into Park Avenue traffic—and death by taxi.

Over turkey and dressing, the skateboarding confessions and remembrances of Sally, Marty, and Danny took our breath away as they recounted their close calls and minor collisions.

June said, "If you had been seriously hurt, it would have been our fault. We told you never to talk to strangers. We told you never to let a kid ride your bike—you'll never see it again. We told you never to wise off to a policeman. But we flat forgot to tell you not to fly into Park Avenue traffic on your skateboard."

———

IF YOU LET THEM, your self-appointed Manhattan sophisticates can put you down for your questionable taste. This never bothered me. They thought I was joking anyhow when I'd say I was under doctor's orders not to read Susan Sontag, I hated talk-songs in Broadway musicals, and I laughed out loud at everything I saw in the Guggenheim.

But our son Danny was put down—or one-upped—in P.S. 6. when the class was into a show-and-tell session.

Danny proudly related how his parents had taken the family on a ski trip in New Mexico over the Christmas holidays, and he had started learning how to ski.

How exciting, Danny. Next?

The next boy stood, and said, "My daddy wrote *Man of La Mancha*." It was Mitch Leigh's kid.

THERE WAS THIS DINNER AT ELAINE'S with Sugar Ray Robinson and his wife, Millie. They were in town from L.A. Sugar Ray Robinson—not Leonard—is the greatest prizefighter who ever lived. That's my opinion and I'm sticking to it. Many wise men agree.

Allen DeLynn, a friend of Sugar Ray's, arranged the dinner and invited June and me to join them. Allen's dinner date was a mutual friend, Karen Lerner, one of composer Alan Jay Lerner's ex–fair ladies.

I didn't expect to find Robinson a modest, soft-spoken guy, having watched him slaughter people in newsreels—and once in person— with his lethal fists.

I let him know I'd seen him fight in Yankee Stadium. It was on a sweltering 110-degree August night in 1949. His opponent was Steve (Gink) Belloise, "the Bronx Butcher." Robinson decked him in the sixth round, and Belloise didn't come out for the seventh.

Smiling, Sugar Ray said, "It was 200 degrees in the ring. I didn't want to come out for the seventh round myself."

Why was I in New York in August of '49? The trip was a high school graduation present from my mother. Delayed one year because I got the job at the *Press*. I talked three pals into driving with me. Marty McAllister, Al Ryfle, and Dick Spencer.

We made it more than a trip to New York. We hit the Tennessee mountains, we stopped over in Asheville, North Carolina, we did photo ops around the memorials in Washington, D.C., we even went to see Niagara Falls. Which was where we stood on a lookout, and Marty said, "There's your falls . . . can we get a beer now?"

In New York we did more than see Sugar Ray fight. We saw Stan Musial hit a home run against the Dodgers in Ebbets Field. We went to Bop City and saw Louis Armstrong and the All-Stars and George Shearing on the revolving stage. I tracked down June Burrage, future bride, who was spending the summer with her modeling sister Pat. We took her to the Metropole Café in Times Square to hear Charley, Al, and Sally in their straw hats and candy-striped blazers harmonize on "Charley, My Boy," "Heart of My Heart," "Dearie, Please Don't Be Angry," and "I'd Like to See the Kaiser with a Lily on His Chest."

I doubt if anybody ever stopped a room like Sugar Ray Robinson did that night in Elaine's. Women clamored over him, men hugged on him.

Elaine herself beamed at his presence. She patted Sugar Ray on the back, and said, "At last. A real celebrity in the joint."

ON ANOTHER NIGHT AT ELAINE'S, Terry Southern came in a little wobbly, and Elaine sat him at our table, figuring we had something in common—we'd both drink and I'd get the check.

I was delighted to meet Terry Southern, and bragged on his work that had given me so much pleasure, namely *Dr. Strangelove*, *Candy*, and *The Magic Christian*.

I knew he was from Alvarado, Texas. I let him know I was from Fort Worth, only thirty miles from Alvarado.

"Fort Worth!" Terry Southern said. "The cripples!"

He snickered, wiped his nose.

"What?" I said.

"The football school in Fort Worth with the little cripples."

"You mean Masonic Home?"

"That's it. They had these little cripples but they beat everybody. Cripples running for touchdowns. Amazing sight."

I can't recall who else was at the table, other than my astonished wife.

"They were orphans," I said.

"Where?" Terry said, spinning around, glaring.

"Masonic Home was an orphanage."

"Yes! Little cripple orphans. I saw them play."

"So did I. Many times. They had some of the best teams in the state . . . and some great players. Gordy Brown . . . Dewitt Coulter . . . Gene Keel."

"Marvelous thing. Little cripple orphans . . . hunched over, limping . . . arms dangling. But running for touchdowns against teams with no cripples."

"Not a one," I said.

"Wonderful sight," he said.

Terry Southern spotted two people he knew across the room, and abruptly left us. I couldn't tell if they were crippled.

YOU CAN NEVER BE SURE WHO or what you'll get when you're going to meet a showbiz star for the first time. Will he or she be the good, the bad, the impossible, or the loon?

My curiosity was primed the evening David Merrick invited us to join him for dinner at "21" with Mary Tyler Moore.

As I was seated next to her at the dinner table, I couldn't help wondering if I was going to get Mary Richards or Agnes Moorehead setting fire to the drapes.

I got the Mary Tyler Moore I hoped for. She was lovely, natural, friendly—send out for more adjectives. Was she acting? Who cared? I'd once read a quote by her in which she said, "I don't create characters. I just play me."

I mentioned that I liked something her husband, Grant Tinker, had said in a column: "When you're developing a show for TV, remember the network is always wrong."

"That's funny," she said. "I just can't imagine Grant saying it."

Her response took on more meaning a year later when I read that they were divorcing.

In Mary Tyler Moore's presence, *Breakfast at Tiffany's* was never brought up. It was the greatest musical flop in Broadway history. It had been a can't-miss production. Advance sales through the roof. David Merrick producing. Book by Edward Albee. Score by Bob Merrill. Choreography by Michael Kidd. Starring Mary Tyler Moore.

But after weeks of out-of-town tryouts and the fourth night of previews on Broadway, Merrick shockingly closed the show before it officially opened. He then ran an ad in the *New York Times* saying he'd closed the production "rather than subject the public and critics to an excruciatingly boring evening."

Mary Tyler Moore departed "21" after dinner, but June and I stayed on with David for coffee and dessert. I asked him why he had closed *Breakfast at Tiffany's*. Was it the book, the score, the actors, what?

He said, "I've learned it's never a good sign when the audience starts talking back to the actors on stage."

THE BIG CHALLENGE OF DROPPING IN on one of George Plimpton's parties in his Sutton Place apartment on the East River was to conceal your amusement. There would be the usual mix of glitter and scruff. Fashion victims mingling with the jeans crowd. Mousy little women and bearded men in crumpled jackets doing clavicle shots on publishing executives. A new comtemporary artist to meet and wonder if he painted anything that didn't make you dizzy. Somebody claiming to be making a bizarre documentary about a poet living in a jungle, and wondering if anyone cared to help out with the financing. A Candy Bergen might appear to improve the scenery. A Norman Mailer might be in lecture mode in a corner, thinning the herd.

One Sunday afternoon we brought along three Texans from Austin who were visiting us. Among them was Fletcher Boone, an authentic Austin character, sometime artist, but principally known for his lengthy and humorous diatribes on subjects with which he was wholly unfamiliar.

On that Sunday George furnished live music. Over in a corner was Antônio Carlos Jobim. He was strumming tunes on a guitar and not all of them were "The Girl from Ipanema." Most guests at the party were attentively crouched and standing around Jobim.

We, however, were as far away as we could manage. June and I, Bud Shrake, and the Austin friends. And I'm afraid we were talking among ourselves above the acceptable level of one of the mousy little women among the guests. She came over to scold us.

She said with a fierce look, "Don't any of you Texans ever hear someone play the guitar?"

"Yes, ma'am," Fletcher Boone said, "but it's a bit mite more rowdy."

Chapter 22

On the Road with a Plethora
of Names to Drop

LONDON IS ALWAYS A TREAT, once you survive the madness of Heathrow. My job found June and me in London often enough through the years that we sometimes felt like we had an apartment there, but we didn't—we only had Dukes, the Savoy, Claridge's, the Hyde Park, the Dorchester, Brown's, the Cadogan, the Stafford, the Connaught, and back to Dukes.

Yeah, back to the cozy bar in Dukes. To be closer to the first $25 martini I ever came across.

When we pried ourselves away from the hotels, our London consisted of Annabel's, Motcombs, the Grenadier in Belgravia, Green's in St. James's, Langan's in Piccadilly, the White Elephant when it existed, the food halls in Harrods, Les Ambassadeurs when it flourished in the old Rothschild mansion, the Connaught Grill, the Fifth Floor Café in "Harvey Nicks," and the Fountain restaurant in Fortnum and Mason.

We were lunching one noon in the Connaught Grill when I thought I recognized an elderly lady dining alone in a quiet corner. She looked like the lady I'd seen on her book jackets.

A waiter confirmed that it was Agatha Christie.

"One of our regulars," he said smugly.

As we left, I noticed she was reading one of her own mysteries.

Well, why the hell not? She obviously preferred the company of her own people.

Quite by accident on one trip, we wound up in London at the same time as David Merrick. We ran into him in the lobby of the Savoy, where we'd gone to dine. We were staying at Claridge's, home of the $100 room service breakfast long before its time. But that included juice and a copy of the *International Herald Tribune*.

I was in town covering the World Match Play golf tournament at Wentworth for *SI*, and David was there on business. He was going to have dinner with Glenda Jackson that night and insisted we join him.

When Glenda arrived at the Savoy we had a drink. Then she guided us in Merrick's limo to a Chinese restaurant in Covent Garden. She ordered for us. I ate the only thing I could identify, the egg rolls.

One of her remarks has stayed with me. I'd expressed the honest opinion that with few exceptions I thought British actors were better than American actors, and asked her why this might be true?

She said, "It's simple, dear. We care more about our craft than we do our celebrity."

London for us was at its merriest during Wimbledon. I wouldn't be working—we'd be there as spectators. Going to a sports event without having to type was a rare pleasure. I'd be on the way to the British Open, and we'd be tying it in with a vacation in the Cotswalds or Cornwall or Kent or the Isle of Eriska in Scotland. Lot of good neighborhoods over there.

These were the years when Wimbledon was alive and well. The days of McEnroe-Borg and Martina-Chris.

Before tennis died, in other words.

Mark McCormack, giant among sports agents, did what he could to make our London visits interesting through the two weeks of Wimbledon. We'd been friends since I ghostwrote Mark's first book, *Arnie*. Going to his flat off Cadogan Square was a good place to spend an evening if you wanted to stock up on names to drop.

One evening at Mark's we hobnobbed with Sean Connery and Paul McCartney, but in June's opinion they were upstaged by Dame

Kiri Te Kanawa, the renowned operatic soprano from New Zealand, a client of Mark's in the IMG empire he built.

McCormack's hospitality marquee at Wimbledon was in a more convenient location than the regular hospitality tents, which were about as close to Centre Court as the Yorkshire moors.

Mark's marquee was a daily mosaic of celebs doing damage to platters of smoked salmon, mounds of caviar, and champagne. Next door on marquee row was NBC, usually offering hot dogs and ad agency slugs.

Sally Jenkins was covering those Wimbledons, and she was dining with us the day of a marquee moment.

Mark was table-hopping as Christopher Reeve, the actor, then known for his *Superman* roles, was leaving.

Unfortunately, the actor encountered trouble trying to open the marquee door. It wouldn't budge no matter how hard he kept jerking on it. The noise clattered through the tent.

Unable to control her laughter, Sally hollered, "Hey, Mark! You got anybody who can help Superman with the door?"

I enjoyed a marquee moment the day Mark introduced me to a new client. He was a tall, handsome Swede with a name like Ralf or Per or Kjell. That ballpark. As we shook, Mark informed me that the Swedish gent was chairman of the committee for the Nobel Prize in Literature.

I said, "The Nobel Prize for Literature? Really? Listen, if you guys ever dabble in sports, I have some of my books in the car, and—"

"Ho, ha!" he roared. "I see, yes! Sports! Ha, ho, ha!"

ONCE UPON A TIME THERE WAS something called the World Cup of Golf, and from the mid-'50s through the early '70s it was looked upon as a worthwhile event. Fred Corcoran ran it, took it to exotic locales every year, and managed to have the USA represented by the imposing two-man teams of Snead-Hogan (once), Snead-Demaret, Snead-Palmer, Palmer-Nicklaus (four times), Nicklaus-Trevino, and Nicklaus-Miller.

I carefully selected four World Cups to cover—'68 in Rome, '70 in Buenos Aires, '71 in Palm Beach, and '73 in Marbella.

Fred Corcoran spent the week in Marbella, as he did elsewhere, introducing me to sponsors and patrons and dozens of other people I didn't care to meet, and would never see again.

Jack Nicklaus and Johnny Miller won that tournament, and after talking to them I went striding across the clubhouse veranda on the way to the press room to write my story.

As I passed by Fred, who was in a conversation with a Spanish fellow, he grabbed my arm. "Dan, I want to introduce you to . . ."

I irritably pulled my arm away.

"Damn it, Fred," I said. "You've already made me meet 10,000 people I don't want to know. I gotta go. I'm on deadline."

I hurried away, but I'd barely taken two steps when I heard the plaintive voice of Fred saying, ". . . the king of Spain."

I stopped. My head hung with embarrassment. I slowly turned around and with a look of apology I walked back to shake hands with His Majesty Juan Carlos.

COLLECTING NETWORK PRESIDENTS was never a hobby, but if it had been a hobby my pick of the bunch would have been Bob Wood when he ran CBS.

I can't remember exactly how we became friends, but it may have been that we had a good mutual pal in USC coach John McKay. Bob Wood was a bleeding-cardinal-and-gold Trojan.

He was also a good friend and disciple of Don Rickles. There were moments when Bob thought he *was* Don Rickles. One evening he took June and me to a front-row table at the Copa to see Rickles.

The comedian picked on Wood throughout his act. Early into it, he pointed to June, who sat between us, and said to Bob, "This the new one? You're moving up."

One winter month Bob Wood came to visit us for two days in Kauai after he'd made a speech to affiliates in Honolulu. We took him to see the sights. The waterfalls, the blue grottoes, the natural slippery slide, the nude beach on the Na Pali coast where all the wrong people get naked.

We took him to dinner at the Dolphin, one of our hangouts in thriving downtown Hanalei, which consisted of the Dolphin, the Rice Mill, the Tahiti Nui bar, Ching Yung's store, and a small church.

The Dolphin was a ceiling-fan-bamboo-wicker joint with good food. Through the magic of its plumbing system, the bar provided falling rain outside the windows for the customers who liked to pretend they were South Sea island derelicts.

Bob and I took stools at the bar while June sat at a table with local friends. On Bob's right was a huge, muscular Hawaiian thug. The thug wasn't amused when Bob made a wisecrack and nudged him with his elbow, saying, "Pretty funny, huh, big guy?"

The thug rapidly backhanded Bob on the cheek. It was a serious smack. June could hear it.

Bob calmly turned to me, and said: "Dan. He slapped the president."

"I know," I said.

We were whispering.

"What are we going to do about it?"

"Nothing," I said.

"Nothing?" said Bob. "I can't let this go."

"We're letting it go."

"Why are we letting it go, Dan?"

I said, "I know this guy. He has a reputation for beating up haoles."

"What is a howly?"

"A haole is us. People from the mainland. H-a-o-l-e. Haole."

"Fucking Hawaiians," Bob Wood said. "They can't even spell."

IF SUGAR RAY ROBINSON STOPPED A room that night at Elaine's, Sonny Jurgensen stopped a city. This was in Washington, D.C.

The forty-year-old quarterback, making a stunning comeback that day in 1974, threw three touchdown passes for the Washington Redskins to beat the New York Giants 24–3. Then while I was typing in the press box, June went ahead to dinner with Sonny and Margo, Sonny's all-star wife. I caught up with them later.

June marveled at the fans trying to commandeer Sonny's car as he worked his way through the crowds in the RFK Stadium parking lot. She marveled even more when they pulled into a station for gas. The fans recognized Sonny and tried to crawl in the car windows.

When they reached the Palm restaurant, Yasser Arafat in his head-dress couldn't have gotten a table quicker than Sonny.

After dinner, the four of us went to a cocktail party in Ben Bradlee's apartment in the Watergate complex. Every person in the room was somebody. The first five people I saw were Henry Kissinger, Katharine Graham, David Brinkley, Ben Bradlee, and our friend Barbara Howar, who'd gotten us invited in the first place.

Barbara was a Southern blond beauty with a salty wit, and a good writer in spite of it.

Mrs. Graham made an effort to talk to us, the New York visitors, about President Nixon's resignation two months ago, and President Ford pardoning Nixon one month ago, and how frightened she'd been throughout the whole Watergate business.

In the meantime, the men in the room wanted to talk to Sonny about football. This did not escape me.

I mentioned it to Barbara Howar, and she said: "Honey, don't you know about our nation's capital? It's just another little old Southern town where the men aren't interested in anything but sports and women."

Later in the evening, I'm sure I overheard Henry Kissinger say to Sonny Jurgensen: "Ve need linebackers."

Chapter 23

The Short Happy Life of a
Man Covering Ski Racing

I WAS SITTING ON a Swiss Alp the day I decided to write a novel.

Not right that minute.

Right that minute I was having a ham and cheese baguette and a café au lait on the sundeck of a restaurant in Kleine Scheidegg, a tiny outpost beneath the Eiger and Jungfrau. It was a bright day in 1970 and I'd ridden the cog-rail up from Wengen and was waiting for a pack of ski racers to finish the Lauberhorn downhill, dead or alive.

An Austrian, German, or Frenchman would win the race, and through a translator I would obtain the usual penetrating quote for my piece. Like: "The winning is better than the losing."

Such was my plight as the ski writer at *SI* for seven years. Every winter the assignment fell between my other two beats, college football and pro golf.

The sport may have been given to me in the first place—along with the '64 Winter Olympics in Innsbruck and the '68 Winter Olympics in Grenoble—because the magazine decided it wanted to cover ski racing as an athletic event, not a fashion show.

No complaints. It was a plush assignment. Six weeks in Europe every winter. Not skiing on the slopes of Kitzbuehel, St. Moritz,

St. Anton, Garmisch, Wengen, Grindelwald, Val d'Isère, Val Gardena, and back home to not ski on the slopes of Sun Valley, Aspen, and Vail.

I'd tried recreational skiing in New Mexico and found nothing normal about leaning *down* a mountain. A person could get killed doing that. It was helpful to discover that if you could ride the lift up the mountain, you could ride it back down.

In Europe it didn't take long to recognize what a competitive sport Alpine ski racing is. I covered it as such. As for some of the other Olympic winter sports, I'm still a little baffled.

Is cross-country skiing a sport or how a Swede goes to the 7-Eleven?

Is ski jumping from the top of the big hill what Finns do when they can't qualify as airline pilots?

Curling may be popular in England and Canada, but to everyone else it looks like cleaning up after your dog.

Bobsled strikes me as less of a sport than an exercise in which two to four people gather together and mutually agree to commit suicide.

Speed skating. Here's a sport where men and women congregate every four years to decide who has the biggest thighs.

Isn't the biathlon nearly always won by the guy who can cross-country ski, stop to fire a rifle, and spell "biathlon"?

But I like figure skating. Don't gasp.

When Sonja Henie invented it and hopped around on icy ponds, I agreed with whoever it was that said figure skating isn't a sport, it's dinner theater. But once I covered it, I was fascinated. It does require incredible athleticism.

I particularly like the pairs—and I don't care if the guys dress like Lancashire Fusiliers on parade before they go off to the Sudan.

The first night in the ice stadium in Innsbruck I didn't know which Russian was Belousova and which one was Protopopov, but I did know which German was Kilius and which was Bäumler. Marika Kilius was the one who looked like Marilyn Monroe on skates with her skirt blowing up.

The pairs have changed since my era. Now I watch TV as the Lancashire Fusiliers toss rag dolls halfway across the ice. If the rag dolls are Russian they land the "throw triples," but if the rag dolls are

American, they land on their heads somewhere behind the scoring table.

Ice dancing has become my preference. Torvill and Dean and Klimova and Ponomarenko did it for me.

THE BEST THING ABOUT MY SKI lift years was becoming good friends with Bob Beattie, the U.S. ski coach. His competitive motto was, "Screw the French and Austrians, make 'em speak English."

The first ski race I covered was the ladies' giant slalom in Grindelwald. It became an exercise in stupidity. My own. I had foolishly asked a French writer for *L'Equipe* how to cover the race. He said go up to watch the start, ski down to the finish. I said I couldn't ski too good. He said, "But you can stem christie, yes? You will be fine."

Fine to him must have meant ruptured spleen.

I boarded a train with a group of foreign journalists. The train went up and up some more and stopped on a ledge. The foreign journalists hopped off and swooshed away. I got off and looked around. The start of the giant slalom was over there. The finish was way down there. Before I could get my boot in my left ski, it accidentally slid away from me and out of sight down the mountain. I said what I thought of skiing for a moment, then threw away my other ski, and started hiking down the mountain.

Soon I was sliding down the mountain parallel to the race course. Sliding on my side, on my back, on my stomach.

Halfway down I grabbed on to a root poking up out of the snow, held on, and lit a Winston. A ski patrol guy schussed to a stop, sprayed me with ice. He looked at my cigarette, laughed, and schussed away.

When I reached the bottom, I brushed off the snow and ice, and trudged over to the finish tent, where I ran into a friend. It was Fred Casotti, the SID at the University of Colorado. He was the U.S. ski team manager. He'd been watching me stumble and slide down the mountain.

Fred said, "I figured it had to be somebody from *Sports Illustrated,* but I didn't know it would be you."

June had flown over to meet me in Innsbruck halfway through the Olympics, but first she'd taken our kids to Lafayette, Louisiana, to stay with her other sister, Anne, and her husband, Rex Alford, and their two cousins, Amy and Bryan. Rex was in the oil well supply business. They spoiled our kids as rotten as I ever was.

June arrived in time for the men's slalom where the two of us were thrilled to watch Billy Kidd and Jimmy Heuga win the silver and bronze, taking the USA's first men's medals—ever—in Olympic Alpine ski racing. We celebrated that night with Bob Beattie, Fred Casotti, and the team, and everyone got boxed on patriotism and grown-up beverages.

There was unpleasantness. In Innsbruck I was manhandled by the Austrian army everywhere I tried to go. Why? Because it's in their genes. They'd growl something as they pushed me around. When they growled in broken English, it sounded like: "Your papers, please."

JUNE AND I RECUPERATED FROM INNSBRUCK at La Belle Aurore in St. Maxime on the French Riviera—André Laguerre's recommendation. It was as romantic a place as the name sounds, right out of a movie. Our room came with a balcony overlooking the blue Med. It was where we were introduced to scrambled eggs with truffles served in an egg shell for a breakfast dish.

We were sure that hadn't got to Texas yet.

I'm moved to pause and list other tasteful delights we came upon in our travels. Grub that rates almost as many stars as Shanghai Jimmy's chili-rice in Dallas, the bacon cheeseburger in Clarke's, and the McCarthy Salad at the Beverly Hills Hotel.

Last time I looked, the list included:

The steak and *pommes frites* at Café de Paris in Geneva. Choose your fresh fish at Sabatini in Trestavere, Rome. Barbecued goat in Fez, Morocco. Rainbow trout out of the river at the Huka Lodge in New Zealand. Steak sandwich on any street corner in Buenos Aires. The perfect omelets at the Hotel Valrose in Rougemont, Switzerland. The bay lobsters in Sidney, Australia. Cornish pasty on any corner in Penzance. The bread pudding at a farm outside Capetown, South Africa. Raclette or fondue anywhere in Switzerland. Shepherd's pie in rural Scotland. Cottage pie in rural England. And bacon and eggs at Camp David, very nice resort, on the two weekends I spent there when President George H. W. Bush was the resident.

We would update the list from time to time, and at one point years back our son Danny insisted on contributing two items—the mixed green salad with bleu cheese dressing on Braniff, and the chicken soup out of the vending machine in the Minneapolis air terminal.

ROBERT REDFORD HELPED ME COVER the Grenoble Olympics. That may be overstating it. He *was* with us. We'd met and got to know each other when we were living in the same Manhattan apartment building at the corner of 86th and Madison.

Through *SI*, I'd arranged an Olympic press credential for Bob and got him his own bedroom in the pension the magazine arranged for our staff in Grenoble. He'd wanted to go to the Olympics to research *Downhill Racer*, a film that was going to be made because he would star in it.

We dined together a few times in Grenoble and I'd be disappointed if he didn't remember the Trois Rose, which was where I teamed up with Mac Hemion, a director for ABC-TV, to money-whip the chef into preparing steak tartare well done.

It was a puzzling thing. Aside from June and I and Beattie, nobody appeared to know who Redford was. They evidently hadn't seen *Barefoot in the Park*, *This Property Is Condemned*, or *The Chase*. I kept telling people he was a movie star. They'd look blank.

But about a year later, after *Butch Cassidy and the Sundance Kid* came out, Nancy Williamson, one of our reporters at the Olympics, came up to me in the hall at *SI*, and said, "That blond guy who was with us in Grenoble? Wasn't that . . . ?"

My coverage of ski racing didn't amount to much, but André was overly pleased with the cover story I wrote on France's Jean-Claude Killy. André being half French may have had something to do with it.

I proclaimed Killy the sport's greatest racer before he won all three golds in Grenoble:

> He has that lonely, soulful, semi-tragic, slightly tortured, sit-down-and-I-will-tell-you-stories-of-betrayal-and-suffering look that makes most women 5 to 1 underdogs. He is young and as French as truffles in your scrambled eggs. With his obsessive love of speed and daring and that *look* of his, you get illusions just seeing him. You get the idea that if he had come along 25 years earlier he would have been one of those Frenchmen who stuck knives in Gestapo agents, tapped out radio messages to the Allies in a reeking Paris cellar, and left Michèle Morgan dripping tears on her loaf of bread by a foggy bank of the Seine. But Jean-Claude Killy is fighting a far less dramatic war. It's the war of men on skis against snow on mountains, and what you should know about him is that right now he is probably the best ski racer in the world.

Bob Beattie introduced me to Norma Shearer one evening in the Sun Valley Lodge. I was there for an international ski race. Once the Queen of Hollywood, she was nearing seventy years of age. She had entered the lodge ballroom with her husband, Marty Arrouge, a former ski instructor. The orchestra instantly struck up "It Happened in Sun Valley," and, no kidding, the couple danced twice around the floor before taking their table.

I was told they made this entrance every night during ski season.

When I met her later in the evening, I said, "Mary Haines, I'd know that voice anywhere." It was her role in *The Women.*

Norma Shearer took on a glow. Movie stars tend to glow when you remember a role they played.

On another evening in the lodge I met a movie star who didn't take on a glow when I made a wisecrack. Ann Sothern wound up at the dinner table with Beattie and me and some of the American racers. It was known that Karl Schranz, the brash Austrian ski racer, was Ann Sothern's house guest that week. All I said was, "How's it going with the storm trooper at home?" She slapped my face. Yes. Maisie slapped me. She felt she had the right, being a movie star. I only smiled. She later apologized. Stuff happens.

THE SPORT WOULD HAVE BEEN IMPOSSIBLE for me to cover without Anita Verschoth, an *SI* reporter. Anita was an attractive brunette, a native of Germany, spoke half a dozen languages. She knew all about winter sports, and knew the athletes, officials, and foreign journalists.

When we were getting to know each other in Innsbruck, I got her lit in a bar and she confessed that she'd grown up in a little town near Düsseldorf, and at the age of ten she'd been forced to become a Hitler Youth.

She should never have told me that. On another evening in an Austrian tavern I got her lit up enough to make her sing "The Horst Wessel Song."

"Die fahne hoch!" she began to sang. *"Die reihen fest geschblossen!"*

"Good, you remember the words," I said. "But I guess we'd better hold it down a little—some locals might want to join in."

As you might guess, that wasn't the only time we got lit and I made her sing it.

Chapter 24

"I'd Buy a Novel Called *Semi-Tough* If There Was Nothing in It but Blank Pages"

I HAD THE TITLE before I had the novel. The title came easy. Growing up in Texas, I'd spent a lifetime listening to guys say, "I'm semi-tired . . . I'm semi-hungry . . . I'm semi-horny . . . He's a semi-sorry excuse for a football player . . . I could be two-thirds in love with her if she wasn't about half slut and semi-dumb."

What could I write a novel about?

I'd never been to war, never been to sea, never been to a shrink, never been poor, never been black, never been in prison, never been in politics, never even been gay.

Also, I'd never been up close and personal with anxiety, depression, depravity, and despair. That was for book authors who liked to brood and introspect. Never had time for it myself. Too busy with deadlines.

When a book author broods and introspects, it better be short, is what I say, otherwise I toss the dude.

The little corporal limped out of the foxhole holding his purple guts in his hands, and all he could think about was how he'd only joined up because his mother got so mad that day she threw away his Dinky Toys.

Toss.

I can still see the copy of Nietzsche on the bedside table and feel the slab of liver my mother had strapped to my chest.

Toss.

Thad was late.

Slam shut.

Okay, what about football? I'd been to football. I'd been to coaches, players, locker rooms, sidelines, press boxes, bars, restaurants, hotel suites, dormitories. I'd kept secrets and protected sources. But this would be fiction. I could make stuff up and use words that would never make the cut in a family newspaper.

Inspiration had been all around me in high school and college.

I'd known a pulling guard who stole the refrigerator out of his mother's home and sold it to get poker money. I'd known a linebacker who could out-fart a city bus. I'd known a tackle who kept a mad dog chained up in his dorm room to keep away thieves and fags. I'd known a fullback who pushed a Coke machine down two flights of dormitory stairs because his girlfriend broke up with him. I'd known a halfback who didn't bathe or brush his teeth for eight weeks because he couldn't get a date with Priscilla Alice Dodge. He thought she must be rich with a name like that.

I borrowed or stole lines from gridiron heroes who became friends—Bobby Layne, Doak Walker, Don Meredith, Sonny Jurgensen, Frank Gifford, Billy Kilmer, Jake Scott, Alex Hawkins, Paul Hornung, Billy Vessels, Tucker Frederickson, Bubba Smith. A cast of thousands, really.

Most of them contributed unknowingly.

You can find a tip on how to write behind any tree stump or in any magazine rack, and a lot more from creative writing professors, most of whom have never creatively written. Those you toss.

But three tips I clutch to my heart.

Dorothy Parker: "Wit has truth in it. Jokes are simply calisthenics with words."

Elmore Leonard: "If it sounds like writing, I rewrite it."

I may be partial to the one that came from a sit-around friend in Clarke's, Freddy Finklehoffe. Freddy had conquered Broadway *and* Hollywood. His best-known work was *Brother Rat*, the play and movie. Freddy said there was only one rule in fiction, and his tip was: "Get 'em up a tree. Throw rocks at 'em. Get 'em down again."

No doubt there are book authors who'd scoff at the way I went about it in novels. I never did outlines. That would make it carpentry. I'd have in my mind who the main characters were, how it would start and how it would end, but I liked to surprise myself in the middle.

If you're interested, I've never written standing up in a gazebo with a pencil and yellow legal pad. Or dipping my pen in the blood of a Cape buffalo and scratching words on the sleeve of my safari jacket.

I type. I write clean. I was once the Wite-Out king. I worked on a Remington desk machine and Smith-Corona portable in my early newspaper days. The Smith-Corona weighed 500 pounds when I lugged it up the steps of a stadium.

I graduated to an Olympia standard for the office and a lightweight Olivetti for the road. The Olivetti was a gift from God, although there were occasions when its obstinate ribbon reverse could turn into a rat vermin saboteur. There was an era when I had an Olympia desk model at *SI*, another one in the office at home, and a third one at the house in Hawaii.

I came late to computers, and only after a bypass in the late '90s. I had a triple. It was supposed to have been a quad, but I birdied one.

I had to quit smoking. To give me something to help take my mind off losing one of my best friends, June and my son Marty slipped into my office at home and replaced the Olympia with a desktop computer and printer. For three weeks, the computer made me want to beat it to death with a hammer. I slowly wrestled it to the ground and let it know who was boss, but there's still one thing about it. I can lose a column or an entire manuscript if I accidentally hit a key I didn't know existed.

I've decided that if science seriously wanted to do something for the sake of journalism and literature, it would invent one click that tells the little Asian inside the computer: "Put all my stuff back where it was before you jacked around with it."

Semi-Tough was written on the three Olympias. I just got Billy Clyde Puckett talking and went where he took me.

I SOLD THE NOVEL AT P. J. Clarke's. On an evening in the spring of '71, June and I had gone there to sit around with Jack Whitaker, Danny Lavezzo, Jimmy Martin, Jones Harris, Toby Stone, and other regulars. We stopped to speak to Willie Morris, who was at another table with someone. Willie was the editor of *Harper's* in that historical period, and it was a time when Willie referred to himself after the third cocktail as "this little old Southern boy."

Willie asked what I was working on. *The Dogged Victims* and *Saturday's America*, two collections, had come out a year earlier, and although I'd become a hardcover book author, those books hadn't bought us any new furniture.

I said I was trying to write a pro football novel, and I was calling it *Semi-Tough*.

The fellow with Willie perked up.

"*Semi-Tough?*" he said. "I'd buy a novel called *Semi-Tough* if there was nothing in it but blank pages."

That's how I met and became friends with Herman Gollob, the editor of Atheneum, who would later hold the same position at Simon & Schuster and Doubleday. Herman Gollob would be my editor on five other novels, including *Semi's* sequels, *Life Its Ownself* and *Rude Behavior*.

Herman was a Texas A&M grad, had grown up in Houston, and understood the language of Billy Clyde Puckett.

I admire A&M's corps of cadets. I have a son named for a Texas Aggie. It was a Texas Aggie on Omaha Beach on D-Day—Lieutenant Colonel Earl Rudder—who led the 2nd Ranger Battalion up the cliffs of Pointe du Hoc and held it against a German counterattack. I enjoy a good "Aggie joke" as much as the next Texan, but I've often thought they'd work better on Arkansas people who wear pigs on their heads.

Herman said, "How far along are you?"

"Around 200 pages."

"When will you be finished?"

He seemed serious.

I said, "Before the night's over if you're really interested."

"Send me what you have tomorrow."

He *was* serious.

The up-front offer wasn't anything to shout out of our apartment window, but I was going to get a novel published. Me. A sportswriter.

Herman made a key suggestion out of the blocks. I had Billy Clyde telling the story into a tape recorder, and Barbara Jane Bookman was transcribing it.

Herman said, "Athletes writing books have a mechanic. Come up with an as-told-to guy. A sportswriter, maybe."

It took me all of five minutes to come up with Jim Tom Pinch of the *Fort Worth Light & Shopper*.

I finished the book in the spring of '72. It came out in the early fall—and ran away with me.

THEY HADN'T OFFERED A COURSE AT TCU on how to act like a big-time author. I could have used some advice after *Semi* took flight. It leaped onto all the best-seller lists—and stayed. It sold to paperback for what was a minor fortune to us, but the number wouldn't make a blister on John Grisham's ass today. David Merrick bought it for Broadway or a movie. I went on a nationwide book tour.

Herman went with me on three stops, and heard me say such things as, "I'm just a sportswriter, I don't know how this happened."

"You don't know how to sell a book, do you?" Herman said. "When you talk to people, tell them you wanted to take the reader *inside* pro football. Behind the scenes in this great American sport. It's what you've done. Stop apologizing for your damn book."

Ben Hogan's words came back to me. *Never apologize for winning.*

By the time the tour led to Fort Worth, I was trying to act like the

serious novelist whose jacket photo has him gazing out over the Bos-
phorus and contemplating what other service he can provide for man-
kind. The line was long, but one customer in it, standing patiently,
caught my eye and caused me to jump out of my chair.

The person was Dr. Lorraine Sherley, one of my professors at
TCU, who I liked tremendously. I hadn't seen her in twenty years.
She'd had me in her "Interrelation of the Arts" class, and she had
given me a passing grade even though she was quick to realize that I
didn't much give a shit about the things that Botticelli had in common
with Brahms.

I gave Lorraine a hug, and said, "This book might be a little too
advanced for you."

All she said was, "Congratulations. Good characters. Excellent
dialogue. But now we go on to the next one, don't we?"

It was a sobering moment.

I received a lot of fan letters. A good many of them came from
people who wanted to know how to get their own books published.
Some asked if I would like to collaborate with them. One guy said
he had this really funny uncle who could tell stories forever about
his job selling aluminum siding. Another guy said he could keep me
up all night laughing about his life as an insurance salesman—mainly
Casualty, Disaster, and Theft. A lady said she had some hilarious tales
to tell about her thirty years as a secretary for the Firestone tire company.

I replied to some of them that I was moving to Londolozi, South
Africa, and if they were ever in the region we could discuss their literary ideas in more detail. But call first. I might have gone down to the
river to watch the rhinoceroses bathe.

Although it may be insufferably self-serving to bring it up, I did
receive one fan letter I particularly cherish. It came from a writer
I'd never met, Alex Haley, a black man, the author of *Roots* and *The
Autobiography of Malcolm X.*

He explained that he often wrote while traveling on a freighter
bound for anywhere. His letter to me was written on board the

SS *President Polk* and was postmarked from Keelung, Taiwan, China. He further explained that my novel had been handed to him by the captain of the ship, and it had robbed him of a day and night's work. It was highly complimentary.

I embrace Alex Haley's letter as testimony that *Semi-Tough* wasn't written by a redneck in a white hood.

David Merrick gave me a shot at writing the "libretto" for what might become a Broadway musical. I had no idea how to go about it, so I went to Freddy Finklehoffe at Clarke's for advice.

"Two acts, sixty pages," Freddy said. "The book for a musical is children's literature."

"I can't do children's literature," I said.

"Somebody will," said Freddy. "Don't matter. The score will sell the show, or it won't."

While I was cramping the novel into sixty pages of locker rooms, hotel rooms, bars, and sidelines—the score became a problem. Merrick couldn't hire who he first wanted, and second wanted, and never told me who they were, leaving me to figure that Cole Porter and Jerome Kern were still dead.

Merrick wound up hiring the songwriting team of Will Holt and Gary Friedman. They'd been a part of one Broadway hit, *The Me Nobody Knows.* I hadn't seen it.

At our first meeting, Will Holt opened up a folder and pulled out a newspaper clipping about Evel Knievel.

I stopped him right there. "Evel Knievel? We're talking about Evel Knievel here? If *Evel Knievel* winds up in this musical, it'll be after he gets killed trying to jump his motorcycle over my apartment building."

When Holt and Friedman had written the first four songs, I was summoned to Merrick's office on 46th Street, a short putt from Sardi's, to join David, Allen DeLynn, and a secretary to give the songs a listen.

We sat and faced the piano across the carpeted room with our backs to the shelf with the 5,000 Tony Awards on it.

The first song was a ballad that had something to do with apples and acorns. I fought off a killer sigh. The next two I don't remember—I was still trying to stay in my chair.

The last song was introduced by Will Holt, who said, "This is the number Barbara Jane sings while she's roller-skating through Bloomingdale's."

I fought off an urge to shout, "Where's my hat?"

But relief was on the way. In the middle of the song, David Merrick leaned over to me and whispered, "We're making a movie."

LOVED THE MONEY, hated the movie.

I should rephrase that. I liked watching the movie being shot, then I hated it. I liked getting to know Burt Reynolds and Kris Kristofferson and Jill Clayburgh and Brian Dennehy, and seeing my longtime Fort Worth pal Norm Alden play the role of the coach. I liked sitting at picnic tables and having lunch with the cast and crew. I liked getting to know Ring Lardner Jr., who wrote the first script. It was faithful to the book. But in the end, I didn't like knowing Michael Ritchie, the director. He was one of those guys who never lost a conversation.

I should probably say I didn't hate the movie as much as I simply got tired of looking for *Semi-Tough* on the screen.

Michael Ritchie brought in Walter Bernstein, another screenwriter, to throw away Ring Lardner's script and write the movie the director wanted to make. Which in my opinion was a remake of *Bob & Carol & Ted & Alice*, the group therapy comedy of a few years in the past.

The movie turned out to be nowhere as entertaining as the review John Schulian wrote for the *Chicago Daily News*. John Schulian, for those unaware, is the best sportswriter who ever left our business to get rich writing for TV. The highlight of John's review:

"Ritchie wound up putting Burt Reynolds and Kris Kristofferson in a movie about the consciousness movement. If you aren't familiar with the consciousness movement, the premise on which it is built is that nobody's hemorrhoids are more important than yours."

Chapter 25

Learning to Love the Game That
Ate Our Sports Pages

YOU COULD CALL IT covering pro football, or you could call it waiting for Burt. It took four years for Burt Reynolds to become available so *Semi-Tough* could be a movie. But I wasn't idle. I had my day job.

André Laguerre retired as the ME of *SI* in the winter of '74 and it was an emotional night for many of us when we closed his last issue. The night ran into dawn. Hangovers the next day set records.

Roy Terrell took over as our leader, and this was a good news–bad news thing for me personally. The good news was that Roy was a fellow Texan and had been an accomplished writer for the magazine and appreciated good writing. The bad news was he made me cover pro football.

Tex Maule had been covering the pros for fifteen years, but he retired with André, and Roy wanted to capitalize on my *Semi* success, whatever it was.

I had never liked pro football as much as college football. I still don't. Certainly not since the nation's newspapers have turned the NFL into the most overcovered activity in history. If you live in the Metroplex, for one example, you can find a story on the Dallas Cowboys in the Fort Worth and Dallas papers 365 days a year.

Tell me why this makes sense? Better yet, tell me when pro football fans started to read. They watch the games on TV and listen to the NFL shills who fancy themselves broadcast journalists. They listen to babbling sports talk on the radio. They save up for a year to take the kid to one game. But if you piled up the number of college degrees among pro fans in the entire country, it wouldn't reach the roof of a Walgreens.

Beyond all that, I've never understood how a team can lose four, five, six games during the season and be called the world champion of anything.

Yeah, I'm aware the college game has its share of sillies. But the college sillies aren't just cheering for the team. They're cheering for the campus, the drag, the old school colors, the memories.

In the pros, players come and go, become heroes, get defrocked, suffer injury, retire. Coaches are fired and rehired somewhere else as head coaches or coordinators. I'm sorry to break this news to pro fans, but the "team" they're cheering for consists of the owner, the general manager, and a flock of attorneys and accountants.

I'll walk you through the six Super Bowls I covered. The big challenge was surviving the social week leading up to the game.

1975 SUPER BOWL. NEW ORLEANS. STEELERS 16, VIKINGS 6.

My colleague Roy Blount Jr., single at the moment, bought flowers from a hippie flower girl on a street corner in the Quarter. Then he bought the hippie flower girl. But he couldn't get rid of her for two days. She'd grown accustomed to clean sheets and room service.

Now for an encore the Pittsburgh Steelers' defense will pick up Tulane Stadium and throw it into the middle of Bourbon Street. And L. C. Greenwood and Mean Joe Greene will swallow what is left of Fran Tarkenton in a crawfish bisque. Why not? Along with Ernie Holmes and Dwight White they have already dined on the Minnesota running game—has anyone else tasted Chuck Foreman's jersey lately?

1976 SUPER BOWL. MIAMI. STEELERS 21, COWBOYS 17.

Bud Shrake brought Jerry Jeff Walker and his guitar to the press hospitality room in the Fontainebleau on Miami Beach. Jerry Jeff sang and picked far into the night, topping anything we would see at halftime. In those years, getting Jerry Jeff out of there was another problem.

> For all the gaudy things that happened, like a decent Super
> Bowl game for a change, memories of this one will keep going
> back to the Pittsburgh Steelers' Lynn Swann climbing into the
> air like the boy in the Indian rope trick, and coming down with
> the football.

1977 SUPER BOWL. PASADENA. RAIDERS 32, VIKINGS 14.

We headquartered at the Beverly Hills Hotel with our showbiz friends. I got us invited to the network parties. David Merrick got us invited to the Hollywood parties. We saw a luxurious display of cleavage and gold shit hanging around guys' necks. We limoed to the game, and June didn't have to wait long for me to file.

> For your halftime stunt, ladies and gentlemen in the stands,
> write down on your cards what you think of the Minnesota
> Vikings so far. Now hold up your cards. Uh, sorry. It would
> never pass the censors. The game was essentially over by then,
> as so many Super Bowls have been concluded by the Vikings,
> who somehow seem to save their worst effort for Pete Rozelle's
> answer to urban strife set to music and pigeons.

1978 SUPER BOWL. NEW ORLEANS. COWBOYS 27, BRONCOS 10.

Galatoire's and Manale's managed to fit into our busy schedule, which largely consisted of socializing in the Old Absinthe House.

My wife proved herself a real trouper. She hung in there in the

Absinthe bar through the wee hours all week with me and Pete Axthelm, the *Newsweek* poet, Roy Blount, Sonny Jurgensen, Jake Scott, and other NFL immortals, and some members of my personal PR Hall of Honor, one of whom was Max McGowan. Max had worked for Al McGuire at Marquette and now ran his own advertising and public relations firm in Chicago.

While I'm at it, others in my all-time publicity-guy lineup were Doug Todd, Dallas Cowboys; Bill Brendle, CBS; Jones Ramsey, University of Texas; Beano Cook, Pitt; Jim Brock, TCU and Cotton Bowl; Roger Valdiserri, Notre Dame; Don Bryant, Nebraska; Johnny Keith, Oklahoma; Fred Casotti, Colorado; and Don Klosterman, a PR man in the cloak of a GM for Lamar Hunt, Bud Adams, and Carroll Rosenbloom.

It was nearing daylight in the Absinthe bar, the game only hours away, when Max McGowan ordered another round.

I cried out, "Jesus, no, Max! I have to get some sleep. I've had four dozen J&Bs and smoked six cartons of Winstons!"

Max said, "I didn't know we came down here to try to quit smoking."

As Super Bowls go, the one played indoors in New Orleans last Sunday was way up there for Mosts. It had the most fumbles, the most noise, the most penalties, the most trick plays, and the most X's and O's stamped on a coach's forehead. Dallas's Tom Landry nailed Denver's Red Miller to the blackboard and left him there.

1979 SUPER BOWL. MIAMI. STEELERS 35, COWBOYS 31.

It was the week we received the news that André Laguerre had died, which was the worst thing, but it was also the time my wife had her ticket stolen outside the Orange Bowl, and the day a zebra won the game.

I called Roy Terrell to ask if the Time-Life Gulfstream could come pick us up so we could attend André's funeral, and bring us back. Roy said, "Are you kidding?" I dropped the subject and hosted a dinner for twenty writers and other friends in honor of André at the Jockey Club. The tab was in the neighborhood of $2,000. I put it on the expense account. André would have smiled. Roy didn't.

A month later, when Roy saw my expense report, his inner CPA came out in him. He called me into his office.

His face red, he said, "If you want to live like King Farouk, you're going to have to pay half of it yourself!"

I said, "I can do that."

Then I added, "But Roy . . . *King Farouk*?"

Up in the press box roughly forty minutes before the kickoff, I was paged to the elevator. An NFL executive said, "There's a lady down-stairs who says she's your wife and she's lost her ticket."

I said, "Somebody's playing a trick. My wife's been to sports events all over the world. She's never lost her credential. She knows to guard it."

Ten minutes later I was getting coffee when the elevator doors opened and out stepped June Jenkins with our friend Pat Summerall. Pat had rescued her and brought her upstairs, as only a TV personality could have.

"It *was* you!" I said, nearly spilling the coffee.

The thief had lifted the ticket out of her shoulder bag as she was about to enter the portal with two friends from Gotham. Fortunately, June knew where the seats were. A policeman escorted her to her seat in the stadium, and I settled in to watch a zebra ruin a good football game with a despicable pass interference call.

For three quarters and six minutes of the fourth last Sunday, Super Bowl XIII was everything pro football's championship game is supposed to be, but rarely is. It had the NFL's two best teams, the Pittsburgh Steelers and Dallas Cowboys, doing things in heroic fashion. It had Roger Staubach and Tony Dorsett. It had Terry Bradshaw and John Stallworth. And then it had Field Judge Fred Swearingen and his yellow flag.

1980 SUPER BOWL. PASADENA. STEELERS 31, RAMS 19.

My last NFL rodeo. The magazine wanted more X's and O's in its pro football coverage. Paul Zimmerman was hired from a New York tabloid to provide it. In an X's and O's contest, Paul Zimmerman would lap the field. I would only write a piece if the Rams won, due to my connections with Don Klosterman and Georgia Rosenbloom, Carroll's widow. This put me back in the Polo Lounge having a Junior and water while "Dr. Z" was still doing his X's and O's.

In reality, my farewell to pro football came two nights before at a Hollywood Super Bowl party. It was held in one of those hot restaurants where tents are pitched on the side to accommodate all the tits and ass. Milling about among movie stars and people trying to look like movie stars, I was introduced to Ned Tannen, a studio mogul.

"*Semi-Tough*," he said, shaking my hand.

"Guilty," I said.

"Football don't do foreign," he said, and moved on.

My one regret in leaving pro football is that I wasn't in New Orleans for the '81 Super Bowl. Not the game. The pregame press conference with Jim Plunkett, the Oakland Raiders' quarterback.

Many friends were there—Blackie Sherrod, Jim Murray, Ed Pope, Furman Bisher, Tom Callahan. For years, they laughed about a question Plunkett was asked by a writer from a New Jersey paper. The question: "Help me out here, Jim. Is it dead father, blind mother, or dead mother, blind father?"

A memorable moment in media history.

WHILE COVERING GOLF AND THE NFL, the game that ate America's sports pages, and while waiting for Burt, I somehow managed to squeeze two more novels out of the typewriter.

I wrote *Dead Solid Perfect*, saw the title enter the language of golf, chased it around the country, and watched it cling for a spell to the roof gutter of the *New York Times* best-seller list. That was in '74.

Next, Bud Shrake and I collaborated on *Limo*, another romantic comedy in my mind but a comment on marriage in Bud's. In the novel the term "Left Coast" was introduced to America, and reality TV was invented. Not the Loud family experiment. The kind of reality TV you see today on a broad scale. We've never been given credit for creating it. I won't say this still makes me hot, but like the Israelis, I keep a list.

People asked how two people could write a novel in the first person of one character. I only know how we did it. Since the project was my idea, Bud said, "You start, I'll follow." I wrote the first chapter, and off we went. The network TV material became mostly mine, the Hollywood material mostly Bud's. The girlfriend became mine, the ex-wife his. When we finished, I edited the manuscript and made sure it sounded like the same person talking.

We wrote the reality TV show together over three days while pacing the living room floor of our house in Hawaii. We chain-smoked, swilled coffee, paused to eat June's lunches and dinners, and howled with laughter at our own wit.

What *Limo* did, if nothing else, was lead the authors into one of the most engaging interviews in the annals of local TV. On our book tour, we covered the country and ended up in Dallas.

The night before the interview we paid our respects to some old haunts—the Point After, the End Zone, the Chateaubriand. The Chateau was known for its good steaks, but more for its bar, where talk-big guys in business suits went to meet homewreckers and discuss world events.

It was a long night of socializing, we didn't get much sleep, and felt like we'd been thrown away when we arrived at the TV station at 6:30 a.m.

I've forgotten which network affiliate it was, or the name of the interviewer. She was attractive if you like the kind that doesn't smile.

We were placed on a sofa, wired up, given mugs of coffee, and she faced us in a chair next to a cameraman. Rolling.

She said, "I'm sorry, but I have to open this by saying I hated your book. I didn't find one thing funny in it."

"That's a joke or it's not a joke?" I said, smiling.

"It's not a joke," she said.

Determined to win her over, I said, "Which parts did you think were the least funny?"

"I know a bit about network TV and Hollywood, and I don't find a ring of truth in any of this," she said.

I said, "Don't tell me you didn't laugh at the reality TV show."

"It was stupid," she said. "The idea that anything like that could ever happen . . . I mean, *really*."

Now she turned to Bud, who hadn't spoken a word. She said, "You don't talk much, do you? Did you have anything to do with this at all?"

The twice divorced and brutally hungover Bud Shrake ended the interview. He looked at her painfully and said: "I can't believe I was never married to you."

Chapter 26

Hooray for Hollywood, That Silly, Dippy, Goofy Hollywood

THE '80S FOUND ME WRITING three more novels, a half-dozen movie scripts, two of which actually made it to the screen, while I kept covering sports. Oh, and I changed employers—from *Sports Illustrated* to *Golf Digest* and *Playboy*. Did I just bury the lead?

The novel *Baja Oklahoma* was a love letter to Fort Worth and country music. *Life Its Ownself* was a sequel to *Semi-Tough*. Then came *Fast Copy*, a newspaper novel set in the '30s in which I selfishly enjoyed creating my own Martha Gellhorn.

My scripts that reached all the way to the screen were *Baja Oklahoma* and *Dead Solid Perfect*, a couple of HBO productions that almost made moviemaking fun.

I labored over three other projects that would have bought some groceries if they'd worked out.

One was an effort to make *Semi* into a sitcom. It would have had a better chance if the network hadn't hired two Faulkner scholars to "punch up" my pilot. They inserted jokes for morons, and made Barbara Jane into a gift shop owner or a perfume saleslady—I forget which, some dumb-ass thing. I knew it was doomed for sure when the producer said, "Can't we turn Tex-Mex into Chinese food? Something funny? You know. Chopsticks and noodles?"

I went racing back to the sanity of New York. The show was canceled after four weeks.

Kay O'Brien, a medical drama for TV, was another project I somehow got involved in. I researched the pilot by hanging out at night with the doctors and nurses in the trauma center in a New York City hospital. The first thing I told the producers was that we should call it *Never Get Sick*. The drama ran a number of episodes but never caught on. It couldn't decide whether it wanted to deal with measles or bullet wounds.

The third project might have been our retirement run if Bud Shrake and I had received the screen credit we deserved as the first writers on *Beverly Hills Cop II*. When our names were left off the credits for whatever evil reasons, we sued Paramount, the Writers Guild, the memory of Irving Thalberg, and everybody else we could think of in Hollywood. We won a settlement, but the whip-out we collected wouldn't have made an IRS auditor's head swim.

I did all of that while keeping a bounce in my step supporting my wife's venture into the restaurant business.

Summerhouse was at the corner of 91st and Madison. The food was delicious and identifiable. The recipes came from mothers, grandmothers, aunts. Nowhere would you have found sliced elk with goose liver and blueberry sauce on a layer of seaweed.

The partnership at Summerhouse consisted of six attractive ladies—June, Angelique Graziano, Susan McAllister (the former Mrs. Dave Marr), Eloise Rowan O'Connell (now Mrs. Bernard Riviere), Cynthia Walsh, and Dina Schmidt. June, Angelique, and Eloise were transplanted Texans and good friends from back home.

A flattering article in *New York* magazine labeled them "the Lunch Bunch," identifying them as a group of Manhattan friends who got together and decided to do something creative and profitable—and succeeded.

Before Summerhouse opened, I was in the place one afternoon lobbying for navy bean soup on the menu. You couldn't expect me to forget the response of Dina Schmidt, who said, "I can't imagine anybody eating a *blue* bean."

From my perspective, it was an eyes-closed-thumb-and-forefinger-on-the-bridge-of-the-nose moment.

The grand opening was a hit, and I think you have to say the highlight was when Eloise, playing hostess, ran back to the kitchen in a panic, and said, "Every table is full and the passengers are lined up halfway down the block."

Passengers. All of a sudden, the customers had a name that would brand them forever.

In that first year, when the winter holidays approached, Cynthia Walsh announced to the partners that she couldn't work Thanksgiving weekend. She explained, "Thanksgiving is a tradition in our family."

The others could only stare at her.

Seconds later it was Angelique who said, "That is such a coincidence, Cynthia. Thanksgiving has always been a tradition in our family, too."

And they all fell about laughing.

The wait staffs were comprised of struggling actors, actresses, and singers. There was one success story. A pretty little blond waitress at Summerhouse landed a prominent role in a daytime soap. She bought a fur coat and came around to show off herself and the coat. It was with the greatest of restraint that her onetime coworkers managed not to choke her to death and rip the coat into balls of fur.

Summerhouse basked in the glow of celebrity clients. One afternoon a solemn man and tearful woman sat in the side room by themselves for over four hours to discuss their lives. Their privacy was protected by the staff. The solemn man was James Taylor and the tearful woman was Carly Simon.

Only the three Texas ladies participated in Juanita's, at the corner of 75th and Third. The recipes came from June and Angelique. They spent weeks learning to re-create the Tex-Mex dishes a Texan grows up on.

The significant celebs who dined at Juanita's included Don Imus, the striking and friendly Ali MacGraw, the Dan Rathers, the Tom Brokaws, Frank Gifford, Howard Cosell, and the Alistair Cookes, who lived nearby and frequently required a Tex-Mex fix.

BACK AT MY CAREER, it was probably time for me to leave *Sports Illustrated* after twenty-four years. Go on to another life. But I'd never have guessed that a certain individual would make it so easy to do.

For most of my stay I'd known *SI* as a happy place. I still keep up with those who were good friends *and* coworkers—Walt Bingham, best college football editor I ever had; Sarah Ballard, city dweller who introduced June and me to the Village and other Manhattan challenges; and Myra Gelband, who played Ginger to my Fred as we covered so many golf tournaments together. I couldn't begin to count the laughs I had with Ray Cave, Andy Crichton, Bob Creamer, Bill Leggett, Ron Fimrite, Stephanie Salter, Mike Del Nagro, Morrie Werner, and Demmie Stathoplos. Demmie had a standard line each time she entered the Ho Ho at the end of the workday. To one or the other of us, she'd say, "Hi, sailor—want to buy a lady a champagne cocktail?"

It was fun to be around the crowd on the twentieth floor when I'd return from the road. It was a friendly encampment to come back to. Well, all but the northwest corner, which was often joked about. Demmie gave it two names—"the Bermuda Triangle" and "the Boulevard of Broken Dreams." I never knew anyone who occupied a desk in that dreary corner, other than the morose Mark Kram.

But the genial atmosphere changed on a day in '79 when Gil Rogin crawled out of a dark cloud to become managing editor.

Gil was a strange individual, and appeared to take pride in it. You never knew which mood you'd find him in. Worse, in my opinion, he surrounded himself with a comedy lineup of sycophants. They carried clipboards down the halls and tried to look concerned about something. You got the feeling that they were capable of stabbing anyone in the back if they thought it would elevate them on the masthead. Together with Rogin, they acted as if they alone could save the week's issue from the sabotage being inflicted on it by the rest of the staff.

Gil had sold short stories to *The New Yorker*. I confess I never read one, having been told that I wouldn't appreciate it unless I was interested in his inner demons and body parts. But that success fueled his notion that no other writer's words were worth reading compared to his own, particularly if the writer had received a shred of public acclaim.

In an interview with the *New York Observer* in 2010, he said of Frank Deford, one of *SI*'s best and most decorated writers, "Frank was a very good writer, but not as good as he thought he was. . . . His stories were well thought out, but artificial."

It was difficult to imagine who he had in mind—Herb Wind, maybe—when he said of me in the same article, "He missed deadlines and covered golf as if it was played not on a course but in a cathedral."

That was so far from the truth, it was incredibly stupid. I'd never missed a newspaper or magazine deadline in my life. Usually I filed earlier than any editor anticipated. And if I wanted to go looking for a golf writer who covered the sport as if it were NOT played in a cathedral, I would start with your basic me:

From where Tom Watson was on the 71st hole of the U.S. Open golf championship Sunday at Pebble Beach—in the rough, on a downslope, looking at a slick green—you don't simply chip the ball into the cup for a birdie to beat Jack Nicklaus, who is already in the scorer's tent with a total good enough to win. First, you throw up.

If that's cathedral writing, tell the white suits to come get me.

He is a known Communist. He kidnapped the Lindbergh baby. He attacked Pearl Harbor. He peddles dope to kids, and—what? Oh, sorry. We were just sitting around here at the PGA in Akron trying to think of something new to say about Jack Nicklaus.

Yeah, there I went—on the loose again. The old cathedral writer.

I suppose it was what I should have expected from Rogin, who only liked track and field, pro basketball, and swimming, a man whose idea of lunch was to swim a mile at the West Side Y, then sit on the same stool at the same lunch counter and eat the same tunafish sandwich every day.

Rogin had referred to me behind my back as a "casual" writer. He said it to a lady *SI* reporter, who couldn't wait to repeat it to me.

I laughed, and said, "Gil thinks everybody is a casual writer, except himself and Proust."

In July of '84 I returned from the British Open at St. Andrews to find a shocking note waiting for me from Rogin. He said my British Open story *greatly disappointed* him and that he was *benching me* as the golf writer and assigning someone else to cover the PGA at Shoal Creek in Birmingham, Alabama, and I needed to see him in his office immediately, where we would *discuss my future* with the magazine.

Gil? Dude.

First thought: if my story had so "greatly disappointed" him, how come it ran in the magazine practically word for word?

But after reading Rogin's note, I knew I was out of there. The minute my wife read it, she *wanted* me out of there.

First, I asked my agent, Esther Newberg, to call our friends at *Playboy* and ask if they could use a sports columnist. They said yes. I called friends at *Golf Digest* and asked if they could use a golf columnist. They said yes.

Following that, I spoke with a lady in the Benefits Department at Time, Inc., to ask what early retirement looked like.

She said, "It's a good deal. You can walk off with half the store and go to work for somebody else."

In my case, that meant I could walk off with two years salary at its peak, a huge lump of stock, and lifetime medical for June and me.

"Sign me up," I said.

All that done, my future secure, my take-home enhanced, I sat in my *SI* office, lit a Winston, and wrote the reply to Rogin.

Gil:

Your letter of July 23 of course makes it impossible for me to continue working at Sports Illustrated. Consequently, I'll have to decline the invitation to discuss my future with you. Rather,

*I think I'll take up the subject with the editors of another
publication.*

*This, then, is to inform you of my decision to take early
retirement from Time, Inc. in December of this year, that
retirement to be preceded by a 3-month sabbatical. I find that
I'm eligible for both under company policy.*

*Naturally, it saddens me to have to make this decision after
24 years. I truly relished all of those deadlines, including the
last one. But at least it's satisfying to know I'm leaving behind
a body of work that a good many of SI's readers have enjoyed,
understood, and certainly admired far more than you ever did.*

Dan Jenkins

In Texas, that's known as a *"Buenas noches,* coaches."

This was a Tuesday. Nobody was around. We worked a Thursday–
Monday week in those days. I made a copy of the note and pinned
it on the prominent bulletin board in the southeast hall. I put the
original in an envelope and placed it on the desk of Rogin's secretary.

I awarded myself a stroll around the halls, pausing here and there
at areas that brought a smile. I returned to my office and collected
some photos off the walls, took the elevator down to the ground floor,
and walked out of the Time-Life Building for the last time.

It wasn't raining.

Chapter 27

Goodbye to All That and Hello
to the Rest of My Life

FOR A MONTHLY MAGAZINE you write a piece in September for the January issue, and write a piece in October for the February issue, and so on and so forth, and a man can lose track of what year it is, or what meal it is, if he doesn't keep a sharp eye on things.

While working on books and movies throughout the rest of the '80s and beyond, I had to adjust to writing on a monthly deadline for both *Playboy* and *Golf Digest*.

All in all, I found it safer to confine my column topics in *Playboy* to issues that weren't likely to go away soon, or dead people. Events of the day rarely overtake dead people.

For *Golf Digest*, I wrote features but covered the majors "live," on deadline, as I had for *SI*. It was good of the magazine to hold open for my reports. It was sort of like nothing had changed, only I was around smarter golf editors and nicer people as a whole.

I had friends who wondered if writing for *Playboy* meant sitting in an office and dictating the prose to Pamela Anderson, and having Hef drop by in his robe and slippers to invite me to dinner at the mansion with a dozen centerfolds.

That wasn't my experience in the five years I helped fill space in the magazine. For one thing, I wrote at home in New York and faxed the copy to Chicago. For another, Hef lived in L.A. I did go out to Chicago a few times for meetings, lunches, and drinks with Arthur Kretchmer, the editorial director.

Kretchmer was a boy wonder who ran the magazine successfully for thirty years. He retired at the age of sixty-one in 2004. He gave an interesting quote to the press when he hung it up, saying, "It was a good ride, but I finally got tired of chasing after the next new thing."

He didn't mean a Playmate. He meant a trend in the arts, popular music, and lifestyle.

The biggest favor *Playboy* did for me was permit Billy Clyde Puckett to sit with me at the typewriter. If political correctness had appeared anywhere near the Michigan Avenue Bridge or Lake Shore Drive in the late '80s, he'd have been shot like a moose and gutted and skinned.

A brief history of my typing life at *Playboy* . . .

You hear a lot about mambas, hippos, rhinos, even terrorists and Commies, but I say Africa gets a bad rap. In basketball, you can't win without the big guy who can work on top of the iron. When I can't find a prospect in Africa, I look in Yugoslavia, Sweden, Germany, maybe Russia. A scout never knows where he'll have to be. But I always start in Africa. They're taller. The kid in Belgrade who's 7-2 comes in at 7-6 in Ubangi. All I do is find 'em and place 'em. It's the coaches who have to teach 'em how to piss indoors.

For indiscriminate killing, it's hard to beat a Latin American country. They take soccer seriously down there. It shows up in their riots and stadium collapses. But they enjoy it, knowing the only thing they have to lose is an ascendance of bad waiters.

I went over to the condo to visit Wendiel Hamielton, our 6-10 forward who carries a 3.4 in physical sciences, a successful program we patterned after the ones at Michigan, Penn State, Arkansas, North Carolina, UCLA, Alabama, and LSU.

"How's school, Wendiel," I asked.

"School be up on that hill?"

"Yes, those buildings up there by the bell tower."

"I been up there once, baby. They got some funny shit goin' on."

It's been said that no sport is worthwhile unless it has a literature. Personally I believe every sport is worthwhile to one group or another, it's just that certain sports have a more obscure literature. Only those who follow wrestling as closely as I do know how much it meant when *The Great Pansy* by Scotty Fitz came out.

In my younger and more vulnerable years, I wore a gold cape with sequins, and my father gave me some advice that I've been turning over in my mind ever since.

"Whenever you feel like wearing that cape in public," he told me, "just remember there are plumbers, carpenters, and construction workers in this world who don't have a sense of humor."

PEOPLE WHO PUT DOWN *PLAYBOY* IN my day were generally those who never picked it up. They didn't know it was a literary magazine with skin. Not since *The Saturday Evening Post* in its glory years had a magazine published as many well-known authors. I was flattered to have my byline in there with your Nabokovs and Updikes.

I'm reminded of the times when *Sports Illustrated* tried to lure famous authors into its pages.

One of the earliest attempts involved Kurt Vonnegut. I once met Kurt Vonnegut at a "literary" cocktail party in some skinny woman's Greenwich Village apartment. I introduced myself. I was eager to find out if the story was true about his one week at *SI*. He confirmed it.

It seems that Vonnegut was given a set of photos of an equestrian event and was told to write a 100-word textblock to go with the photos. Vonnegut couldn't think of 100 words to go with the act, so he wrote a simple note to the editor, which said: "The horses jumped over the fucking hedge. I quit."

It was in 1955, the second year of *SI's* existence, that someone got the bright idea to send William Faulkner to cover the Kentucky Derby. The result was a literary ode to the smell of liniment, ammonia, straw, horses, and Kentucky itself, with no mention that Swaps won the race with Shoemaker up. But Faulkner's lead remained a source of amusement with staff members for years. I quote: "This saw Boone:"

I think John Steinbeck topped it. Some years later Ray Cave was editing "outside text," and he managed to talk Steinbeck into contributing a piece. Steinbeck stipulated that if he wrote the piece not a single word could be touched. Not one. The piece he submitted was a long letter about how he couldn't write about sports. His haunting lead: "Dear Ray Cave:"

Far be it for me to make sport of two Nobel laureates in literature, but I've often wondered if they'd liked to have reworked those leads.

THE NOVEL *BAJA OKLAHOMA* FOUGHT ITS way onto the screen in 1988 ahead of *Dead Solid Perfect*, but it almost didn't get there. To begin with, I was made to suffer the kind of disappointment that's common among writers who toil in Hollywood.

I had a studio, Rastar Productions. I had a director, George Roy Hill, one of the greats—among other things, he'd done *Butch, Sting, Garp,* and *Slap Shot,* funniest sports movie ever. I had a script George Roy Hill liked, mine, and George Roy Hill said Shirley MacLaine was eager to play Juanita. All we needed was Paul Newman for Shirley's costar. Was it any wonder I stood on our Park Avenue terrace and envisioned dollar signs drifting toward me from Central Park?

I was in on meetings with George Roy Hill in his apartment—he lived nearby. Me, the director, and Paul Newman, genial guy, brilliant actor. The "property" was discussed. Newman's role was discussed.

Then one afternoon I was called to the director's apartment to learn that Paul Newman had decided not to do *Baja.* Instead, he was going to do *Fat Man and Little Boy*, a film about the making of the atomic bomb.

Since Newman wasn't available, George Roy Hill said, he was afraid he himself had lost interest in the "project." Sorry. But good luck with it.

I like to think I took the news like a man.

I said, "George, it's been great to meet you and work with you. I only wish we'd changed the title to *Baja Hiroshima*."

THANKS TO A TERRIFIC LADY, Marykay Powell, a producer who worked for Ray Stark, the "project" was rescued. It became an HBO Picture in association with Rastar. A young director, Bobby Roth, proved to be a good choice for the material. He did some cosmetics on my script.

I was happy with Bobby's casting of Lesley Ann Warren, the fabulous Swoosie Kurtz, and Peter Coyote in the leading roles. Happy we got Willie Nelson to appear in the concert scene, which was shot before 2,000 people at Billy Bob's gigantic saloon in Fort Worth, a musical night to remember, if you stayed sober. And I was more than happy with Bobby's casting of a nineteen-year-old unknown actress for the part of the daughter.

You may have heard of her by now. Julia Roberts.

Bobby Roth wore jeans, sneakers, and a beard, but he played to a five handicap on the golf course, and soon after *Baja* world premiered in Fort Worth at the Ridglea Theatre—a rewarding evening for me personally—he brought *Dead Solid Perfect* to the screen.

I was pleased when Bobby rounded up Kathryn Harrold, Randy Quaid, Jack Warden, and Corinne Bohrer for the movie. They did the novel's characters proud. Kathryn was the perfect Beverly, and Randy, as Kenny, had a believable golf swing. He played to a six.

Most of the golf action was shot around Colonial, Mira Vista, and Glen Garden country clubs in Fort Worth. Indoor scenes were shot in Joe T. Garcia's, the Cattlemen's Steak House, and the Stockyards Hotel.

Our friends have discussed one scene in the movie more than any other. It's the one in which Corinne Bohrer, as the bimbo Janie Ruth, strides down the hall in the Stockyards Hotel completely nude. If you've seen the film, I don't need to point out that Corinne's body did honor to all pronunciations of "shapely adorable."

That's me and the missus in the hallway. We had lines that were left on the cutting room floor. Interruptive, the director concluded.

As the naked Corinne walks past us, June says, "What is *that*?"

I shrug and say, "Somebody's daughter."

Film work is not all drudgery. The crew felt they had to shoot the Janie Ruth hallway scene three times.

THINKING MY FLINGS IN HOLLYWOOD were over, I returned to covering golf and writing another novel, *You Gotta Play Hurt*. It had been trying to climb out of my head since I'd left *Sports Illustrated*. It came out in '91 and did good, and I was particularly pleased that so many in the journalism lodge enjoyed the send-up of what may or may not have been a magazine like *SI*. People still ask who certain editors, writers, and bosses are, or were, and would I confirm their suspicions? My standard answer is: "I've never known any people like that in my whole life."

But none of that has anything to do with the phone call that came out of the blue from John Frankenheimer, another of the immortal film directors. He'd made scores of brilliant films that included *The Manchurian Candidate*, *Seven Days in May*, and *Black Sunday*. He said he had two sports projects in mind that I would be perfect to write. He wanted me to do a *Semi* dance with both of them.

Getting to know John Frankenheimer was an honor and a privilege, almost as enjoyable as the up-front development money from Universal, thanks to my Hollywood agent at the time, Jim Wiatt.

Frankenheimer was a friendly, witty guy. He had recently directed the movie *Dead Bang*, starring Don Johnson, and shared this with me: "If I were doing a movie on the life of Don Johnson, Don Johnson wouldn't play it." John was a delight to dine with and work with, but he had a drawback. He was a tennis fan. He was longing to make a tennis movie.

Well, okay. I wrote a script for him titled *The Break*. It was about a stud tennis star who gambles and drinks his way to the bottom, but slowly fights his way back to Wimbledon—with the help of, say, a Demi Moore.

It was never made because the studio decided nobody wanted to see a tennis movie. Maybe a decade ago, but not now. I sort of agreed.

John's other passions were fast cars and auto racing. He'd made *Grand Prix* in 1966. Now he wanted to do it again twenty-five years later. This involved my spending considerable time on the Left Coast, going to a Formula One race in Vegas, and loitering around Universal.

I was loitering one day when I ran into Lew Wasserman, last of the powerful Hollywood moguls. He'd built MCA-Universal into a monolithic ATM machine. A gray-haired, dignified man in a black suit, he remembered me from my friendship with Carroll Rosenbloom, one-time owner of the Colts and the Rams. I'd been at a dinner party with Lew Wasserman at Rosenbloom's house in Bel Air. I'd been with him in Rosenbloom's suite in the L.A. Coliseum for a Ram game.

He was friendly in our conversation, and before it ended he felt the need to let me know "this cotillion season" was wearing him down.

I wrote a script for Frankenheimer titled *Flat-Out*. He liked both the story and the title. Flat-out was the speed with which hell-bent Formula One guys drive in a race. They drive flat-out.

I was in a meeting at Universal with a junior mogul who said, "Who do you see in this film?" They always ask that.

I said, "I don't know. Michelle Pfeiffer and Clint Eastwood?"

We were just spitballing here, as they say.

"That would be a hot mix," he said, gazing up at the ceiling.

Hot mix.

The only person who didn't like the script was Ned Tannen, who was now an independent producer with Universal backing. He'd been recognized as a genius in the past for producing multiple hits for Universal and Paramount.

"I don't know what to do with this piece of shit," he said to Frankenheimer and me in a meeting. I wasn't insulted. Producers call every script "a piece of shit" until it beckons a star and reaches the screen.

He liked the idea of throwing any Clint Eastwood, Jeff Bridges, or Harrison Ford he could round up behind the wheel of a Formula One car, but he hated the female lead, who in my mind was a gorgeous, sharp-tonged magazine journalist.

"The bitch is too perfect," Ned Tannen said. "Can't she fall down and roll around in the grease?"

The movie never saw the screen for several different reasons. But that meeting told me I was headed back to real life.

I was emotionally incapable of making Michelle Pfeiffer fall down and roll around in the grease.

Chapter 28

Is It Granada I See or Merely
Camp David?

ALTHOUGH IT WAS NEVER a goal in life, it has occurred to me that I've met six presidents of the United States. It also has occurred to me that six is no record for a sportswriter. Grantland Rice knew every White House occupant from Taft to Ike.

My list is a cheat anyway. I first met George W. Bush, Old 43, when he was the governor of Texas. It was backstage in a big hall in Houston. That evening Barbara Bush, his mother and my favorite first lady, was holding her inaugural "Celebration of Reading" event.

Any patron of the arts looking at a group photo of the four speakers that night would have said, "I know Jenkins, but who are those other people?"

They were Mary Higgins Clark, John Grisham, and Larry McMurtry.

I was introduced to Ronald Reagan when he was governor of California in 1974. It was in an ABC broadcast booth in the L.A. Coliseum. I was keeping Meredith, Gifford, and Cosell company during a Monday Night Football telecast. The governor dropped in with two aides to welcome the broadcast celebs to L.A. I happened to be there.

Richard Nixon shook my hand on an occasion before he became president and wasn't even a governor. It was in that '60s period when the political press didn't have "Nixon to kick around anymore." He had spoken to the Football Writers Association in Chicago during All-Star Game Week, and came around to greet all of us personally.

I bumped into President Gerald Ford in the spring of '76 in the White House when my old Paschal friend Dick Growald was covering the Ford White House for UP. Dick was showing me around when Ford popped up in a hallway in the vicinity of press secretary Ron Nessen's office.

The first president I met was LBJ. June and I and five or six other TCU exes living in the New York area were selected to accompany Lyndon on Air Force One to Fort Worth, where he would make the commencement address at TCU's graduation ceremony.

We flew from Andrews Air Force Base to Carswell Air Force Base, and quite smoothly, I might add. There was a moment during the flight when LBJ came down the aisle and greeted everyone, after which he retired to his office and bedroom behind the door with the presidential seal on it, and ate his chili.

We were told by a staff person on board that we were welcome to take souvenirs off the plane. We took cigarettes, candy bars, match-books, and napkins to scatter among friends.

I kept three packs of cigarettes. I still have one unopened. It sits on a bookshelf, a reminder of the days when smoking was more impor-tant to me than world peace.

When our kids reached junior high age they couldn't resist the temptation. They smoked two of the packs with the presidential seal on them one evening while we were out to dinner. They confessed.

Sally said, "Marty and Danny and Eric Olson did it."

Marty said, "Sally and Vivien Zak and Sarah Graves did it."

Danny said, "What cigarettes?"

The president I came to know best was George Herbert Walker Bush. No. 41 in your program, No. 1 on your list of fast-playing golfers.

We met when the wife, daughter, and I were surprisingly invited to the White House on an afternoon in late May of '89 for the unveil-ing of 41's horseshoe pit. There were buffets of food, beverages for the thirsty, a small military band playing country music. In the crowd,

I spotted meandering U.S. senators, Vice President Dan Quayle, Rupert Murdoch, several ladies who could have been Lesley Stahl but probably weren't, and I ran into a sportswriting pal, Mo Siegel, once a pillar of the old *Washington Star.*

We were milling about when I noticed the president motioning to me to come over where he stood in a cluster of well-wishers. I pulled June and Sally along. The well-wishers parted the sea for us.

The prez was relaxed and friendly. I managed to keep a grip on my nonchalance when 41 began to quote passages from my novels, laughing as they came to mind. He asked who certain characters were based on. So began a friendship.

We stayed at the party for an hour and a half, then walked across Pennsylvania Avenue to the venerable Willard Hotel, had drinks in the Round Robin bar, and made general observations on the events of the day.

Sally said, "Pop, do you realize the leader of the free world was quoting your books to you?"

I said, "Walter Cronkite was there today?"

THE PRESIDENT AND I EXCHANGED WRITTEN notes over the next several months. His were brief. A word about his golf game. The latest golf joke. A comment on national politics.

Like many who know him, I have a collection of correspondence from him that fills a three-inch-thick loose-leaf notebook.

I was covering the 1990 U.S. Open at Medinah when he tracked me down. I was sitting in the press lounge with Blackie Sherrod and Jim Murray. A USGA volunteer came over to tell me I had a phone call from the president of the United States. Blackie and Jim gave me a look.

I said, "Somebody's playing a joke. Ignore it."

Twenty minutes later the volunteer returned. "Mr. Jenkins, it really is the White House. President Bush is trying to reach you."

"This better be important," I said to Blackie and Jim, who were giving me another look.

I walked to the phone at the media operations desk.

President Bush said, "Dan, where did they find you?"

"I'm at the U.S. Open at Medinah in Chicago, Mr. President."

He said, "Of course you are. I'm watching it."

This was the phone call that led to my first round of golf with a president of the United States. But before the golf it led to coffee in the Oval Office, lunch on the residence floor of the White House, and a ride on Marine One, the presidential chopper. The carpeted interior was decorated no more comfortably than a room at a Ritz-Carlton.

It was the first of my two weekends at Camp David.

We dined in a small area of the White House across the hall from the boss's master suite. As we were leaving for the golf game, an elevator door opened, a door I hadn't noticed before, and out stepped Brent Scowcroft, the national security advisor.

The president introduced me. I didn't have to be told that the two of them needed to have a private conversation.

"Is there anyplace I can smoke around here?" I asked 41. He said, "Sure. Go out on the Truman Balcony down there by the Lincoln Bedroom."

In the five minutes I spent on the balcony, I wondered what crisis was going to cancel my golf game with the president. I was reminded of a morning in October in a previous decade when Tom Brokaw was hosting the *Today* show and invited me on to plug my novel *Baja Oklahoma*.

We'd barely begun to discuss the book when Tom got a message through his earpiece. He turned to me with a grim look.

He said, "Anwar Sadat's been assassinated. They're saying it was an Islamist group in his own army."

"They did this in *my* time slot?" I said hilariously.

Brokaw said, "*News* is taking over the rest of the hour. I'll be on a plane to Cairo in the morning."

I said, "If you need something to read on the flight . . ."

Brent Scowcroft was gone when I returned to the hall.

"No red phone deal?" I said to the president.

"No," he smiled. "No red phone deal."

On the ground floor we were heading for a door to the back lawn where Marine One was waiting. The prez saw a tour group at the end of the hall, and said, "I want to go say hello to these people. It's their house."

Marine One dropped us off in Frederick, Maryland, where a motorcade took us to Holly Hills Country Club. Two people who would complete our foursome were waiting there. One was U.S. congressman Marty Russo, a Democrat from Illinois, known as the best golfer in the House of Representatives. The other was Walter Payton, "Sweetness" himself, who had retired from the Chicago Bears in '87.

Holly Hills was a strong layout with a number of unique holes, but aren't they all when you reach geezerdom?

Marty Russo was too good a golfer to be a servant of the people. Payton was monstrously long, when we could find his tee shots.

The prez played extremely fast but enjoyed himself, even when he flubbed a chip shot and three-putted, and heard an onlooker on the other side of a fence holler, "Does your husband play golf, too?"

He laughed. "I hadn't heard that one."

My game showed the rust of living in Manhattan. That I can think of, there is no greater pain in the ass for a Manhattan dweller than to be invited to play a round of golf in the suburbs. I'd learned to turn down most invitations, unless it involved Pine Valley. It required taking a taxi to a car rental agency, getting lost going to Long Island, Westchester, Connecticut, or New Jersey, and getting lost coming back.

I had sold the Olds 88 when we moved from Westchester to Manhattan, having keenly observed that it was insanity to keep a car in the city. If you didn't spend $4 million a month on a garage, you spent hours out of your day looking for parking spaces twelve blocks away from where you live, or were going, and you hoped and prayed the car would still be there when you went back to get it.

The president invited me to play golf with him on other occasions. Some I was forced to skip—journalism intruded. But we did play in Manassas, Virginia, on the Robert Trent Jones course, at Jupiter Hills in Palm Beach, Florida, at Marsh Landing in Ponte Vedra, Florida, at Cape Arundel in Kennebunkport, Maine, and we hit balls at Camp David.

The prez and I were playing a hole in Manassas when I glanced down a cliff and saw a boat cruising slowly along the Potomac. On it were three people, two with weapons, and one looking up at us through high-powered binoculars.

"Are those our guys?" I asked him.

"Those are our guys," he said.

I felt sure the person with the high-powered binoculars was staring at me. I blamed him for the double bogey.

June and I were house guests of 41 and Barbara's on a weekend in Kennebunkport when the boss let me try out a golf club in his bag as we were playing Cape Arundel. It was a new kind of metal wood—and I've never been able to refer to a metal wood as a 3-metal or 4-metal. Too old.

I hit a 180-yard screamer with the club that found the green close to the pin for a birdie. I said to the prez, "This club is mine now."

"Keep it," he said. "They send me clubs all the time. I have closetsful. They all go the same distance."

The club was a Tight Lies. A Barney Adams creation. It may or may not have been the forerunner of the hybrid. I only know it helped extend my recreational golf life.

Camp David, for those who don't know, is located in the Catoctin Mountains of Maryland. Catoctin. There's a word I challenge you to spell correctly if you're typing in a hurry. The camp is run by the Navy, guarded by the Marines, and the Army handles transportation.

You might not care for it unless you like squandering your time in beautiful woods with trails for walking, biking, horseback riding, and discovering tennis courts, swimming pools, handball courts, a practice range for golf, a skeet range, and all the well-appointed, rustic cabins named for trees—Aspen, the president's residence, Birch, Dogwood, Holly, and Laurel Lodge, where you have breakfast, and where meetings are held. And Hickory Lodge, where you find a café, gift shop, bar, and bowling alley.

"This is good duty," a naval officer told me. "But I have to go to sea. You can't make rank if you don't go to sea."

June was with me on my second weekend at the retreat. We dined in the residence with the prez and Barbara, and later one evening sat in front of a fire and watched a Tom Berenger movie yet to be released. Just folks doing what folks do on an average evening at home.

It took that one visit for world traveler June Jenkins to put Camp David in her list of exquisite hotels. In there with the Mamounia in Marrakech for exotic, the Hotel du Palais in Biarritz for grand, and the Baur au Lac in Zurich for charm.

My golf with 41 at Camp David consisted of hitting balls from the three different sets of tees—long, middle, short—to the green that President Eisenhower had ordered installed below Aspen Cabin.

It started off as a match, but deteriorated into us raining mulligans down on Ike's well-manicured bent green.

On that Sunday morning after breakfast, June went for a walk with Barbara. Before they started out, Barbara said to us, "We're going to the eleven o'clock church service. George says you don't have to go, but I say you do."

We were thinking of going anyhow. Evergreen Chapel had been added to the grounds by President Reagan and dedicated by 41. Every president adds something. The choir was comprised of Navy personnel and Navy wives. Their hymns were beautifully done, and they brought tears of pride to our eyes when they closed with "God Bless America."

Another keeper moment came on my first visit. It reflected on what a decent and thoughtful man this forty-first president was, a man who had served his country in more capacities than perhaps anyone ever had—decorated pilot of a torpedo bomber in World War II, U.S. congressman, U.N. ambassador, chief of U.S. liaison office to China, CIA chief, vice president of the United States, president of the United States.

He was taking me on a tour of the grounds in a golf cart when he stopped in front of Holly Cabin, one of the oldest in the camp.

He said, "Go up on the porch and sit on that bench for a moment."

"Why?" I asked.

He said, "That's where Roosevelt and Churchill sat when they were planning the D-Day invasion."

I went up on the porch of Holly Cabin, lit a Winston, and sat on the bench where FDR had smoked his Camel in the ivory cigarette holder and Churchill had puffed on his Cuban cigar.

When 41 lost the '92 election to Bill Clinton, we exchanged a couple of emails on the subject. Intending to cheer him up, one of mine said: "YOU feel bad? I just blew Camp David."

Chapter 29

What I Gave I Kept, What I Kept I Lost.
Have I Got That Right?

IT HAS NEVER TAKEN MUCH to boggle my mind—human beings are good at it—and it happened again recently when I realized I'd been writing for *Golf Digest* for twenty-eight years, which is four years longer than I wrote for *Sports Illustrated*. It doesn't seem possible, but ah, yes, there you have it.

One thing it's done is get me to the total of 220 majors I've covered, starting with the first one in 1951 when I was a newspaper lad. I want to be clear. That's just the Masters tournaments, U.S. Opens, British Opens, and PGAs. It doesn't count all the Ryder Cups, TPCs, L.A. Opens, Crosbys, Colonials, Harbor Towns, Hawaiian Opens, Tucsons, T of Cs, Dorals, Akrons—had enough?

I'm sure I've set the bar so high it can't be topped. For one thing, there may not be any more newspapers in another five or ten minutes.

I plan to keep on writing for *Golf Digest* as long as the magazine will have me. As an editor and boss, *Digest's* Jerry Tarde, prince among humans, Northwestern grad, low handicapper, ranks up there on the pedestal with Blackie Sherrod and André Laguerre. Jerry does his best to let me be me.

You can lay a lot of the blame on Jerry for my induction into the World Golf Hall of Fame. He must have been a dogged lobbyist.

That's a fabulous facility and museum down there in St. Augustine, Florida. It's the Louvre of the game. Every golf victim should make a pilgrimage to see it.

I was touched, I confess, at the induction ceremony when I went into the Hall with the rest of the class of 2012—Phil Mickelson, Peter Alliss, Sandy Lyle, and Hollis Stacy.

They start giving you these lifetime achievement things when you live too long. But being taken into that exclusive club, one where Ben Hogan and Jack Nicklaus dwell with the other greats of the game, and where only two other working golf writers have been inducted—England's Bernard Darwin and America's Herbert Warren Wind—was awfully nice.

I'm wearing the robe and hoisting the scepter with pride, but only rarely in public.

When I topple over—while typing, would be my preference—I'll leave the epitaph up to the wife and kids, but I made a facetious suggestion in my Hall of Fame acceptance speech:

"I KNEW THIS WOULD HAPPEN."

Meantime, I wouldn't trade the friendships I've made with the folks at *Digest* for a Yorkshire terrier that speaks English. Tempting . . .

Not only Jerry Tarde, but Mike O'Malley, Nick Seitz, Jaime Diaz, Guy Yocom, Ron Sirak, Tom Callahan, Dave Kindred, Jim Moriarity, John Huggan, Bill Fields, Tim Rosaforte, Pete Finch, Matt Rudy, and Dom Furore, world's greatest photographer.

Among the footprints I've left at *Digest* through the years, these seem to have disturbed readers the most:

How many times do you have to be reminded that the Masters doesn't start until the back nine Sunday? Arnie's charge was born there. Sarazen double-eagled there. Byron caught Guldahl there. Nicklaus beat Miller and Weiskopf there. Roberto failed arithmetic there. This time, Curtis Strange went back there with a four-stroke lead but before he got back up

the hill he was nursing a two-stroke loss to—*Gott in Himmel*—
the son of a Bavarian laborer. Here was a guy, Bernhard
Langer, who had only won tournaments in Germany, Japan,
France, Italy, Holland, and Spain, places where wars were
more popular than golf.

What do you do if you're Greg Norman in the 18th fairway of
the Masters on Sunday and you're trying to get Jack Nicklaus
into a playoff? You hit a half-shank, push-fade, semi-slice 4-iron
that guarantees the proper result for the history books. Oh,
well, Greg Norman has always looked like the guy you send out
to kill James Bond, not Jack Nicklaus.

Tiger Woods, like Arnold Palmer and Jack Nicklaus before him,
went to the British Open chasing a Grand Slam, but he saw it
flutter away over Scotland like a wounded seagull, as Arnold
and Jack did. Meanwhile, scads of writers when last seen were
pestering Ernie Els to let them write a best-seller for him titled
Watch Out for Your Lap, a British Open Might Fall in It.

Bury my laptop at Wounded Foot. Sorry. Make that Winged
Foot, and put it next to Phil Mickelson. The 2006 U.S. Open
was grim from start to finish, and Mickelson will be saying, "I
am such an idiot," for months to come, having given away this
Open with the worst driving exhibition since the Greyhound
bus ran into Ben Hogan.

Retief Goosen's first name is relatively common in South
Africa, as it is in Arkansas, but of course in Arkansas everyone
is trying to spell Ralph.

Ask yourself this about Kemper Lakes. Is the clubhouse
for a PGA Championship supposed to look like the
tourist information center you find after crossing the
state line?

The FedEx Cup still needs work. The way it is, the USA can win World War I and World War II, then lose to Greenland.

AS SO MANY GIANTS OF MY trade have gradually passed on—John Lardner, Red Smith, Jimmy Cannon, Jim Murray—and while others like Blackie Sherrod have entered retirement, I began to think that the future of sportswriting looked bleak.

But today I think it's in very good hands.

Some of the best you can still hold in your hand to crinkle as you read, but others require a series of clicks. At any rate, there's plenty of devilish, spirited sportswriting around today.

If you've read her, you won't consider it an upset if I start with my own daughter. Sally Jenkins, sports columnist at the *Washington Post*. She's been the best writer in the family for a while now, and one of the best in the country. She's written twelve books, most of them best-sellers, and she could walk around with a shopping bag filled with column-of-the-year awards.

I delight in quoting some of her work:

From the moment he arrived in Washington, Albert Haynesworth has expected to be cooled with palm fronds and fed another grape. He has been consistently uncooperative, refused to practice hard, argued with his coaches, and we all know the reason why, deep down. He doesn't care. He would be just as happy if the Redskins cut or released him next season, so he can move on down the river, like Cleopatra's barge, to plunder another community.

According to NCAA bylaws, I have violated the rules of amateurism. I am therefore ineligible to continue writing this column. Fortunately, however, I have just been fully reinstated. An exhaustive NCAA inquiry of several seconds has found that while rules were clearly violated, none was broken. Hence, my ineligibility has resulted in the following punishment: I am eligible again. But I wish to make clear these actions are unacceptable. There is no place for them in intercollegiate athletics, except at Auburn.

A locker room is not the Lux Lounge, and it's not Clinton Portis's private den, either. It's a weird hybrid room, a public space where private things happen, crowded and stinking, littered with dirty adhesive tape that sticks to your shoes, and packed with bodies, starting with the un-deodorized athletes in various states of dress and undress, some of them picking their feet or putting salve on their back acne, but also including equipment managers collecting sweat-soaked laundry, and TV anchors and radio announcers jostling each other. Anyone who argues that women reporters don't belong in a locker room because they might see something private had better kick the cameras and microphones out first. Personally, I don't interview naked men. That's just my policy.

I'll spit this out quick, before the armies of feminism try to gag me and strap electrodes to my forehead: Tim Tebow is one of the better things to happen to young women in some time. I realize this stance won't endear me to the Dwindling Organizations of Ladies in Lockstep, otherwise known as DOLL, but I'll try to pick up the shards of my shattered feminist credentials and go on.

Sally has good company at the *Post*. Here's Barry Svrluga at the most electrifying contest of the 2012 London Olympics.

MANCHESTER, England—The match was so old, past 10 p.m. at historic Old Trafford, that Hope Solo walked back to her own goal line, stared at a spot on the ground in front of her, and prepared for penalty kicks. The U.S. women's soccer team had won games that way before, and if that's the wildest way to end things . . . then this match, this crazy match against Canada in the Olympic semifinals, must end that way. But moments before Solo settled in, Heather O'Reilly settled the ball on the right side, and with her fresh legs sent a cross into the box in hopes that it might find an American head, an American foot, something. And Alex Morgan jumped.

"I couldn't wrap my head around what just happened," Solo said.

Here's Rick Maese at the *Post*:

> KEY WEST, Fla.—There are palm trees in purgatory. He walks by them without paying much attention. Here, each is a pixel on a postcard designed as paradise. Mike Leach stops at a wooden shack for a Cuban coffee. "What was I talking about?" he asks. Doesn't matter. He hops topics like lily pads. The Cuban caffeine only makes matters worse. The need for a college playoff system. Unemployment. Hunting pigs. Sarah Palin. Eating fast food in Japan . . .

Gene Wojciechowski at ESPN.com nails any topic he approaches:

> We were . . . Penn State. In the 3 minutes and 14 seconds it took NCAA president Mark Emmert to announce the details of the NCAA's surgical and devastating sanctions Monday morning, the Penn State that Joe Paterno once ruled for decades ceased to exist. It was removed as if it were a years-old wart, too unsightly to endure anymore. The NCAA, with Penn State's blessing, didn't impose the death penalty. It went further than that. It ordered the university and the people who run it to transform its soul.

Geno again on golf:

> PONTE VEDRA, Fla.—The man who leads the so-called Fifth Major is harder to watch than a circumcision at an IMAX

theater. Kevin Na plays slow. He plays so slow his five o'clock shadow doesn't show up until midnight. Glaciers ask for his autograph.

Jim Moriarty in *Golf World* stole my heart with his piece on the last major of 2012:

> South of a genteel city that drips history from its hominy, on a Pete Dye golf course that was awarded a Ryder Cup before it got its first bulldozer, Rory McIlroy's ascending star helped snatch credibility from the jaws of folly in a PGA Championship that will be talked about for as long as humans wait in queues. And wait. And wait. The only thing quick about Kiawah Island was how fast McIlroy became a multiple major champion, and that required 23 years, three months and eight days—or roughly the time it took to go from Charleston to the Ocean Course and back.

Dan Wetzel at Yahoo.com is consistently compelling:

> LONDON—They came from Cork and Kerry. They flew in from Dublin. They came for a 5-foot-5, 132-pound woman whose hands deliver hammer swings, happiness, and hope. They came because Katie Taylor—Ireland's Katie Taylor—was boxing for the gold medal. They came because, back home, the recession drags on and drags down. And when Katie Taylor hits someone in the mouth it feels, even for a brief moment, like Ireland, too, can hit back.

Rick Reilly at ESPN.com on why you can't watch baseball:

> Things nobody reads in America today: Major League baseball's "Pace of Play Procedures." Not that baseball games don't have a pace. They do: snails escaping a freezer.

I knew I was in trouble in the first inning of the Reds-Giants game on TV when the Reds' Brandon Phillips stepped up. Strike: steps out, examines the trademark on his bat at length. Ball: steps out, grabs barrel of bat, seems to be talking to it. Ball: steps out, takes three practice swings, taps corner of batter's box, steps one foot in, taps plate, places other foot in, stretches, fiddles, looks at pitcher, calls timeout, does it all again. Swing and miss: steps way out, adjusts belt, re-wraps glove, addresses barrel again.

Grounds out to short.

Will Leitch founded Deadspin.com, but he's moved on. Here he is on *New York* magazine's website:

It's strange: Roger Clemens hasn't really been around for the last three years, and still, we're sick of him. Clemens's comeback tour kicks off tomorrow night with the Sugar Land Skeeters against the Bridgeport Bluefish. It'll be a circus, but everything with Roger always is. We just want to know if the 50-year-old is still frosting his tips.

Mike Lupica of the *New York Daily News* is as good a man as you'd want on a late-night deadline:

In the kind of moment when great Yankees are supposed to stand up at Yankee Stadium, Alex Rodriguez sat down.

Joe Girardi let Rodriguez bat No. 3 all night, watched him go 0-for-3, watched him strike out twice. Then Girardi sent 40-year-old Raul Ibanez up to hit for A-Rod with one out in the bottom of the ninth, Yankees down a run to the Orioles. And Ibanez hit one over the right-field wall to tie the game. Rodriguez was one of the first to greet Ibanez in the dugout. Good teammate. Great $30 million dollar cheerleader in that moment. The night Ibanez stood up and A-Rod sat down.

And here is Tommy Craggs, after he took over as the editor of Dead-spin.com, being dead right on a segment of the workforce:

> The World Anti-Doping Agency, the people who once banned
> caffeine, now demands that baseball violate federal labor law
> and unilaterally impose a testing regime of dubious efficacy
> for a substance of uncertain benefits. It's an organization of
> professional hysterics. These are lunatics and hucksters, and
> it's not the job of sportswriters to give credulous coverage to
> their medicine shows. At some point this will cease to be news,
> and journalists will realize that quoting a WADA official on
> anything is like quoting the town crazy on the fluoride content
> of his water. They are just a gang of moralizing cranks running
> around with needles and piss cups.

MY REAL HEROES HAVE ALWAYS BEEN sportswriters. That was why
I was proud to become a member of a group known neither far
nor wide but only to ourselves as, simply, the Geezers. Aging, cynical sportswriters is what we were. But so many have departed from
the press boxes we've stopped having the annual meeting, where
we would sit around for three days to drink and smoke and tell
the same stories. We'd curse the same enemies, and laugh at the
same Point Missers, Time Bandits, Rally Killers, and Room Clear-
ers. Which, when I stop to think about it, would be a good title for
something.

Members of the original crew were Blackie Sherrod, Jim Murray,
Ed Pope, Furman Bisher, Bill Millsaps, Dan Foster, and Dan Cook.
I was the first invitee to join, and then came Dave Kindred, Frank
Luksa, and Tom Callahan.

Six of those gentlemen—Murray, Sherrod, Bisher, Pope, Kindred,
and Millsaps—had won the Red Smith Award, the highest honor one
can receive in the sportswriting profession. But in the spring of 2013
another one joined them when the Associated Press Sports Editors,

who originated the award thirty-three years ago, bestowed it upon this typist, his ownself.

I emailed the survivors of our club the following headline: "Seventh Geezer Nabs Red Smith Award."

The last few gatherings of the Geezers were held in a Dallas hotel because Blackie had retired and refused to travel. We went to him. In his nineties, he still consumed adult beverages and was happy to have discovered a long slender cigarette that, he claimed, "cured emphysema." He'd sit back and tell us how thankful he was that he never had to interview another "rich, arrogant jerk," a reference to the godlike, billionaire professional athletes who populate today's sports world.

Since the Geezers no longer congregate, it's hard to attract Blackie's attention either by phone or computer, but a while back I received an email response from him. In part, it said: "I'm doing all right here in my Museum of Prehistoric Culture, but if you wish to speak to me of Cowboys, Rangers, or Mavericks, I must say you have apparently overestimated my curiosity in such matters."

Another email circulated in which Blackie paid respects to his last public drinking tavern in Dallas, a place called the Loon, and his local friends who would congregate with him there—Barry K., Hendrix, Whiskey, and others. His message: "Tell them they will always be in my concern, like athlete's foot and constipation."

It was good to know he was still Blackie.

NOW AS I TRY TO WIND UP THIS BOOK, you don't need to ask if I've noticed any big changes in sports during my years on the scene. My answer would be, "Are pinto beans maroon?"

Greed, of course, has been the biggest change. A particular word should be inserted into the name of every event and sporting institution today. The Corporate University of Notre Dame. The University of Corporate Texas. The Dallas Corporate Cowboys. The Corporate Olympics. The Corporate Super Bowl, presented by TV commercials and hip-hop halftimes.

You've heard the slogan "Winning is not the best thing, it's the

ONLY thing." The man who said it first lived in a different world. A world in which the athlete built character and tested his heart by competing for a trophy, a wristwatch, a ring. Today the athlete tries to win at any cost for his mansion, twenty-car garage, and portfolio.

But if I was once saddened by that condition, I'm only amused now. When you reach my age, you realize it's kid stuff compared to what goes on in the deplorable world of politics.

A final word about sportswriting.

A sportswriter's life means never sitting with your wife or family at the games. Still working after everyone else has gone to the party. Waiting for a coach or an athlete to return a phone call. Digging beneath a coach's lies, not to forget those of athletic directors and general managers and owners of pro teams. Keeping a confidence. Risking it. The necessity of injuring a person with a comment or joke in the pursuit of truth. Constantly thinking about the next event, dreading the next plane ride, but looking forward to a place you've never been.

It means listening to sports as much as writing about it. Listening to those who know more about it than you do. It's the angry letter from somebody who didn't understand what you wrote. A compliment from someone who didn't understand what you meant. Knowing that your social acceptability most likely corresponds with the size and repetition of your byline. And too often building heroes out of the undeserving—and for the good of something you've never quite known how to define.

It's been all of that for me, but waves of laughter came with it.

Now I'm thinking back to a day in 1972. June was with me on part of the book tour when I was chasing *Semi-Tough* around. I was back in Fort Worth in the house on Travis Avenue where I grew up, sitting at the kitchen table with the three women who'd meant the most to me in my life—June, Mimmie, and Sister.

The novel had been a little too advanced for Mimmie, as I'd thought it was for my old TCU professor. But my aunt told my grandmother she could simply put it on the shelf and look at it.

This was where the phone call came from an elated Herman

Gollob, my editor in New York. He called to tell me that my novel was coming on the *New York Times* best-seller list, near the top, and on all of the other lists. In fact, I would see it linger on the *Times* list for six months.

My victory lap consisted of walking outside and sitting in the swing on my grandmother's front porch. I lit a cigarette and thought about all of the people who'd helped raise me and encouraged my interest in sports. I thought of grabbing the morning paper on that porch and cutting out the football pictures before anybody had a chance to read it—and nobody complaining.

I thought about all the bars and restaurants I'd sat in, from Herb's and Jack's in Fort Worth to Clarke's and Elaine's and Toots Shor's in Manhattan. None of my books could have been written without all that loss of sleep.

Now I'm thinking back to *Semi*, the book that changed my life.

You'd call me a sap if I didn't say I liked the financial rewards and the comfort it provided the family. But what pleased me as much was the novel's honesty that went along with the attempted humor. Beneath the idiom of the athlete as I knew him—and the locker room language in which the story is told—there are sincere feelings about friendship and loyalty. True friends are a priceless commodity in this world, and I've been blessed with many. And there are other things intended: a vitality of existence, a hopeful view of life, and a tender attitude about love.

After all, Billy Clyde won the game and got the girl—and so did I.

Acknowledgments

Typing through the laughter is more or less what my life has been, and to help refresh my memory on this journey I obviously needed to dip into the files of the *Fort Worth Press, Dallas Times Herald, Sports Illustrated, Playboy,* and *Golf Digest.* I'm happy those files still exist and haven't been destroyed by electricity or some "quality control" genius. Of all the books I prowled to refresh my memory, the one I'm most indebted to is John Dunning's *On the Air: The Encyclopedia of Old Time Radio.*

Now to thank a bunch of people. First June Jenkins, of course, a constant inspiration, and not a bad in-house editor. Next, Sally Jenkins, Marty Jenkins, and Danny Jenkins—your memories and the joy you bring are irreplaceable. And to complete the family photo op: Nicole, Julie and Tom, Amy, Sheila, Sarah, Paulina, and Noah.

Special thanks to Jerre and Melba Todd for their sixty years of friendship, laughter, and memories. Same for Bud Shrake and Marty McAllister, even though you've crossed the river. We blazed many a happy trail together from grade school on, and you enter my thoughts almost every day. As for you, Blackie Sherrod, you have only yourself to blame for a lot of what's in these pages.

Friends have always been more important to me than cigarettes, believe it or not. So, in random fashion—and no bonus points for accidentally being listed ahead of somebody else—I wish to thank the following for enriching my life along the way with friendship, company, and kindnesses: Dr. Don and Helen Matheson, Joe and Mary Sue Coffman, Tally Marr, Janet Danford, Jack Whitaker, Anabel Stripling, Walt Bingham, Sarah Ballard, Myra Gelband Wilson, Herman Gollob, Bev Norwood, Jean Boone, Eloise and Bernie Riviere, Vance and Belinda Minter, Clifton and Sheridan Morris, Jerry and Beth Tarde, Mike and Margaret O'Malley, Hunter and Shirley Enis, Dick and Mary Lowe, Bob Beattie, Gary Cartwright, Roy Blount Jr., Tom Callahan, Guy Yocom, Ron Sirak, Jaime Diaz, Nick Seitz, Dave Kindred, John Feinstein, Jim Moriarty, Dom Furore, Barry and Barbara Kerrane, Dr. Tom and Joan Rogers, Frances Trimble, Mark Cohen, Mark Mourer, Buddy Martin, Loran Smith, Dave Burgin and Judy, Dr. Billie Pugh and Paula, Susan and Kent Nix, Iva Green, T. R. Reinman, Cecil Morgan, Sandra and Butch Luskey, Diana Reid Chazaud, Kitty Thompson Olson, Karen Lerner, Joyce Sherrod, Barbara McColm, Walter Rainwater, Dr. Lee Anderson and Sherry, Sandra and Michael Brown, Case Herring, Ginger and Huston Frailey, Jim and Marilyn Hoener, Larry Dorman, Michael MacCambridge, Mike Lupica, David Israel, Bill Creasy, Bill Millsaps, Ed Pope, Steve Reid, Ed Sneed, Marty Leonard, George Solomon, Coach Gary Patterson and Kelsey, Ben and Kay Fortson, Jo Ann Walker, Gail Rawl, Buck McLean, Jim Rich, Barry Switzer, David Fay, Julius Mason, Melanie Hauser, Nell and Jim Branch, Joy and Grant Begley, Scott Corpening, Vernon Averett, Dan Roberts, and for special reasons Ben Matheson, Dr. Wally Schmuck, Steve Hatchell, John Walsh, Jack Peter, Brodie Waters, and Dr. O. S. Hawkins and Susie, who I'm counting on to get me to the peaceful shore someday.

Finally, Esther Newberg, my friend and agent for forty years; Bill Thomas, editor in chief at Doubleday; and Peter Gethers, skillful editor whose savvy made this a better book than the one I thought I'd finished.

Thanks again, one and all.

ABOUT THE AUTHOR

Dan Jenkins is one of America's most acclaimed sportswriters as well as a bestselling novelist. A native Texan, he has spent a lifetime at the typewriter and computer. He might best be known for his twenty-four years of stories in *Sports Illustrated* and now at *Golf Digest.* Three of his bestselling novels, *Semi-Tough, Dead Solid Perfect,* and *Baja Oklahoma,* were made into movies. His sportswriting has won him many awards. In 2012 he was inducted into the World Golf Hall of Fame—one of only three writers to be honored thus far—and he is the 2013 winner of the Red Smith Award, the highest honor in his sportswriting profession.